Harrington on Online Cash Games

6-Max No-Limit Hold 'em

By
DAN HARRINGTON
1995 World Champion

BILL ROBERTIE

**A product of
Two Plus Two Publishing LLC**

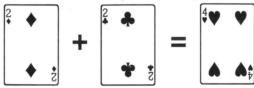

FIRST EDITION

FIRST PRINTING
June 2010

Printing and Binding
Creel Printers, Inc.
Las Vegas, Nevada

Printed in the United States of America

Harrington on
Online Cash Games
6-Max No-Limit Hold 'em

ISBN: 1-880685-49-3
ISBN13: 978-1-880685-49-5

"When a man with money meets a man with experience,
the man with experience leaves with money
and the man with money leaves with experience."

— *Anonymous*

Table of Contents

i

About Dan Harrington

Dan Harrington began playing poker professionally in 1982. On the circuit he is known as "Action Dan," an ironic reference to his solid but effective style. He has won several major no-limit hold 'em tournaments, including the European Poker Championships (1995), the $2,500 No-Limit Hold 'em event at the 1995 World Series of Poker, and the Four Queens No-Limit Hold 'em Championship (1996).

Dan began his serious games-playing with chess where he quickly became a master and one of the strongest players in the New England area. In 1972 he won the Massachusetts Chess Championship, ahead of most of the top players in the area. In 1976 he started playing backgammon, a game which he also quickly mastered. He was soon one of the top money players in the Boston area, and in 1981 he won the World Cup of backgammon in Washington D.C., ahead of a field that included most of the world's top players.

He first played in the $10,000 No-Limit Hold 'em Championship Event of the World Series of Poker in 1987. He has played in the Championship a total of 20 times and has reached the final table in four of those tournaments, an amazing record. Besides winning the World Championship in 1995, he finished sixth in 1987, third in 2003, and fourth in 2004. In 2006 he finished second at the Doyle Brunson North American Championships at the Bellagio, while in 2007 he won the Legends of Poker Tournament at the Bicycle Club. He is widely recognized as one of the greatest and most respected no-limit hold 'em players, as well as a feared opponent in both no-limit and limit hold 'em side games. He lives in Santa Monica, California where he is a partner in Anchor Loans, a real estate business.

About Bill Robertie

Bill Robertie has spent his life playing and writing about chess, backgammon, and now poker. He began playing chess as a boy, inspired by Bobby Fischer's feats on the international chess scene. While attending Harvard as an undergraduate, he became a chess master and helped the Harvard chess team win several intercollegiate titles. After graduation he won a number of chess tournaments, including the United States Championship at speed chess in 1970. He also established a reputation at blindfold chess, giving exhibitions on as many as eight boards simultaneously.

In 1976 he switched from chess to backgammon, becoming one of the top players in the world. His major titles include the World Championship in Monte Carlo in 1983 and 1987, the Black & White Championship in Boston in 1979, the Las Vegas tournaments in 1980 and 2001, the Bahamas Pro-Am in 1993, and the Istanbul World Open in 1994.

He has written several well-regarded backgammon books, the most noted of which are *Advanced Backgammon* (1991), a two-volume collection of 400 problems, and *Modern Backgammon* (2002), a new look at the underlying theory of the game. He has also written a set of three books for the beginning player: *Backgammon for Winners* (1994), *Backgammon for Serious Players* (1995), and *501 Essential Backgammon Problems* (1997).

He has cashed twice in the Main Event of the World Series of Poker (2006 & 2009). Currently, he owns a publishing company, the Gammon Press (www.thegammonpress.com), and lives in Arlington, Massachusetts with his wife Patrice.

Introduction

In our two-part series, *Harrington on Cash Games, Volumes 1 and 2*, Bill Robertie and I explained the theory and practice of full-ring, deep stacked cash games. For the most part, we chose examples from live full ring games played in casinos, where stakes might range from small $1/$2 or $2/$5 blinds to as much as $5/$10 or $10/$20, or even higher, and buy-ins might be several hundred big blinds. The focus of the books was on playing solid, tight-aggressive no-limit hold 'em against competent, thinking opponents.

In this new book we're going to look at the world of online no-limit hold 'em. For most players looking to become good at no-limit cash games, the online world is where the journey will begin. It is, however, a very different world from that of live casino poker, and requires a different treatment and a somewhat different mindset.

What are the differences between live cash games and online cash games? While there are many, here's a quick summary of the most important.

1. **No tells:** In live games, you can look at your opponents, watch their body language, and sometimes get a clue as to what they think of their hand and whether they've gone on tilt or not. They, of course, can look at you for the same information. When playing online, your opponents are silent and faceless.

2. **Databases and heads-up displays:** In the online world, you have access to database programs which track all the hands you play, keeping records of myriads of statistics on both you and your opponents and in between sessions, you can study your statistics to find leaks in your game. The main feature of

1

databases, however, is the heads-up display, or HUD, which enables you to display selected statistics on screen for both you and your opponents. By choosing the statistics carefully, you can learn and remember far more about your opponents than is possible in live games.

3. **More games and stakes:** There are many sites which offer online cash games, and the more active sites might have thousands of tables open at any one time. The stakes at a large site might range from tiny micro-stakes games with $0.01/$0.02 blinds where a full buy-in is $2 to a high-stakes $25/$50 game with a full buy-in of $5,000. You can begin playing at amazingly tiny stakes and, while risking very little, slowly work your way up the ladder.

4. **Different kinds of games:** Casinos typically spread only full ring tables with nine or ten players. From the casino's point of view, this decision makes complete sense. Floor space is expensive and limited, and dealers have to be paid, so each table should be as full as possible. In cyberspace, tables and dealers are free, so sites can spread many different variations of no-limit hold 'em. While full ring games are still popular, 6-max games (six players per table) are also common and growing in popularity. Some sites now spread 4-max games, and heads-up sessions are possible at higher stakes.

5. **Multi-tabling:** In a live casino, you can only be in one seat at a time because there's only one of you. Most online sites will let you play up to 24 tables at a time. (Whether it's wise to do so is another matter.) If you have a significant edge in the games at a given stake, multi-tabling is a way to increase your win rate.

6. **Better players at smaller stakes:** In general, online players are better than live players at similar stakes by a wide margin.

The play in a typical live $1/$2 game at a casino is roughly equivalent to the play in a $0.05/$0.10 game online. As a result, you can practice for very small stakes online and expect to do reasonably well when you graduate to a live casino game.

In this book, we're going to concentrate on the play of 6-max games. There's a simple reason for this focus. If you can play 6-max well, the transition to full ring is easy. However, the reverse isn't true. A successful full ring player can struggle for awhile in 6-max until he adapts to the increased aggression in those games. So 6-max is the right place to start for mastering online poker.

Organization of the Book

"Part One: Basic No-Limit Hold 'em Concepts" is an outline of the basic elements of no-limit hold 'em cash games. We understand that the audience for this book will range from almost complete beginners to players with considerable experience. In this section, we'll discuss a lot of basic ideas like starting hands, analyzing the flop, and estimating odds. More experienced players can skim this section while beginners will want to pay careful attention. All of the ideas outlined here will be revisited in more detail in later sections.

"Part Two: Playing Online" explains the key elements that make online poker different from live poker. We'll show how to use databases and HUDs, how to take notes, how to decide on a multi-tabling strategy, and how to select sites, tables, and seats.

"Part Three: Ranges and Distributions" shows how to estimate your opponent's range from their HUD statistics, and how to use these estimates in deciding whether to open-raise, call, or 3-bet. After the flop, his range plus the flop cards create a distribution of possible hands. We'll show how to plan your post-flop strategy based on his distribution and the actions you've seen so far.

"Part Four: Beating Micro-Stakes Games" covers games up to a blind level of about $0.10/$0.25. We'll outline two different strategies for these games: a conservative strategy that's ideal for the beginner and which will enable you to show a profit while getting your feet wet, and an aggressive strategy that more accurately exploits the weaknesses of the typical players in these games.

"Part Five: Beating Small Stakes Games" covers games with blinds ranging from $0.25/$0.50 to $1/$2. Players in these games are generally better than in the micro-stakes games, although the games are still very beatable. We'll discuss what adaptations have to be made in making the transition from micro stakes to small stakes, and how to adapt to the increased aggression you'll see at this level.

Online hold 'em has evolved its own vocabulary and nomenclature, so we've included a glossary of terms after Part Five. Look there first if we use any term that seems unfamiliar.

Part One

Basic No-Limit
Hold 'em Concepts

Basic No-Limit
Hold 'em Concepts

Introduction

There are certain basic ideas that every poker player has to understand. If you've read any of our earlier books, *Harrington on Hold 'em* or *Harrington on Cash Games*, then you've encountered these ideas already and you can move on to "Part Two: Playing Online."

If you haven't, or if you need a quick review, then "Part One: Basic No-Limit Hold 'em Concepts," is for you. We'll use these concepts explained here throughout the rest of the book, so make sure you understand them before moving on.

Some of the general ideas to be discussed, like pot odds, implied odds, and types of bets, apply to all forms of poker, not just no-limit hold 'em. And while you may have encountered many of these ideas before, their application to no-limit hold 'em might be slightly different from what you've previously seen, so don't pass over these sections too quickly. While these concepts have a mathematical basis, the mathematics are not difficult. No-limit hold 'em is about clear-headed thinking and logical reasoning, not equations.

Other ideas, like structure, hand ranges, and flop texture, are unique to no-limit hold 'em. Understanding them are crucial to playing the game well, and if they're unfamiliar to you, concentrate on these sections because what we explain in Part One provides the necessary foundation for extracting the most value from the rest of this book.

Structure:
Full Ring versus 6-Max

Online cash games come in two main forms: full ring, usually
with nine players, and 6-max, with just six players. (Heads-up,
which is spread at some sites for the higher limits, plays very
differently and we won't consider it in this book.) Given a choice,
should you play full ring or 6-max? Let's consider some of the
differences between the two games.

The first point to notice is that, in a theoretical sense, 6-max
is simply a full ring game in which the first three players have
folded. If this isn't clear, imagine that you're in a full ring game,
sitting in the fourth seat at the table, and the players in seats one
through three all fold. Is your situation in any way different from
sitting at a 6-max table with the same players and stacks and being
first to act? Clearly, the answer is no. The blinds are identical, the
same number of players remain to act behind you, and all the
players have the same stacks. Nothing has changed except that
three players no longer in the hand have elected to throw their
hands away.

One could argue that since three players elected to fold rather
than play, those hands were likely to have held small cards and
therefore the remaining deck should be richer in high cards,
making strong hands more likely. But even this argument is very
weak. Suppose, for instance, the first player elected to fold ace-
ten, the second player folded ace-four, and the third player folded
king-six. These are all standard plays in a full ring game, but the
effect is to remove three-eights of the aces and kings from the
deck. Rather than being heavy with high cards, the remaining deck
is in fact quite weak! Since starting requirements are so high in
early position in a full ring, most hands containing high cards
won't, in fact, qualify as opening hands and will be folded.

7

Therefore, what's known as the *card removal effect* is in this case very small.

Although there might not be any theoretical difference between 6-max games and that subset of full ring games where the first three players have folded, that doesn't mean that the games have a similar feel. In fact, they play quite differently for some very good reasons.

Reason No. 1: Players have wider ranges in 6-max. A *range* is simply the set of hands that you choose to play in a given situation. If you're under the gun at a full ring table, your opening range is probably narrow. Many players might choose to open only 5 to 7 percent of their hands in this situation. Why so few? The reason is simple. When you open the betting, you'd like there to be a good chance that your hand is actually the best hand at the table.

With eight players to act behind you, what's the chance that a hand that's better than 95 percent of all hands but worse than 5 percent is actually the best hand at the table? In order for your hand to be the best, each of the eight players still to act needs to have a hand drawn from the group of inferior hands. For one player, that chance is 0.95. For two players, the chance is about 90 percent.

$$0.9025 = (0.95)(0.95)$$

For eight players, the chance is about 66 percent.

$$0.6634 = (0.95)^8$$

So opening a top-5 percent range under the gun makes you a solid favorite to have the best hand at the table. (Hands like a pair of nines or eights, ace-jack suited, or any better hand, fit this category.)

If you're willing to open a top-10 percent hand, however, the odds aren't quite as favorable. Now the chance that you actually hold the best hand is about 43 percent.

$$0.4305 = (0.90)^8$$

So if you open with a hand that's at the bottom of a top-10 percent range, (say a hand like ace-nine suited or queen-ten suited) you're actually an underdog to be holding the best hand at the table.

As more players fold in front of you, the card strength required to have the best hand at the table steadily drops, so you can open more and with weaker hands. By the time everyone folds to the small blind, a hand of exactly average strength, say queen-seven offsuit, is even money to be better than whatever hand the big blind may have.

In full ring games, players who open in early position are marked with narrow ranges and pretty strong hands. As a result, most players are going to be reluctant to call, even in position, without reasonably strong hands themselves. The result is a tight game.

In 6-max, however, the under the gun player faces only five opponents and thus has a much wider opening range. This in turn allows players to call his bets with a wider range of hands. In addition, a wider opening range permits players acting behind to reraise with a wider range of hands, or even bluff with a reraise, hoping the opener had a marginal opening hand and will fold. (This reraise is also known as a 3-bet.) As a result of the wider opening ranges, the game generates much more action, which in turn calls for better decision-making, which puts more pressure on weaker players.

Shouldn't full ring tables exhibit the same level of action and aggression in that subset of hands where the first three players fold? They should because theoretically the situations are identical. But in practice they don't, except in the highest-level games. Most full ring players become used to a slower, tighter game, and don't adjust properly when the first few players fold, or when the table becomes short-handed.

Reason No. 2: Multi-tabling is more difficult in 6-max. When you play online, you're not restricted to playing a single table. You're free to sit down at many tables if you wish, a practice known as *multi-tabling*. Since full ring hands take longer to play than 6-max hands, a multi-tabler can comfortably play more full ring tables simultaneously than 6-max tables. Someone who can manage eight full ring tables with relative ease might want to restrict themselves to five or six 6-max tables.

Reason No. 3: The blinds are at less disadvantage in 6-max. In a full ring game, the blinds lose money, while the other seven positions have a net positive expectation since they are never required to put money into any pot. In a 6-max game, the same general relationship is true: the blinds lose money, while the other positions make money.

However, in a 6-max game the blinds lose less money than at full ring. The reason is simple: Any particular hand in the blinds is in a relatively better position at 6-max since there is less likelihood that a stronger hand is out against them. But in order to demonstrate this, the blinds must be more active with the hands they have. This leads to the final point, namely

Reason No. 4: There is more skill in 6-max. A tight, somewhat mechanical style (also known as *ABC poker*) can survive and even show a decent profit in a full ring game unless the opponents are quite good. Six-max games, however, require much more skill because of the heightened levels of action and aggression, and a simple tight style won't do nearly as well.

Now we come to the real question: If you aspire to be a successful online player, should you play 6-max or full ring?

We've explained why 6-max requires more skill than full ring, but does this mean you should just run out and play 6-max poker? Not really. The problem is that although 6-max requires more skill, skillful players generally gravitate to 6-max, making the games tougher. The net result is close to a wash.

If you're a skilled player at a given level, you should probably show about the same level of profit playing full ring as playing 6-max. (But your results will show a higher level of variance at 6-max than at full ring because the wider hand ranges will result in more all-in showdowns.)

So if you want to be a good player, concentrate on 6-max first. Once you've mastered these games, you can then decide which of the two forms you prefer. Even if you eventually decide to play full ring, your skill at 6-max will prove to be a huge benefit since full ring games often don't fill all the seats. As players come and go, the table may have long periods of time when the play is in fact seven- or six-handed. At these times, the experienced 6-max player has a solid edge over the solely full ring players who often aren't able to adapt to the increased aggressiveness and action of shorter tables.

Seat Names

In this book, we'll use certain conventions for naming seats in both full ring and 6-max games. We'll list them here in the order of action preflop.

Full Ring Game

Seat	Name
UTG	Under the Gun
UTG + 1	
MP	Middle Position
MP + 1	
HJ	Hijack
CO	Cutoff
BTN	Button
SB	Small Blind
BB	Big Blind

6-Max Game

Seat	Name
UTG	Under the Gun
MP	Middle Position
CO	Cutoff
BTN	Button
SB	Small Blind
BB	Big Blind

The 6-max names are the same as the full ring names except that three positions have been dropped: UTG+1, MP+1, and Hijack. Throughout the book, we'll refer to seating positions using the names given here.

Style: Tight and Loose, Aggressive and Passive

In general, we like to classify poker players along two axes: tight versus loose, and aggressive versus passive. Since these terms are used constantly, let's make sure we know exactly what we mean.

Tight and loose refer to how many hands a player is willing to play before the flop. A tight player will play a relatively narrow range of starting hands. He wants solid values before entering a pot. A loose player, on the other hand, will play a wider range of starting hands, sometimes much wider. Loose players like playing pots and seeing flops, and are willing to play more speculative hands in order to do so.

Aggressive and passive describe how a player will play a hand once he's entered a pot. An aggressive player likes to bet and raise. He's always putting pressure on his opponents, trying to force them out of the pot. A passive player is more likely to check and call. Passive players don't like creating a big pot unless they're relatively sure they have the best hand. On the other hand, they don't like getting bluffed if they have something, so they'll often stick around with medium values or if they hit the flop in some way.

With these two axes, we can create four broad categories of players as follows:

1. Tight & Aggressive
2. Tight & Passive
3. Loose & Aggressive
4. Loose & Passive

The tight-aggressive player plays only good hands and will bet and raise with them. When he's attacking a pot, he usually has something.

The tight-passive player likewise plays only good hands, but will only raise with real monsters since he doesn't like losing money. Because he's rarely involved and easy to read, it's hard to lose a lot of money to a tight-passive player.

Loose-aggressive players are dangerous. They play a lot of hands, see a lot of flops, and are always attacking with their bets and raises. When they do hit a monster, it's frequently well concealed and will often get paid off. A loose-aggressive player who is also a good hand reader and skilled at extracting himself from dangerous situations will often be the biggest winner at the table.

Loose-passive players also play lots of hands but only bet and raise with their best ones. They like being involved and, when they hit a flop, like to hang around and see if their hand is good. They become easy targets because it's so easy to extract value when they hit a hand and you have a better one.

You can be a winner with either a tight style or a loose style. However, it's hard to be a winner with a passive style. A passive player only has one way to win a hand: He has to get to showdown and then show the best hand. An aggressive player has two ways to win: He can win by pushing his opponent out of the pot at some earlier stage, or he can win at showdown. Since most players don't have huge hands most of the time, winning by chasing your opponent out of the pot is a real option in most hands.

Passivity has another significant drawback. When you play passively, you allow your opponents to see more cards for free. If you're ahead in the hand but you check, your opponent may check as well and then catch a free card that beats you. Had you bet, you might have forced him to fold, thus protecting your hand. Passive players tend to win fewer pots than aggressive players, and their wins tend to be smaller. That's why most successful players play some version of an aggressive style.

Straightforward Players and Tricky Players

In addition to aggressive and passive, we can also categorize players by just how straightforwardly they play their hands. A straightforward player, also known as an *ABC player*, likes to play according to the strength of his hand. When he is strong, he bets and raises. When he is weak, he checks, and perhaps calls a bet. With a very weak hand, he'll check and fold to a bet.

An ABC player is easy to play against since he's usually telling you by his actions just what sort of hand he has. Nonetheless, this style of play can be successful in low-level games because many loose-passive players will ignore the signals, stick around with weak hands, and lose a lot of money. Since the ABC player is constantly betting his good hands and getting paid, he can show a nice profit. In higher-level games, ABC players are vulnerable because their more alert opponents observe what they're doing and react to it.

The other side of the coin is the tricky or 'opposite' player. The opposite player delights in fooling his opponents. He checks and calls when he has a monster hand, and bets when he has nothing. He loves the thrill of revealing his big hand on the river, or stealing a pot with a well-timed bluff.

In micro-stakes games, this approach is mostly a waste of money. Your weak opponents will be happy to pay off when they have a hand and you have a better one, so give them every opportunity to do so. As you move up to higher-stakes games, your opponents won't be so generous. Now you'll have to mix some opposite plays with straightforward ones so you can't be easily read. Remember, however, that when you fail to bet a big hand, you are in effect charging yourself in order to be unreadable, and the idea is to charge yourself no more than is necessary to accomplish this goal.

Ranges

Before we proceed any further, we need to expand on the idea of a range. As we said earlier, a range is just the set of hands with which a player might take a particular action. Suppose, for instance, that you're sitting at a 6-max table and you're under the gun. If you don't know much about your opponents, there's probably a set of hands with which you're comfortable opening for a raise. Let's say that set consists of any pair, plus ace-king and ace-queen, suited or unsuited. That's a very tight but perfectly good range for this situation. If you pick up one of those hands, you'll raise. Otherwise, you're going to fold.

To describe specific ranges in this book, we'll use a shorthand notation which has become commonplace throughout the poker world. Here's how it works.

To describe an individual hand, we'll use the letters A, K, Q, J, and T for the ranks aces through tens. We use the numbers 9 through 2 for the lower ranks.

We'll describe a range of pairs by using the top and bottom pairs in the range, or just the bottom pair with a '+' sign if the range extends to aces. For example, a range of aces through fives would appear as either

'AA through 55' or '55+'

However, a range of jacks through sixes would only appear as

'JJ through 66'

We'll describe non-paired hands in a similar way. We'll use the letters 's' and 'o' for 'suited' and 'offsuit.' A range consisting of all the suited aces would be written as either

'AKs through A2s' or 'A2s+'

Notice that 'A2s+' means all the hands of this specific type (suited aces), up to the highest possible example of the type (AKs). Likewise, a range of offsuit aces from ace-nine or higher would appear as

'AKo through A9o' or 'A9o+'

Broadway cards are non-paired hands with both cards ranked between a ten and a king. 'All the suited Broadways' would refer to this range:

'KQs through KTs, QJs, QTs, JTs'

It's also worth noting that there are 1,326 ways to be dealt a two-card hold 'em hand. Any pair can be dealt in six ways, and any non-pair can be dealt in 16 ways, four of which are suited and 12 of which are offsuit.

The range notation enables us to quickly and easily describe any set of hands we want.

Position

Position simply refers to the order in which players act in the hand. You have position on your opponent if you act after him. He has position if he acts after you.

Fundamentally, poker is a game of information. The more information you have about an opponent, the more closely you can estimate his hand, and the better your subsequent decisions will be. When you have position on your opponent, he must act before you, thereby giving you information. With position, you will win more pots, and on average the pots you win will be bigger. Without position, you win fewer pots, and the pots are smaller.

In no-limit hold 'em, you want to have position on your opponents when you play a hand. If you're not going to have position later in the hand, you need some compensating advantage. That's why starting hand requirements are higher for early position than for later position. If you raise in early position and get called, you're likely to be out of position for the rest of the hand, so you need better cards to balance your positional disadvantage. If instead you're on the button and everyone in an earlier position folds, you can open a wide array of holdings because you'll have position if the hand is played out.

Without position, every phase of poker is more difficult.

- It's harder to extract money with your strong hands because you have to announce your strength first, and your opponent makes his decision with that knowledge.

- Draws are harder to play because in order to get a free card, you first have to check and reveal weakness. Betting instead of checking, however, puts money in the pot when you may be the underdog, and allows the possibility of being raised off the hand.

- Bluffing is more difficult because you have to bluff before your opponent has had a chance to check and show weakness.

As much as possible, you want to play hands in position.

The Four
Basic Principles
of No-Limit Hold 'em

While there are lots of rules and generalizations for playing good poker, there are four simple rules that are more important than all the others. I call them the four basic principles. Once you understand these ideas, your game will be on a sound basis. We'll see these principles recur over and over as we explain other concepts and problems, but we'll state them here in their purest form.

No. 1: The Strength Principle

> In general, you want to bet your strong hands, check or call with your hands of middling strength, and fold or bluff with your weak hands.

The idea that you'd want to bet your strong hands should be fairly obvious. These are your most profitable hands, so it's important to get money into the pot.

Checking rather than betting with your middle strength hands is less obvious, but here's the main reason. A middle strength hand has value and could win the pot if you can get it to showdown. If you bet with one of these hands and your opponent folds a weak hand, you haven't actually gained much since you would have beaten that hand anyway. But if you bet and you're raised, you're going to fold, and you may have had to lay down a hand that could have won at showdown.

Folding most of your weak hands is clear. Choosing some of these hands as your bluffs is less clear until you look at the alternative. If you bluff with a worthless hand and get raised, you can fold at no extra cost. If you bluff instead with a hand with some value and get raised, you'll still throw it away, but now you've had to discard a hand that might have won at showdown.

No. 2: The Aggression Principle

> In general, aggression (betting and raising) is better than passivity (checking and calling).

When you play passively, you are in essence trying to get to showdown. Playing passively gives you only one way to win: having the best hand at showdown.

Playing aggressively, on the other hand, gives you two ways to win: You can push your opponent out of the pot at some point when he refuses to call your bet, or you can win at showdown. Having two ways to win is better than having one way, so in general, aggressive play wins more pots.

We refer to the value we gain when we make our opponent give up as *folding equity*. All bets, even small ones, will have some folding equity, but checks and calls have none.

No. 3: The Betting Principle

> In general, a good bet should do one of three things:
>
> 1. Force a better hand to fold.
>
> 2. Force a weaker hand to call.
>
> 3. Force drawing hands to put more money in the pot to see another card.

Although aggression is good, your bets still need to be made with some purpose in mind. A bet which forces a better hand to fold will win a pot that otherwise would probably have been lost. A bet which makes a weaker hand call builds a pot which you're favored to win. If your opponent has a drawing hand, you don't want to let him have another card for free; betting charges him to see that card.

Situations arise frequently on the turn and river where you have a hand that may be best, but the board is dangerous enough so that weaker hands than yours will certainly fold to your bet, while better hands will call or raise. In that case, betting usually isn't profitable, and your goal is to reach showdown as cheaply as possible.

No. 4: The Deception Principle

> In general, you never want to do anything all of the time.

To win at poker, you can't allow your opponents to be sure about what you have. Playing in a rigid style allows them to get a clear line on your strategy, so you need to make an effort to vary your play making your hands more difficult to read.

The better your opponents, the more important this principle becomes. In weak games where they aren't paying attention, playing in a straightforward manner may actually be close to optimal.

Opening Hand Ranges

You're playing at a 6-max table and you're sitting under the gun. With what hands are you happy opening the pot for a raise?

First, let's note that there is no simple answer to this question. What hands you're willing to play should be a function of your own style, how you perceive the other players at the table, and, perhaps more important, how they perceive you. While you might have a certain default set of hands that you're comfortable opening under the gun, you need to be prepared to widen or narrow that set depending on what you've seen so far in your session. Let's start by taking a look at a typical hand range for both a tight player and a somewhat looser player, and then see how these players should adjust their range depending on circumstances.

A moderately tight player sitting under the gun might choose to open with only about 10 percent of his hands. Here's one such collection of starting hands, which we'll call Range No. 1:

> All pairs: AA through 22
> Suited aces: AKs through ATs
> Unsuited aces: AKo through AJo
> KQs

This isn't the only possible collection of top-10 percent hands. Here's Range No. 2, a slightly different one:

> Pairs from AA through 66
> Suited aces: AKs through A9s
> Unsuited aces: AKo through AJo
> Suited kings: KQs through KTs
> QJs, QTs, and JTs

These two sets have almost the same number of hands, but they play somewhat differently. The first set, which includes all pairs, has the advantage that it can make a credible threat on any kind of flop since it has the ability to flop a set no matter what cards are showing. It's also a hand range which is a little easier to play for beginners because its high card hands will usually make top pair or nothing at all, instead of middle pair hands whose play requires more judgment.

The second set eliminates the low pair hands and replaces them with suited Broadway cards like KJs and QTs. This group creates fewer sets on the flop, but more strong drawing hands, as well as a lot of top pair and middle pair hands. However, the presence of more drawing hands requires more post-flop skill than the first group.

A somewhat looser player might open with a wider range of hands under the gun. Here's an example of a range that might suit such a player, comprising about 17 percent of all hands (Range No. 3):

All pairs
Suited aces: AKs through A8s
Unsuited aces: AKo through ATo
All suited Broadways: KQs, KJs, KTs, QJs, QTs, and JTs
Offsuit Broadways: KQo, KJo, QJo, and JTo
Suited connectors: T9s, 98s, 87s

Which of these three hand ranges is "correct" for opening under the gun?

A key concept in poker is that there are often no correct answers to certain kinds of questions. Under the right circumstances, any of these hand ranges (and others as well) could be considered "correct" in the sense that they might be the best hand range for a certain type of player at a certain type of table. Instead of trying to label one range as best, what we want to do is describe situations where one range is better than others.

For example, if you were a beginner at a micro-stakes table, just getting started with no-limit hold 'em cash games, we'd certainly recommend using Range No. 1. Compared to the other ranges, it has the great advantage of getting you involved in fewer hands and being much easier to play after the flop. When the flop appears, you'll either have a very strong hand, like an overpair, top pair with a strong kicker, or a set, or you'll have nothing at all. Those are relatively easy situations for a beginner to play.

Range No. 3, on the other hand, contains a lot more hands like lower Broadway cards (king-jack offsuit) and suited connectors. When you play these hands, you'll find yourself with more middle pairs and drawing hands after the flop. Handling these situations correctly requires much more experience and seasoned judgment, qualities not found in most beginners. This is a range for a player who's confident in his post-flop play.

In general, you should open with narrow, relatively strong ranges if you

1. Are a beginner, or
2. Lack confidence in your post-flop play.

If you have confidence in your ability relative to your table, you can favor looser, somewhat more speculative opening ranges.

Your range should also be affected by the table where you're playing. If you've played long enough to see that the other players tend to be tight, you should loosen your opening ranges. The blinds will be easier to steal, the other players will be less likely to reraise you preflop, and you'll encounter less resistance post-flop. If the other players at the table are loose preflop, the opposite advice applies. Play tighter ranges, and try to enter fewer pots but with stronger hands.

Finally, you can adjust your range if the other players seem to be reacting to your current approach. If you've been loose and the other players now seem eager to play pots with you, tighten up. If you've been tight and your opponents are quick to fold to an opening raise, loosen up.

Opening from Later Positions

As you move around the table from under the gun to middle position, the cutoff seat, and the button, you can open raise with wider and wider hand ranges. The reason is twofold:

1. There are fewer players left to act behind you, so there's a better chance that no one has a hand they want to play.

2. There's a better chance that you will have position on any opponent after the flop.

When you open under the gun, for instance, there are five players left to act who might have a hand they want to play. Of those five, three would have position on you after the flop (everyone but the two blinds). But if you open from the cutoff seat, only three players remain to act, and only one of them (the button) can have position on you later in the hand.

While there are no exact rules for widening your ranges, a tight player who opens 10 percent of the time under the gun with Range No. 1 might reasonably expand his range like this:

1. Open 15 percent of his hands from middle position.

2. Open 22 percent of his hands from the cutoff seat.

3. Open 30 percent of his hands from the button.

Let's recall that Range No. 1 consisted of all pairs, suited aces down to ATs, unsuited aces down to AJo, and suited KQ. Here's how he might add hands to create these new, wider ranges:

- To open 15 percent from middle position, add to Range No. 1

  > Suited Broadway cards: KJs, KTs, QJs, QTs, JTs
  > Suited aces: A9s, A8s
  > Offsuit aces: ATo
  > Suited connectors: T9s, 98s
  > Offsuit Broadways: KQo, KJo

- To open 22 percent from the cutoff seat, add to the 15 percent range

  > Suited aces: A7s, A6s, A5s
  > Offsuit Broadways: KTo, QJo, QTo, JTo
  > Suited connectors: 87s, 76s
  > Offsuit aces: A9o, A8o

- To open 30 percent from the button, add to the 22 percent range

  > Suited aces: A4s, A3s, A2s
  > Offsuit aces: A7o through A2o
  > Suited kings: K9s, K8s, K7s
  > Q9s

Opening from the small blind is a little different because although only one player is left to act (the big blind), but he'll have position on you. In this case, you can begin by opening with your button range, but if he calls frequently and uses his position well, consider changing to your cutoff range.

As before, these suggested ranges are for players using a tight style. If you're more comfortable with a looser style, start with the 17 percent range under the gun and increase your hand ranges proportionately.

Bet Sizing for Opening Raises

Let's say you're sitting under the gun in a $1/$2 6-max online game and you pick up a pair of queens. You decide, quite reasonably, that you'll open for a raise. How big should your raise be?

As with the question of opening ranges, there is no single "correct" answer. There are a number of possible raise sizes, any of which could be optimal depending on circumstances. Let's take a look at some different raise sizes and consider their merits and demerits.

1. **A min-raise:** The minimum amount you can raise is to twice the size of the big blind. In our example, that's a raise to $4.

2. **A big raise:** Since it's no-limit hold 'em, you're free to raise to any amount you want. A raise to 5 or 6 big blinds, or $10 to $12 in this case, would be considered a big opening raise.

3. **Standard raise:** The most common raise sizes are to either 3 or 3.5 big blinds. In the case of our game with a $1 small blind and a $2 big blind, a standard raise would be to either $6 or $7.

A raise to $7 is what's known as a *pot-sized raise*. To make a pot-sized raise, first put in enough money to call any existing bet, then add an amount equal to the size of the new pot. In this case, we would have to put in $2 to call the current raise from the big blind, which creates a new pot of $5. Then we would add another $5 to make our raise. The result is a total pot-sized raise of $7.

What's special about a pot-sized raise? In general, a pot-sized raise has two advantages:

1. It's large enough to deny your opponents great calling odds with speculative hands.

2. It's small enough to allow hands of moderate strength to play against you.

These are good reasons, and in no-limit hold 'em, most raises are to the size of the pot or a little less. Let's look at an example and see why this is so.

Example: You're under the gun in an online $1/$2 6-max game. You pick up the

Let's look at what happens with each of three possible raise sizes: a min-raise to $4; a big raise to $10; a pot-sized raise to $7.

The min-raise to $4 creates a $7 pot. Any of the three players sitting behind you can call and enter the pot with position for $4, getting 7-to-4 or 1.75-to-1 odds. The blinds are doing even better, with the big blind getting 3.5-to-1 odds to call. For most hands, those are good odds. A hand like the 8♥7♥, for example, is only a 1.5-to-1 underdog to your hand, while even a completely trash hand like the J♦2♣ is only a 2.3-to-1 underdog. In effect, you've given every reasonable hand the correct odds to call your bet.

The big raise to $10 (five big blinds) eliminates the previous problem but creates a new one. By making such a big raise, you ensure that only good hands will bother to call. You've made yourself a favorite to take down the blinds, but at the cost of probably being either an underdog or just a small favorite whenever you do get called.

The pot-sized raise to $7 creates a nice balance. You're raising enough to deny great odds to all the speculative hands, while not raising so much that all the weaker hands run away.

Varying
Your Raise Sizes

There's nothing wrong with using a constant raise size for all your opening raises. Raising to three or 3.5 big blinds each time you open has the merit of preventing your opponents from getting any possible information from your raise size. That's not terribly important in weak games where your opponents aren't paying much attention. But as you move up the ladder, denying your opponents any information becomes more and more important.

However, there is a reasonable argument to be made for varying your raise size by position. In early position, you tend to have strong hands but you'll often be out of position if called. Both these points favor making bigger raises, partly to discourage players from entering in position, and partly to create bigger pots with better hands. In late position, you tend to have weaker hands but you'll usually be in position when you're called. Both these points favor making smaller raises.

You could combine both these ideas by adopting a different opening raise size for each position at the table. Here's a chart that shows how this approach might work:

Under the gun	Open raise to 4 big blinds
Middle position	Open raise to 3.5 big blinds
Cutoff seat	Open raise to 3 big blinds
Button	Open raise to 2.5 big blinds

Preflop Limping

When everyone has folded to you and it's your turn to act, you have a choice: You can raise, as we described in the previous section, or you can just call the big blind. Calling in this way is better known as limping, and by limping, you enter the pot for the minimum amount of money possible. Usually, players who limp do so because they have a somewhat weak hand, like a small pair or suited connectors; they'd like to see a flop, but they don't think their hand is strong enough to raise. Limping is commonplace in games at low stakes; it becomes less and less common as one moves up the levels to higher stakes.

The best advice concerning limping is — don't do it. If no one has entered the pot, and you have a hand you want to play, just raise. If you raise every time you have a playable hand, you'll win more pots when your opponents don't have anything, and you'll project strength when you get called and actually see a flop. Your opponents won't be able to tell when you have a premium hand and when you're raising with something like a suited connector; you'll be harder to read and a more dangerous player.

Raising with strong hands and limping with weaker ones makes you exploitable. Your opponents who have position behind you can raise your limps, a move known as the *isolation raise*. You'll then have to make a bad choice between folding your weak hand (thereby wasting your call) or calling their raise, in which case you'll be out of position with a weak hand, having put as much money in the pot as if you'd raised to start.

Limping isn't an absurd play for very good players who can employ it occasionally as part of a balanced strategy involving some speculative hands and some strong ones. If you're not in this category, simplify your game and minimize possible mistakes by raising when you enter the pot.

3- and 4-Betting Preflop

If an opponent open-raises in front of us and we have a hand worth playing, we have two choices: call or reraise. Under what circumstances is reraising best?

First, we need to learn some terminology. In no-limit hold 'em, the initial reraise is known as a *3-bet*. This label may seem odd at first, but it's based on the idea that the big blind has already raised the small blind (the *1-bet*), and then the opener raised the big blind (the *2-bet*). The first real reraise thus becomes the 3-bet, and a subsequent reraise would be a *4-bet*. It's a handy terminology because it lets us see just where each reraise fits into the betting order.

Example: In a $100 NL game with each player having a full stack of $100, the blinds are $0.50 and $1.00. The under the gun player open-raises to $3.50. The players in middle position and the cutoff seat fold, but the button 3-bets to $11 making the pot $16. The blinds both fold and the under the gun player now 4-bets to $35 making the pot $47.50. The button can now fold, call, or 5-bet. Given the stack sizes, however, a 5-bet from the button will almost certainly be an all-in push. In games where most players have 100 big blinds, a 5-bet is usually an all-in bet. In games with very deep stacks, like 200 or 300 big blinds, a 5-bet would probably not be an all-in move.

In the early years of no-limit hold 'em where players were mostly tight and an opening raise often signaled a strong hand, 3-bets usually meant an extremely strong hand, while 4-bets and higher often meant a pair of kings or aces. When online no-limit play got started, a lot of players who were looking for action would open with a relatively wide range of hands. However, when they were 3-bet, they tended to tighten up and call or 4-bet only with their best hands, an approach that created a highly exploitable situation.

For example, suppose you're on the button in a 6-max game and the action is folded to the player in the cutoff seat who raises to three big blinds. From observation, you're pretty sure he'll raise in this situation with about 20 percent of his hands. You're also pretty sure that if you 3-bet, he'll call or 4-bet with only about 4 percent of his starting hands (roughly AA through TT, and AK and AQ, suited or not.) You can 3-bet him with any two cards! He'll fold 75 percent of the time, and even if you lose every hand where he doesn't fold, you'll make a profit. (We're assuming the blinds will fold behind you, which is mostly true.) Assuming your 3-bet is to nine big blinds, the calculation looks like this:

- You win 4.5 big blinds 75 percent of the time, for a profit of 3.375 big blinds.

$$3.375 = (0.75)(4.5)$$

- You lose your 3-bet 25 percent of the time, for a loss of 2.25 big blinds.

$$2.25 = (0.25)(-9)$$

On average, you win 1.125 big blinds every time you make this move.

$$1.125 = 3.375 - 2.25$$

This insight led to a new approach to reraising, known as *'light 3-betting.'* The idea was to exploit most players' tendencies to play only premium hands when 3-bet by raising with hands like suited connectors, small pairs, and medium Broadway cards, pocketing a solid profit when the opponent folded, while exploiting the disguised nature of the hand after the flop.

Light 3-betting was soon followed by light 4-betting, which tried to exploit the strategy of light 3-betting by carrying the trend one step further. At first these aggressive strategies were tried mostly in the high-stakes 6-max games, but they gradually filtered down to the mid-stakes games over a period of a few years. Today you can see this approach just starting to inch into the micro-stakes world.

The proper handling of 3- and 4-betting preflop is highly dependent on the stakes you're playing and the kinds of opponents you're likely to meet. Light 3-betting is not hard to counter, but it requires a well thought-out open raising strategy. We'll have much more to say about these in the sections on beating the micro-stakes and small stakes games.

Flop:
Heads-Up or Multiway

Once the preflop betting is finished, the flop is dealt. At this point, you have most of the information needed to evaluate your hand.

Play on the flop depends heavily on the number of players left in the hand. When there are just two players, you have what's called a heads-up flop. More players constitute a multiway flop and they are more common in full ring games because of the larger number of players. In 6-max, most contested flops are heads-up.

Heads-up pots give more scope for creative play because of the greater likelihood that both players have missed the flop. When multiway, there's a greater chance that someone has connected strongly with the flop and now has a good hand. Let's quickly consider each case and see how the number of players affect the play.

Heads-Up on the Flop

When you're heads-up on the flop, your play will be governed by several key factors. Let's look at them one at a time and see how they affect your strategy.

Aggressor: Whoever made the last (or only) raise preflop is considered to be the aggressor. He announced that he had the better hand preflop, and unless his opponent connected with the flop in some way, he probably has the better hand post-flop. If you were the aggressor, you will mostly be betting on the flop. If your opponent was the aggressor, he will mostly be betting the flop and you'll need to decide if your hand is worth playing.

Position: If you act after your opponent you have position. That's almost always advantageous in poker because you get to see his action before you have to respond. If he tries to mislead you, perhaps by checking a strong hand, he has to pay a price. You may elect to check behind, thereby getting a free card. Having position in the hand gives you an extra incentive to continue play beyond the flop where positional advantage may give you an indication that your opponent is willing to give up on the hand.

Hand Strength: Much of your post-flop play is predicated on your hand strength. Let's take a look at hands of different strength and see how they should be handled.

1. **Monster hands (quads, full houses, flushes, and straights):** These hands are almost certainly best now and will most likely be best at showdown. The only disadvantage of these hands is that you may not be able to get much action because a flop that connected with your hand this strongly may not have connected with your opponent at all. These hands are well-suited for playing big pots, but your opponent may not cooperate.

2. **Very strong hands (sets, two pair):** These hands are likely to win and are worth betting on the flop and usually the turn as well. They can run into trouble later in the hand if a draw connects, but in the long run they should win a lot of money.

3. **Strong hands (overpairs and top pairs):** These are your workhorse hands. They're certainly worth a bet on the flop, and may win the pot at that point. For variety, you may elect to check the flop and bet the turn. These hands, however, require a certain amount of caution. If you're betting and your opponent sticks around, it's often because he

A. Can beat these hands
B. Is drawing to a really big hand, or
C. Plans to bluff you off your hand later.

Overpairs and top pairs are mostly good on the flop, but if you get to the river and haven't improved, and a lot of money is going in the pot, you're probably beaten.

4. **Medium hands (pairs below top pair):** These are hands which may be best on the flop, but which are very vulnerable as the hand goes on and overcards appear on the board. Your main goal with a medium pair is to get to showdown cheaply and see if it's best. Medium pairs play well against passive opponents, but much less so against active opponents.

5. **Drawing hands (flush and straight draws, plus combination draws):** Playing these hands well is crucial in no-limit hold 'em because they have the capability of winning your opponent's entire stack when he has a strong hand and your draw connects. In general, you'll have the odds to call a bet on the flop, but if you don't connect there, you may not have the odds to call on the turn.

6. **Nothing hands (no pair, no draw):** Your bluffing hands will come from this group. When you play well, you'll be able to win some of these hands, especially when your opponent has nothing.

Multiway on the Flop

The nature of flop play changes dramatically when you face multiple opponents. Because more players are involved, hands at showdown will tend to be stronger than in a heads-up pot. The likelihood that you'll be facing stronger hands at showdown in turn affects how you play each type of hand on the flop.

Here's a quick summary of the changes you'll need to make in a multiway pot.

1. **With a very strong hand, almost never slowplay.** When you have a strong hand in a multiway pot, there's a better chance that someone at the table has a drawing hand, or at least a hand that can call a bet. If someone can call, you certainly want to bet.

2. **With a strong or medium strength hand, you need a stronger hand than usual to bet.** Hands like top pair, top kicker drop in value both because there is a better chance that someone already has a stronger hand, and because there is a better chance that someone else will improve to a stronger hand by showdown. You will still mostly bet a top pair, top kicker type hand, but you'll need to be extra careful when you encounter resistance. With hands weaker than top pair, top kicker you should be checking more often in a heads-up situation.

3. **With a drawing hand, you can accept smaller odds than usual to draw.** With several opponents, there's a better chance that someone will have a hand that can call when you make your draw. So be inclined to call even if the expressed odds appear a little short.

4. **If you're planning a bluff, circumstances must be better than usual to justify your move.** Even though the pot is larger, the probability of the bluff being successful, due to the fact that more players are involved than heads-up, has most likely gone down more than the pot has grown. Therefore, be less inclined to bet a weak hand as a bluff than you would if the pot was heads-up.

Since more players create an incentive to bet big hands rather than slowplay, and an incentive to check or fold rather than bluff, we can summarize multiway play with a simple rule:

> The likelihood that a player's betting action represents his true strength is directly proportional to the number of players in the pot.

Types of Bets on the Flop

There are many different types of bets on the flop. We might have a strong hand and want to get more money in the pot as soon as possible. We might have a weak hand, but think the flop missed our opponent and we can take it down with a well-timed bluff. We may want to bet because we took the lead preflop and don't want to show weakness. All of these are valid reasons for betting the flop. In addition, there are some good reasons for *not* betting the flop which we need to consider.

Flop bets fall into a number of different groups. Let's look at each type and see when and why we might want to make that kind of bet.

Value Bets

The simplest kind of flop bet is the *value bet*. After the flop comes, you think your hand is probably best. Usually this will be top pair or better. You bet, both to get more money in the pot and to discourage your opponents from drawing to beat you. If someone calls, you've built a pot with what is presumably the best hand. If everyone folds, you've won.

Example: You're under the gun in a $1/$2 6-max game with the

You raise to $6 and get called by both the button and the big blind, creating a $19 pot. The flop is the

You have top pair with a good kicker. The big blind checks and it's your turn to act. You have a strong hand and right now have no reason to think anyone has a better one, so you make a value bet of $14. The button folds and the big blind calls, making the pot $47.

Your value bet accomplished three goals: You built the pot with what is probably the best hand right now, one opponent was eliminated, and you gained position on the last opponent for the rest of the hand. Your opponent's call probably means one of four things:

1.   He has a better hand than you but he called rather than raised to set a trap later in the hand.

2.   He has a pair worse than yours, but he's not sure you actually have anything.

3.   He has two hearts and is drawing to make a heart flush.

4.   He has nothing but he has decided to *float;* he's planning on taking the pot away with a bluff later.

The rest of the hand doesn't concern us right now. How the hand actually plays out depends on the turn and river cards and the skill of the players.

Bluffs

If you take the lead preflop but the flop doesn't help, you can elect to bluff. Flop bluffs are particularly effective if the flop might have helped a lot of the hands you would have raised preflop. Here's a typical case.

Example: You're in the same $1/$2 6-max game as before and pick up the T♥9♥ in middle position. The under the gun player folds and you raise to $7. The cutoff and the button fold. The small blind calls and the big blind folds. The pot becomes $16.

The flop is the A♥J♠4♣. The small blind checks. Although you missed the flop and there are two overcards to your hand, many of the hands with which you might have raised preflop contain an ace, and your opponent might easily believe this flop hit you. You bet $11 and the small blind folds.

Semi-Bluffs

A semi-bluff is a bet (or raise) on the flop or turn with a drawing hand which is usually not best now but which has outs to become the best hand. The combination of your opponent folding immediately plus the chance of improving to the best hand makes the semi-bluff profitable.

Example: In our $1/$2 6-max game, you have 8♥7♥ under the gun and raise to $7. The button calls and the blinds fold, so the pot is $17. The flop comes Q♥J♥4♣. You check. The button bets $10 and you raise to $30. Currently you only have eight-high which is probably not the best hand (although it might be). However, any of the nine remaining hearts give you a flush, and any of the six remaining eights or sevens will give you a pair which might possibly be the best hand. Your raise may win the hand outright, and if it doesn't, you may still make the best hand. Semi-bluffs differ from true bluffs by having outs to a winning hand, whereas a true bluff usually has no outs or very little chance to improve to the best hand.

Continuation Bets

A *continuation bet* is a bet on the flop by the preflop aggressor. You raise preflop, get a caller, the flop comes, and now you bet again. A continuation bet puts a lot of pressure on the opponent. The bet could be a value bet or a bluff, but in either case if the opponent missed the flop or just has a small pair, he'll have difficulty continuing with the hand.

Continuation betting is a standard move in no-limit hold 'em. A typical good player will make a continuation bet between 60 and 70 percent of the time after raising preflop.

Donk Bets

A donk bet is a lead-off bet on the flop made by a player who didn't take the betting lead preflop. Donk bets are generally the mark of a weak and inexperienced player. If you act first post-flop and your hand is strong enough to bet, it's generally best to check to the preflop raiser, let him bet, and then raise, thereby getting more money in the pot.

Example: In our $1/$2 6-max game, the under the gun player makes a standard opening raise to $6. Everyone folds to you in the big blind. You have the and call. The pot is $13. The flop comes the

You have top pair with a weak kicker. The standard play would be to check and see what the preflop raiser does. Instead, you lead out for $10. The under the gun player folds.

Your donk bet informed the preflop raiser that you had hit the flop and liked your hand. The preflop raiser probably had two high cards and decided (wisely) not to fight for the pot. Although you won the hand, your expectation would probably be higher by checking and allowing the under the gun player to make a continuation bet.

Information Bets

An *information bet* is just a bet made to get information about the strength of your hand by gauging your opponent's response. Players who bet this way often have a medium-strength hand and are trying to "see where they stand."

Betting like this used to be popular, but most good players now view such bets as just mistakes. A better strategy is usually to check and gauge your strength by your opponent's play on the flop and the turn. Often you will get the same information at less cost, while keeping the pot small.

Understanding
Flop Texture

A key element in playing the flop is understanding the significance of the *flop texture*. This is just a term for describing the different characteristics of the flop. Are the cards of three different suits (a *rainbow flop*)? Are two suits represented (a *two-tone flop*)? Are all three cards of the same suit (a *monotone flop*)? Are the flop cards connected or are they widely separated? Is there a pair on board? All of these characteristics comprise the texture of the flop.

When the flop arrives, you can combine the flop texture with your knowledge of the preflop betting to answer some key questions:

1. How good a hand do I have now?

2. Given my opponent's preflop action, should the flop have helped him?

3. Given what I did preflop, should my opponent think that this flop helped me?

Once you answer these questions, you can formulate a plan for betting the flop and later streets. If you now have a made hand — a high pair or better — you will mostly bet the flop for value. You expect your hand to be best, and you want to start building the pot while discouraging your opponent from trying to catch a card that beats you. But if you missed the flop, you have a more difficult decision. If you were the aggressor preflop, do you want to make a continuation bet or just check and try to see a turn card?

If you weren't the aggressor preflop, you still have to deal with the same questions. For the most part, your opponent will be betting at you. Do you want to continue with the hand, or should you just fold and cut your losses?

Let's take a look at some sample hands with different flop textures and see how they should be handled:

Example No. 1: The dry flop. We're playing in a $0.10/$0.25 6-max game. You have the

in middle position. The first player folds. You raise to $0.75 and the cutoff folds but the button calls. The blinds fold and the pot is $1.85.

The flop is the

What do we do?

We call this sort of flop a *dry flop*. Dry flops have just one high card which is not an ace, three widely separated cards, and no two cards of the same suit. Very few hands connect to a dry flop and no draws are possible, which makes them ideal flops for a continuation bet from the preflop aggressor because when players call preflop raises, they generally have one of four kinds of hands:

1. Medium to small pairs.

2. An ace with a medium to small kicker, often suited.

3. Medium suited connectors.

4. Two medium suited cards, like jack-nine or nine-seven.

And very few of these hands will connect with a dry flop. No flush draws or straight draws are possible, and unless the caller started with a pair, he probably still doesn't have one. And even if the caller suspects that you missed the flop as well, since you may have started with a high pair, it's too difficult for him to play on after you bet.

Example No. 2: The wet flop: We're in a $0.25/$0.50 6-max game. Under the gun, we pick up the A♠9♠. We're feeling loose and aggressive and raise to $1.75. The player in the cutoff seat calls, and everyone else folds. The pot is $4.25.

The flop is the J♥T♥9♣. What do we do?

Here's the opposite of a dry flop: the *wet flop*. These flops connect strongly with many of the medium-card hands that a caller can be expected to have. If our caller's hand contained a queen, jack, ten, nine, or eight, he now has at least a pair or an open-ended straight draw, and could easily have two pair, a set, or a made straight. In addition, the two hearts mean that a little less than a quarter of his suited hands now have a flush draw.

Although you made bottom pair, the prudent play is to check. A bet won't chase away any of the hands that connected with this flop, and while you could take down the pot if he has a very small pair, the chance isn't worth the investment.

You in fact bet $3.50. The cutoff raises to $11 and you fold.

Example No. 3: The paired flop: We're playing in a $0.25/$0.50 6-max game. The first two players fold and the cutoff raises to

$1.50. We have the 6♥6♣ on the button and call the $1.50. The blinds fold and the pot is $3.75.

The flop is the 8♣8♥2♠. The cutoff bets $2. What do we do?

Paired flops share many of the characteristics of dry flops since very few hands connect with a paired flop, so if the cutoff didn't start with a pair, he probably doesn't have one now. In addition, he can't have a flush draw or a straight draw. Our modest pair of sixes is likely to be the best hand.

If we probably have the best hand, our options are calling or raising. In this case, raising is the better choice. If our opponent has two high cards and is bluffing (the most likely scenario), a raise should win the hand. If we just call, many cards can arrive on the flop which we won't like to see. If we just call and an ace comes on the turn and our opponent bets, we won't know if the ace hit him or not, and we could be setting ourselves up to lose a big pot if we guess wrong.

We raise to $6 and the cutoff folds.

Example No. 4: The ace-high flop. We're in a $0.25/$0.50 6-max game. Under the gun, we pick up the

We raise to $1.50. The player in the small blind calls and everyone else folds. The small blind likes to play a lot of hands. The pot is $3.75.

The flop is the

The small blind checks. What should we do?

Ace-high flops behave a little differently from other kinds of flops. Since the initial raiser often has a hand with a strong ace, these are natural flops for him to continue betting even if (as here) he actually has some other sort of hand. However, whether the flop is likely to connect with the caller depends heavily on what level of players are involved.

In weak games, many loose players call bets with weak aces and will therefore connect with these flops. In general, weak players won't fold a pair or an ace preflop, so the aggressor has no chance of betting them off the hand. He can, however, win his opponent's whole stack if he has a better ace.

In stronger games, the caller rarely has an ace in this spot. Good players will often 3-bet with ace-king and sometimes ace-queen, while they'll usually fold aces with a medium or small kicker for fear of being dominated against an under the gun raiser. In these games, the aggressor generally has a pretty risk-free continuation bet on these flops.

In this case, we know the small blind is loose and the stakes are not especially high, so there's some chance he has an ace. However, most of his possible hands don't have an ace, so betting is slightly better than checking. You bet $2.50 and the small blind folds.

Bet Sizing
on the Flop and Later Streets

So the flop has arrived and now you want to bet. How large a bet should you make?

In general, typical flop bets range between half pot and full pot. Deciding on a bet size hinges on several factors including the strength of your hand, the flop texture, stack sizes, and any knowledge you may have about your opponents. Let's take a look at some typical bet sizes and the logic behind each one.

1. **Bets of less than half the pot:** Players make small bets for different reasons. Players in micro-stakes games will sometimes make the minimum bet possible because they want to bet but don't see any reason to bet more than the minimum. Others will make a small bet for information ("to see where they stand"), although as we've seen, this is usually a bad reason for betting.

    The most sensible reason for a small bet is as a blocking bet. You believe that your opponent will bet if you check, and your hand is good enough to call that bet. Rather than wait, you make a small bet first in the hope that your opponent will just call that bet, enabling you to see the next card at less cost. Blocking bets are more common on the turn and river, but they can occur on the flop.[1]

2. **Half-pot bets:** A half-pot bet is a typical size for a continuation bet on a dry flop. Since dry flops don't offer drawing chances, and since players who miss dry flops often

---

[1] For more discussion of blocking bets, see *No-Limit Hold 'em: Theory and Practice* by David Sklansky and Ed Miller.

don't continue with the hand, a half-pot bet is big enough to chase away the players who don't want to continue while losing less when the opponent has connected with the flop and wants to raise. Half-pot bets offer a good risk-reward ratio since if your opponent folds more than one time in three, you will show a profit.

3. **Bets of two-thirds to three-quarters of the pot:** These are good bet sizes for value bets, designed to build the pot, or continuation bets on boards that are not so dry. For instance, a board like the 9♣8♦3♣ (with two cards of one suit) offers some drawing chances, so a larger bet cuts down on the odds being offered.

4. **Full pot bets:** Full pot bets are usually reserved for very wet flops where you have a hand and you want to charge players for trying to draw. For example, suppose you have the Q♥J♦ and the flop is the Q♠J♣T♠ (with two spades). While your hand is strong (top two pair), many hands could have a draw to beat you. In this case, a pot-size bet charges them to play while still not overcommitting you to the hand.

5. **More than the pot:** Betting more than the pot on the flop is an unusual move. Bets like this are usually driven by consideration of stack sizes rather than board texture. For instance, suppose the pot on the flop is $20 and you have only $30 left in your stack while your opponent has much more. If you have a hand and make a pot-sized bet and get called, the pot would become $60 and you'd only have $10 left. On the turn, you'd be pot-committed — if your opponent bet, you would automatically call for the rest of your stack getting such good odds. In that case, you might as well bet your whole stack right away even though this means making a larger than pot-sized bet.

Whatever the situation, these are not fixed guidelines. You'll need to vary your bet sizes so your opponents can't deduce exactly what your bet means. But in general, bets intended for a given purpose should average something like the amounts suggested here.

One final point: These suggestions are intended for flops where you're heads-up against a single opponent. If you intend to bet, and you're facing multiple opponents, you should plan on making a larger bet. With multiple opponents, there's a greater likelihood that someone has a made hand that can call (in which case, if you have a hand, you'd like to get more money in the pot), and also a greater chance that someone has a drawing hand (in which case you'd like to cut down on their odds).

Playing the Turn

By the time you reach the turn, four of the five board cards have been dealt. You know a lot about your final hand, and if you've been paying attention to what your opponent has done, you probably have some good guesses about his hand. The most important feature of the turn is that only one card remains to come. If you have the better hand now, you're a much bigger favorite than you were on the flop because your opponent has only one chance left to catch a card that beats you. For the same reason, if you thought you were an underdog on the flop, and you didn't hit your hand, then you're a bigger underdog now.

The fact that the leader is in a better situation than before has some important implications for turn play. Let's look carefully at two of the most important.

1. **Value betting is stronger than before.** Let's say that after the flop the pot was $10, you had a high pair, and your opponent had a flush draw. With two cards to come, your high pair is about a 2-to-1 favorite over a flush draw with no other outs. You bet $8 and your opponent calls, making the pot $26. Both actions are reasonable. You're a favorite, so you're happy to get more money in the pot. He thinks his flush draw makes him a 2-to-1 underdog right now, and the pot is offering him 18-to-8 odds, or 2.25-to-1. (In addition, he might win more money if he hits his flush.)

    Now suppose the turn card arrives and it doesn't help anyone. With only one card to come, he's now about a 4-to-1 underdog to hit his flush. While he should fold to a bet at this point, any bet you make will have much higher equity than before.

2. **Drawing hands are weaker than before.** From the above example, we can see that any drawing hand that hasn't connected by the turn will probably not get the odds it needs to continue. Even a half pot bet on the turn will be giving a drawing hand only 3-to-1 odds, whereas the odds of hitting a flush or an open-ended straight draw with no extra outs will be between 4-to-1 and 5-to-1. The holder of a drawing hand would need to feel that it was likely that he could win extra money on the river to continue.

Betting the Turn

With these ideas in mind, let's look at several concrete reasons for betting on the turn.

1. **Bet for value with a strong enough hand.** If you have a hand that's strong enough, you mostly want to bet to get more money in a pot you expect to win. The key words are "strong enough." How strong a hand has to be to qualify as strong enough depends on a number of factors. Let's take a look.

    On the flop, a hand like an overpair; top pair, top kicker; or top pair, good kicker will mostly be the best hand and is certainly worth betting. Awkward situations can occur where the board is especially dangerous or several players are involved in the hand. For instance, if you hold the

you're against three players, and the flop is the

you can't be very confident that your top pair, top kicker is in fact best. You might bet anyway just because it could be your best (or only) chance to win the hand, but if you get raised or otherwise run into resistance, you're unlikely to get more money involved on later streets.

As the hand develops and your opponent indicates that he's willing to get a lot of money committed, it becomes less and less likely that a hand like top pair, top kicker is in fact the best hand. By the river, a top pair type hand has become a hand of medium strength — good for catching bluffs, but somewhat dangerous for betting or raising.

You should make adjustments once you have some information about your opponent. Against a tight opponent, you should be extra cautious. Tight players don't play deep into the hand without a good hand to back them up. Against a loose passive player, you can bet more liberally. They can go deep into the hand without anything better than bottom pair, especially at low stakes.

2. **Build the pot if you checked the flop with a hand.** You won't always bet when you have a hand on the flop. Sometimes, just to mix up your play, you won't bet the flop; this way your opponent won't know that if you check the flop, he can bet with impunity and take the pot away from you. So check a few good hands on the flop.

Also, sometimes you won't bet the flop because, although you like your hand, you think it's a hand that's only good for winning a small pot. Checking the flop is a way to keep the pot small.

But if you have a hand and you check the flop, and your opponent checks as well, then you mostly want to bet the turn. At this point you need to start earning some money on the hand, as well as preventing your opponent from hitting a random two pair that beats you.

3. **Bet if the flop was checked around and you don't have a hand.** If everyone checked the flop, then it's likely that no one has much of a hand. Even without a hand, betting the turn is now frequently reasonable, and may be your only chance of winning the pot.

4. **Bet if you made a continuation bet bluff on the flop and your opponent just called.** A few years ago the idea of a "continuation bet" on the flop was new to many players who just folded if their opponent bet and they hadn't made a strong hand. As continuation bets became understood, more players were willing to call a bet on the flop with a weak pair, a draw, or even nothing at all to see if they could win the hand later.

    The counter-strategy to this approach is to fire a second bluff on the turn. Known as "double barreling," this second bet shows a lot of strength and is correspondingly harder to call. You should plan on double-barreling at least some of your flop bluffs.

5. **Bet if you have a hand and your opponent is likely to have a draw.** As we saw in the previous chapter, most draws will not have the odds required to call a bet on the turn with only one card to come. If you bet, you can either make these hands fold or force them to make a mistake by calling with incorrect pot odds.

6. **Bet before the "cooler" comes.** Another reason for betting into a potential drawing hand is that your opponent may not,

in fact, have a drawing hand. Suppose you have a pretty strong hand like top pair, good kicker. You bet the flop and your opponent calls. The flop has a couple of potential draws, so you think he may have a drawing hand.

However, that's not the only reason he could have called. He may have a medium strength hand and think you might be betting with a drawing hand. If this is the case, he'll want to get to showdown, but is afraid you may hit your draw.

On the turn, a card comes which doesn't hit the draw. You could bet, and if you do, your opponent will probably call again.

But suppose you don't bet, worried that he may be trapping or that the pot is getting too big. Now comes a river card which seems to complete the draw. You won't bet for fear of being raised by a monster. But if you check, your opponent won't bet for the same reason. At the showdown, your hand will win, but you will have missed winning some extra money that you could have made with a bet on the turn.

We call the card that came on the river a "cooler." By creating a seemingly dangerous board, it froze the action. If you have a good hand and your opponent may or may not have a draw, the possibility of cooler cards gives you another reason to bet the turn.

7.   **Bet to set up an all-in on the river.** When you have a very strong hand, you'd like to win your opponent's entire stack if he has some sort of hand that he's willing to take to showdown. The way to set up an all-in bet on the river is to make a good bet on the turn. Try to bet enough on the turn so that the all-in river bet isn't much larger than your opponent's stack.

For instance, suppose you have made a concealed straight on the turn and your opponent has called your preflop and flop bets. Let's say the pot is now $20, and both you and your opponent have $80 left in your stacks. If you make a half-pot bet of $10 (to keep your opponent in the hand) and he calls, the pot will be $40 and you will both have $70 left in your stacks. If you now push all-in on the river, it will be a massive overbet compared to your stacks, which may scare your opponent away.

However, if you bet $20 instead of $10 on the turn (a pot-sized bet) and your opponent called, the pot would be $60 and so would your two stacks. Now an all-in move is just a pot-sized bet itself, and more likely to be called.

Checking the Turn

We've listed the reasons for betting the turn. What about checking the turn? When is this the best play? Let's take a look at some of the reasons for checking the turn.

1. **Check after a failed continuation bet.** Double-barreling is an option, but not something you can do to excess. If you have nothing and the board is unfavorable, often you should just check and fold to a bet.

2. **Check as a trap.** If you make a lot of continuation bets, you will occasionally need to check the turn with a strong made hand, particularly against an aggressive opponent. He will often bet to win the pot, and you can then respond with a raise or a call. This play not only makes you difficult to read and hence more dangerous, but garners at least one bet you might not otherwise have earned.

3. **Check to induce your opponent to bet or call.** If you have a very strong hand by the turn, a bet threatens your opponent with the potential loss of his whole stack if he calls your turn bet and a subsequent river bet. We call this the principle of *leverage*: You're leveraging a moderate turn bet into a threat

against his whole stack. Checking the turn removes the threat to his stack, and may allow your opponent to call a bet on the river since his risk is then quantifiable and smaller.

4. **Check as a bluff catcher.** A bluff catching hand is a hand with some showdown value, but which you don't want to bet. If you bet, you're afraid that stronger hands will call but weaker hands will go away. But by checking on the turn, you allow your opponent to bluff at the river with some of his weak hands, thinking the pot is up for grabs. You can then pick off these bluffs.

Playing the River

The river is the most important street in no-limit hold 'em. By the time you reach the river, you've seen the preflop, flop, and turn betting, and you've seen the entire board. You now have as much information as you will ever have. In addition, the bets are larger than on any other street, and all-in bets are not unusual.

The combination of large amounts of information combined with large bets means that a good player's edge is greater on the river than on any other street. Mastering river play is a key part of mastering no-limit hold 'em.

How you play the river largely depends on what sort of hand you have. Let's look at some categories of hands and see how they should be handled.

1. **You have the nuts.** Having the nuts on the river is a rare and happy situation, but you still need to play the hand correctly. The simple rule which governs this situation goes as follows: *If you have the nuts on the river, you mostly want to push all-in.*

    This play may seem drastic, but the logic behind the move is actually easy to understand. If you make a normal-sized bet, you'll get called some percentage of the time. If you push all-in, you'll get called less often, but when you do get called, you'll win much more money. The extra money will more than compensate for the times your opponent folds when he would have called a smaller bet.

    Under what circumstances don't you push all-in on the river? Since you need to vary your play, you can't always push with the nuts. Eventually even feeble-minded opponents will figure out what you're up to. So the best time to make a normal-sized bet is when your opponent has shown no real strength, but has indicated he has some kind of hand and he'd like to see a showdown. A typical case would be against a player who checks and calls a couple of bets when no obvious draw is present. That betting pattern indicates some sort of bluff-catcher hand like a medium pair or top pair, decent kicker. In this case, a big bet will probably chase him away, but a half-pot bet might make some money. So go with the smaller bet.

2. **You have a very good hand which is not the nuts.** To handle this situation, ask yourself a simple question: "If I make a good-sized bet, perhaps the size of the pot, and my opponent then puts me all-in, do I call?" If the answer is "yes," then treat this situation as though you had the nuts and play accordingly.

   If your answer is "no" and you're actually going to fold to an all-in raise, then you must believe, from the previous betting action, that there's a decent chance that your opponent could have the nuts. In that case, you should plan on getting to showdown cheaply. You might make a small bet or check with the idea of calling a modest bet by your opponent.

3. **You have a good hand given the board and the betting.** Here we're talking about hands that are not the second nuts or the third nuts, but are nonetheless "pretty good." Exactly what constitutes pretty good in a given situation can vary widely. If the board is paired, then quads and full houses are the nut hands, and straights and flushes could qualify as pretty good. On a non-paired board without three suited cards, straights are the nuts and sets are very strong, but a good two-pair hand qualifies as pretty good.

   The classic (and costly) mistake that many players make is to get cold feet with these hands and refuse to bet the river, thus turning these hands into mere bluff-catchers. It's an easy mistake to make because with five different cards on board, all sorts of strong hands are possible. Your opponent could be trapping with some well-hidden straight, or he could have hit any of five different sets. The sheer number of possible better hands makes betting with a hand like two pair difficult for the inexperienced player.

In general, pretty good hands are worth a good-sized value bet on the river. If you're having trouble making these bets, you need to be diligent about analyzing the hand thoroughly before making your river play. Consider how your opponent played the hand. Would he really have checked a set through two streets? Did he really call the flop and turn with a gutshot straight, only to hit on the river? Remember, for the most part, people's actions reflect their hand strength. If it's unlikely that your opponent has your pretty good hand beaten, you should feel good about betting.

Also, keep in mind that on the river you either have the best hand or you don't. A winning bet on the river that elicits a call can double your overall profit on the hand. Over time, betting well on the river can be one of your biggest money-making skills.

4. **You have a hand with some value.** By the river, a hand with some value is typically something like top pair or even second or third pair. But depending on the board, it could be stronger, like a good two pair. In any case, it's a hand that you believe might be best, but where you'd rather not put any more money in the pot if you don't have to.

The ideal situation is to have a hand like this in position. In that case, if your opponent checks, you can check behind and see if you're best.

If he makes a small bet, you'll probably need to make what's known as a *crying call*. You're most likely beaten, but his bet may be giving you pot odds of as much as 5- or 6-to-1. You don't have to win many of those bets to show a profit by calling.

If your opponent makes a big bet, your odds won't be as good, and it's time to make a tough decision. You'll need to call once in a while or your opponents will learn they can bluff you relentlessly. So here the best strategy is to think back over the hand and ask yourself if he would have played a strong holding that way. If his story is consistent, it's usually best to fold. But for those hands where his story is inconsistent, use them to make your calls. Sometimes you'll get tricked, but your chance of picking off a few bluffs will be improved.

5.   **You have nothing.** When you have nothing on the river, your only options are to fold or bluff. Mostly you're going to fold. However, you'll need to bluff some of the time so that your opponents won't be able to tell whether a river bet from you means a strong hand. Here are a few rules for bluffing on the river.

   A.   **Only bluff with hands that have no showdown value.** If you bluff with nothing and your opponent raises, you can cheerfully throw your hand away. If you bet with a hand like second pair and get raised, you may have to fold a hand that would have won if your opponent decided to raise with nothing! Pick hands that can't win the pot for your bluffs.

   B.   **Don't bluff someone who's already shown a lot of strength.** They'll call you, even if they might not be happy.

   C.   **Don't bluff a calling station.** This should be obvious. Players who rarely lay their hands down will continue to do just that.

    D.   **Don't bluff with an inconsistent story.** If you're representing a strong hand, think back to the turn and see if your action there was consistent with what you're representing now.

    E.   **Bluff if the river is a scare card.** Good scare cards are hands which make a low or medium pair on the board, or cards which seem to fill a straight. The story you're telling is that you had a medium hand or a draw and hit the jackpot. However, weak players often try to bluff when the third card of a suit hits on the river. Good players know that move and they'll figure you do as well.

6.   **Don't bluff with a high card (like an ace) in your hand.** If you and your opponent were both drawing, and you both missed, your high card may be good enough to win.

Expectation
and Expected Value

In poker, all decisions have a value. We refer to this value as the "expected value," or "expectation" of the decision. (The shorthand term for expected value is just "EV.") In some cases, we can calculate this value directly, in other cases, we estimate the value by making educated guesses about our opponent's hand and what he might do in the future. In general, however, when making a decision in poker we're trying to estimate or calculate the value of different courses of action, and picking the choice with the highest expected value.

Let's look at a concrete example and see this decision-making in action. Suppose we hold the

in a game with $1/$2 blinds. Preflop, one player raises to $7, and a second player calls. Our stack is $120 and we call as well. Everyone else folds and the pot is now $24.

The flop comes the

The first player bets $20, the second player folds, and we call with our nut flush draw. The pot is now $64 and we have $93 left.

The turn card is the 2♦. We still have a flush draw with just one card to come. Our opponent now pushes all-in for his last $60. We don't believe he would make this move without a reasonably strong hand, at least top pair. Should we call?

To answer this question, we'll calculate the expected value of calling and compare it to the expected value of folding. In this simple example, these numbers are actually easy to calculate. (In most real-life examples, we have to settle for educated guesses.) Let's see how it's done.

The expected value of folding is just zero. We put no more money into the pot and just go away. Note that the $27 we've already put into the pot doesn't count here in any way. That money is already gone; it belongs to the pot, not to us. We're only looking at new money that we'd have to risk, and folding costs us exactly nothing.

Suppose we call instead. The pot is currently $124 and we have to put in $60 more to see the river. We're risking $60 to win the $124 that's out there. Our best guess is that hitting a king or a queen won't be enough to take down the pot. To win, we'll need to hit the flush. Right now there are nine remaining flush cards that we haven't seen out of a total of 46 remaining cards. So if we call, we think we'll hit the flush 9 times out of 46 (19.5 percent) and win, while we'll miss 37 times out of 46 (80.5 percent) and lose. (Another way of saying the same thing is that we have nine *outs*, where an out is a card that will turn a losing hand into a winner.)

Let's simplify by saying we'll win 20 percent of the time and lose 80 percent of the time. In poker, there's mostly no need to make difficult calculations when a simple approximation will do just as well. So our expected value calculation looks like this:

$$(0.20)(\$124) = \$24.80$$

plus

$$(0.80)(-\$60) = -\$48.00$$

Our net expectation is the sum of $24.80 and -$48.00, or -$23.20. If we call, that's what we rate to lose on average.

In a single trial, of course, we'll never lose that amount. We'll either lose $60 or win $124. But if we were to set up this situation hundreds or thousands of times, our average loss would approach $23.20 per trial. In poker parlance, we would say that calling is 'negative EV,' and folding is the correct play.

Pot Odds

During a poker hand, we rarely try to make expected value calculations as in the previous section. Instead, we use a shortcut method based on *pot odds*.

Pot odds are just the size of the pot compared to the amount required to call a bet. In the previous example, the pot was $124 and we needed $60 to call the last bet, so our pot odds were 2.07-to-1.

$$2.07 = \frac{\$124}{\$60}$$

Big pot odds mean we're being well compensated if we hit our hand, and we can call as an underdog. Low pot odds mean the opposite.

To solve a problem at the table like the previous example, we compare the pot odds being offered to the odds of making our hand. If the pot odds are bigger than the odds of making our hand, then it's profitable to call. If smaller, then we're not being offered enough odds and we should fold.

In the previous example, the odds of making our hand were 4.1-to-1.

$$4.1 = \frac{37}{9}$$

The pot odds are smaller than the odds of making our hand, so we should fold. That's the same conclusion we reached by doing an exact calculation of expected value, but with much less work.

Expressed
and Implied Odds

Let's look at this idea of pot odds a little more closely. Pot odds actually come in two varieties, *expressed odds* and *implied odds*. Expressed odds are the odds which occur when there is no more action in the hand. The odds you see are the only odds you're getting. If you have enough odds to call, you should call, otherwise you should fold. The example in the last section, where your opponent moved all-in on the turn and your call or fold would end the action, is an example of expressed odds.

Implied odds are a little different. Suppose you call a bet but the hand doesn't end. Another street or two is played where more betting can occur. You may be able to win more money later if you hit your hand, but you won't necessarily have to put more money in the pot if you miss. Implied odds are an estimate of the real odds being offered taking into account the money you may win later.

Suppose for instance we're in the big blind at another $1/$2 6-max no-limit hold 'em table. We pick up two red deuces. The under the gun player raises to $6 and two more players call. The others fold and the action is on us. The pot is now $21 and it costs another $4 to call and play the hand.

Since we're out of position (we have to act first after the flop) and facing three other players, it's reasonable to assume that we'll have to improve to at least a set of deuces to win the hand. The odds against hitting at least one deuce on the flop is about 7.5-to-1. Those aren't good odds, but let's check the pot odds we're being offered. With the pot at $21 and needing $4 to call, our pot odds are 5.2-to-1.

$$5.2 = \frac{\$21}{\$4}$$

Those are pretty good odds, but not quite as large as the odds on making our hand, and if we knew that no more money was going into the pot, we'd fold. However, it's very likely that more money will go into the pot if we hit our set.

Here's an example. Suppose the flop comes the

With three other players in the hand, it's certainly possible that at least one player now has a pair of aces and is willing to play. Let's assume we check our set, the preflop raiser goes ahead and bets $16, and the other two players fold. If we then raise to $40, and even if the preflop raiser folds at this point, another $16 went into the pot. That extra money represents the implied odds that we had when we called the initial bet.

This is a simple example, and implied odds can be a complex subject. In many situations, it's easy to overestimate them. You may hit your hand and find that no more money goes in because your opponents have nothing. You might also hit your hand and lose a lot of money. (In the previous example, suppose that the initial raiser actually raised with a pair of queens and was called by someone trapping with a pair of aces. A lot of money is going in this pot, but unfortunately none of it is going to you unless the fourth deuce comes!) Implied odds are real and you need to take them into account, but it's usually best to make conservative estimates. They're more likely to be correct.

Reverse Implied Odds

The concept of implied odds affects hands that are not strong now but can easily become very strong. Small pairs, connected cards, and suited cards are holdings that can improve to sets, straights, and flushes respectively. When one of these holdings makes a strong hand and the opponent has a merely good one like an overpair or two pair, they create a threat to win a large chunk, if not all, of the opponent's stack. We refer to holdings like these as good implied odds hands: they lose a little when they miss the flop, but can win a lot when they connect strongly with the flop.

For other kinds of hands, the opposite situation arises. Let's take a look.

You're in a $100 NL 6-max online game and your stack is $106. You're on the button holding the

The first player folds. The second player raises to $3.50 and the player in the cutoff seat folds. The pot now contains $5 and it costs you $3.50 to call. Your pot odds are 1.4-to-1.

$$1.4 = \frac{\$5.00}{\$3.50}$$

You have an ace and position on the raiser, so you decide to play. You call $3.50, making the pot $8.50, and the blinds fold.

The flop is the

The first player checks. You have top pair, albeit with a weak kicker and decide to bet $5 "to see where you're at." The initial raiser now raises to $15, informing you that you're in a world of hurt. What do you do?

It's smart to fold. In fact, your bet on the flop was unwise. Hands like an ace and a small card are hands that exhibit what we call "reverse implied odds." The more money that goes in the pot with a hand like that, the more likely you are beaten. When you hit a hand like ace-seven unsuited on the flop either by making a pair of aces or a pair of sevens, your best post-flop scenario is that you bet and your opponent folds, and you take down a small pot. If the hand continues and the pot gets large, your top pair, weak kicker type hand becomes more and more likely to be second-best. The logic of an implied odds situation is now working against you, and staying in the hand can become more and more costly.

Stack Sizes

In no-limit hold 'em cash games, whether played online or live, stack sizes determine overall strategy and hand selection. You'll play a very different sort of game with stacks of 20 big blinds than you would with stacks of 200 big blinds. Your initial hand selection will change, and your post-flop strategy will change as well. Let's take a look at some different stack sizes and see what sort of strategy each one favors.

Short Stacks

Stacks that contain 20 to 30 big blinds are known as short stacks. You can get a short stack in one of two ways: voluntarily, by buying in for a small amount, or involuntarily, by losing most, but not all, of your chips.

Involuntary short stacks don't have much independent significance. If you're comfortable playing with a 100 big blind stack, and you then lose 80 big blinds in a big hand, nothing prevents you from immediately rebuying the 80 lost blinds, and in fact most players will do that. A player doesn't have to sit at the table with a 20 big blind stack unless he really wants to.

Players who choose to play with short stacks do so for one of two reasons. Some don't like the idea of losing 100 or 200 big blinds at a time, and play with a short stack to cut down on their risk. Generally, these players are trying to play "normal" poker but with a short stack. Players with this strategy are at a significant disadvantage because short stacks don't allow you to play "normal" no-limit hold 'em; we'll see why in a second.

The other reason for playing a short stack is to pursue a well-defined short stack strategy. This strategy consists of playing only premium hands like high and medium pairs, strong aces, or Broadway cards, but betting these hands very strongly both preflop and on the flop. The idea is to get all-in on the flop either with an overpair or a top pair, top kicker type of hand. This strategy is an effective one, based on solid logic. Small stacks, however, can't take advantage of hands that require implied odds because the odds aren't there.

Example: To see the problem with short stacks and non-premium hands, imagine that you have a stack of 20 big blinds and you're on the button. You pick up a pair of treys. A player in middle position with a full stack of 100 big blinds raises to four big blinds. The cutoff seat folds. Should you call?

Let's imagine you call and the blinds fold. You don't really expect that your pair of treys will be enough to win the pot on their own. You'll need to improve to a set to feel comfortable about getting the rest of your stack involved. Right now you've invested four big blinds, but the most you can win is 20 big blinds from your opponent, plus 1.5 big blinds from the blinds, a total of 21.5 big blinds. The payoff is a little larger than five times your investment, but you're about a 7.5-to-1 underdog to hit your set on the flop, and if you do hit, it's far from a certainty that your opponent will have a hand that can pay you off.

Hands like suited connectors need time to develop, but a small stack is likely to be all-in after just a couple of bets. As a result, small stacks need to play hands that show their strength early; big pairs and big aces are perfect for this purpose.

A short stack strategy is an effective tool for players with limited skills. However, it's hard to develop any of those skills further while playing such a strategy. In addition, online sites are starting to eliminate the small buy-in option, so the small stack strategy may become a historical artifact pretty soon except for those times you lose most of your chips and choose not to buy any more.

Medium Stacks

A medium stack is a stack in the 40 to 60 big blind range. Compared to a short stack, which only allows you to play premium hands, a medium stack is big enough to offer some implied odds, so more speculative hands can be played with these stacks in the right situations.

Full Stacks

In online play, a full stack is usually 100 big blinds. In most cases, that's the maximum amount you can buy-in, and if you think you're a good player, capable of outplaying your opponents at your level, you should buy in for a full stack.

Since a full stack is roughly 25 to 35 times the size of a normal opening raise, provided your opponent(s) also has plenty of chips, you're being offered good enough odds to play some of the speculative hands like small pairs, suited connectors, suited aces, and a few others. Of course, you'll continue to play your premium hands like the high pairs, the big aces, and the Broadway cards, but your hand selection will now contain a mix of speculative hands as well.

Deep Stacks

A deep stack is a stack of 150 big blinds or more. In micro-stakes games, some sites will allow you to buy in for 200 or 250 big blinds, so you can start the game with a deep stack. Sites are starting to allow deep stack buy-ins for higher stake games as well. If you can't make a big buy-in, then you can only accumulate a deep stack by winning some big hands. Deep stacks offer much more scope for skillful play, but also contain many dangers for the unwary player.

Tailoring Your Strategy to the Stack Size

In general, the hands you play preflop and the way you evaluate and play them post-flop will be a function of the *effective stack size*. By effective stack size, we just mean the size of the smaller stack. If you have a stack of 100 big blinds and your preflop raise is called by a stack of 30 big blinds, the effective stack size is just 30 big blinds. The smaller stack represents all the money that can be won or lost in the hand, so that's the stack that controls the overall strategy.

One of your goals in poker is to have the best hand when all the money goes in. If the stacks are small, all the money should be going in fairly quickly, so you want to play hands that rate to be best either preflop or after the flop. These hands, as just stated, are the big pairs and the big Broadway cards. The big pairs don't necessarily need to improve to be the best hand on the flop. The big Broadway cards will make top pair, top kicker on many flops, which will mostly be the best hand.

With big stacks, the money won't go all in until the turn or the river. When the money does go all-in, it's a lot of money. From this observation we can draw two conclusions:

1. Having the money go in later favors hands that take a longer time to develop, like suited connectors, suited aces, one-gappers, and to a lessor degree, small pairs.

2. Because so much money is involved, players won't get their stacks committed unless they have a hand they think is strong. In order to win that money, you need a well-concealed, very strong hand. The best hands for this purpose are hands that form unlikely straights.

Take a look at the next two examples and notice how the effective stack size alters the strength of an apparently good hand.

Example No. 1: You have a stack of 20 big blinds and you're in the big blind. The button, a strong tight-aggressive player who is a regular winner, with a stack of 120 big blinds raises to three big blinds. The small blind folds. Your hand is the

so you 3-bet to 10 big blinds. Your opponent calls. The pot is now 20.5 big blinds and you have 10 big blinds left in your stack.
  The flop is the

You have top pair, top kicker, push all-in for your last 10 big blinds, and your opponent calls. What's the chance that you have the best hand at this point?
  We can't be sure, of course, but the chance is pretty good. Only a few possible hands are currently beating you: a pair of kings, nines, or eights, each of which has made a set, or any of the hands that make two pair, none of which would likely have called preflop. Meanwhile, your opponent could have called with many other hands. Since he was getting 3-to-1 pot odds, he could have a flush draw or a straight draw. He could also have a pair of jacks or tens and think there's some chance you don't have a king or a

higher pair. In short, his set of possible calling hands includes mostly hands that you're currently beating, so you've accomplished your primary objective: getting your money in with the likely best hand.

Example No. 2: This time you have a stack of 150 big blinds, as does the button, who as before is a good, tight-aggressive player. Once again you're in the big blind with the A♦K♦, the button raises to three big blinds, you 3-bet to 10 big blinds, and he calls. The pot is 20.5 big blinds, but now you have 140 big blinds behind.

The flop this time is the A♣8♥6♣ giving you top pair, top kicker. You bet 12 big blinds and the button calls. Now the pot is 44.5 big blinds and the effective stack is 128 big blinds.

The turn is the 5♣. Your hand strength remains the same. So with top pair you now bet 30 big blinds and your opponent calls again. The pot becomes 104.5 big blinds, and the effective stack is now 98 big blinds.

The river is the 9♦. You check and your opponent moves all-in. If you call, what is the chance you have the best hand?

Unlike the previous example, here it's pretty clear that your top pair, top kicker hand is not likely to be good. Your competent opponent called two streets on a draw-heavy board and is now willing to get all his chips involved. With straight and flush draws available, not to mention various sets, and no particular read on your opponent to indicate he's making a move, calling would be a very optimistic play.

Implied Odds

Another way to understand the relationship between hand selection and stack sizes is to consider the ideas of expressed and implied odds. When you enter a hand, it's because you view the combination of the expressed odds offered by your hand strength plus the implied odds offered by the concealed hands you might make as favorable.

$$Playability = Expressed\ Odds + Implied\ Odds$$

When the stacks are short, the expressed odds dominate since the implied odds are bounded by the stack sizes. High pairs and big unpaired cards offer the best expressed odds, so those hands dominate a small stack game.

But with large stacks, the implied odds start to dominate. Now high pairs and big cards are less important because they tend to win small pots, but the medium and small connected cards offer the chance to win huge pots.

Another relationship develops as stacks get larger. Because each hand that you play offers a chance to win a monster stack with the right flop, you want to play more hands. The naïve strategy of waiting only for pairs and big cards and trying to win the pot on a great flop (also known as *set-mining*) turns out to be the opposite of correct deep stack play. The right strategy can be encapsulated in the following relationship:

> Big stacks *imply* big implied odds *which imply* play more hands.

Hand Strength and Pot Size

One of our goals in no-limit hold 'em is to roughly match the strength of our hand with the size of the pot. We even have a shorthand expression to cover this situation: *big hand, big pot; small hand, small pot.* When we have a very strong hand, we want the pot as large as possible. When our hand is modest but still might be best, we want to keep the pot small and get to showdown.

The idea of correlating hand strength and pot size may seem obvious, but it's surprisingly hard to implement in practice. When we have what may be the best hand, like top pair, top kicker on the flop, we have a lot of reasons to bet.

1. We want to bet for value and to get more money in the pot when our hand is best.

2. We want to bet and force drawing hands to receive incorrect odds for the chance of beating us.

3. We want to bet to balance the hands where we miss the flop and bluff with a continuation bet.

That's a lot of good reasons for betting. However, bets and pot sizes in no-limit hold 'em grow geometrically, so it's easy for bets that seem reasonable to quickly create pots that are out of line for a hand's strength.

Example: You're playing at a $200 NL 6-max table. You're on the button with a stack size of $220 and the player in the cutoff (directly on your right) has a stack of $190. You've only been playing a short time and he seems to be a standard tight player who hasn't gotten out of line.

Your hand is the

The first two players fold and the cutoff raises to $6. You have a reasonable hand and think he might be using his position to steal the pot, so you reraise to $15. He calls and the blinds fold. The pot is $33 and you have position on your opponent.

The flop is the

That's a good flop and you now have top pair with the second-best kicker. The cutoff checks and you bet $20, just over half the pot. With no draws available, you think it's likely you'll win right here. Your opponent, however, calls the $20. The pot is now $73 and the effective stack is $155.

The turn card is the 8♦. You still have top pair and your opponent hasn't shown any strength yet. He checks again. You decide to get rid of him for good and bet $60. He raises all-in to $155.

The pot is now $288 and you need to put in $95 to call his last bet. You're getting almost exactly 3-to-1 odds, and with top pair you decide you can't lay your hand down for that price. So you call and he shows the 9♥9♦ for middle set. The river is the A♥, he takes the pot, and you lose $190 or 95 big blinds.

What went wrong? You didn't make any decisions that were ridiculous in themselves. At every decision point you made the most aggressive choice, and each choice was plausible given what you knew at the time. Each decision, however, escalated the pot to the point where you got your whole stack involved with a hand (top pair, second kicker) that only warranted a small pot. This can happen in a game where bet sizes can grow rapidly.

A better way of playing the hand was to check either the flop or, more likely, the turn. On the flop, you have a good top pair on a dry board. If you have the best hand, which is likely, your opponent has very few outs. If he holds, let's say, the 8♦8♣, only the last two eights are outs for him. If he holds the T♠9♠, so that he has a pair of nines, he has five outs, the last three tens and the last two nines. If he holds the K♦J♣, then only the last three jacks are outs. So checking the flop only gives him a small chance to catch up and keeps the pot small.

Betting the flop is all right, of course, but checking behind on the turn was definitely a better play. If your hand is still good, it's likely to be best at showdown, but betting the turn gives the hands that are beating you a chance at winning your whole stack, which is just what happened.

Checking the turn is what's known as a *pot control* move. That is, deliberately limiting the size of the pot when your hand isn't strong enough to play a big pot.

What hands are good enough to happily create a big pot? That's a difficult question which really depends on the opponent, the board, and the betting so far. But very generally, one-pair hands are small pot hands, while sets, straights, and flushes are big pot hands.

Pot Commitment

Closely related to the small hand, small pot/big hand, big pot concept is the idea of pot commitment. Basically, you are committed to the pot when the pot is large enough so that an all-in bet from your opponent will offer you such good pot odds that you are compelled to call given the hand you have and the hand you think your opponent may have. When pot commitment happens, you may elect to move all-in yourself to grab some amount of folding equity (if any still exists).

The example from the previous section is a textbook example of pot commitment. When your opponent moved all-in on the turn, the pot was so large that you were being offered 3-to-1 pot odds to call. Those were big odds, and you thought the chance that he was bluffing, plus the chance that he might have had a hand like king-jack, plus the chance that you might draw out were worth taking in exchange for a possible big payoff.

In no-limit hold'em tournaments, pot commitment decisions arise constantly during the later rounds because so many players have stacks that are relatively small compared to the blind levels. Imagine that you're in a tournament at a nine-handed table, the blinds are T1,000/T2,000, the antes are T300 each, and your stack is only T22,000. If you pick up a pair of jacks, you're committed to the pot before the hand starts. If a player in front of you opens for T6000, your best play is to move all-in.

In cash games, however, pot commitment decisions are rarer and must be considered carefully. In general, you want to assess bets and calls earlier in the hand according to the likelihood that these plays may lead to a pot commitment decision later.

Stack to Pot Ratio

The stack-to-pot ratio, or SPR, is a handy tool for analyzing how the relative stacks and pots affect the play of the hand. It's defined as the ratio of the smaller stack to the pot size after all the preflop betting has occurred.

SPR = (small stack) / (pot after preflop action)

For instance, suppose you're playing at a $1/$2 6-max table. You're on the button with a stack of $250. The under the gun player lost a lot of money a couple of hands ago and hasn't reloaded. His stack is $70.

Preflop, the under the gun player raises to $7 and you call. Everyone else folds. The preflop action is complete. What is the SPR?

The pot now contains $17 ($3 from the blinds and $7 from each of the players). The shorter stack at this point is the under the gun player, who has $63 left. So the SPR is 3.7.

$$3.7 = \frac{\$63}{\$17}$$

Why is this number useful? The SPR is a quick guide to two useful pieces of information:

1. How likely the players are to become committed to the pot if any more action occurs.

2. What hands are likely to play well in this situation.

Obviously, the lower the SPR the more likely that the players will quickly become committed to the pot. An SPR of 3.7 is quite low, which indicates that unless the action on the flop is bet and fold, we'll probably see the short stack get all-in. Intuitively that should be pretty clear. If the short stack makes a reasonable bet on the flop of $15, the pot becomes $32 and he has only $48 left. If you then want to raise, the only reasonable raise is all-in because that's essentially just a pot-sized raise. Even if you just call, the pot becomes $47, and the only sensible bet on the turn is an all-in from either player. Conversely, a high SPR, say 10 or greater, means that the players still have room to make an additional bet without committing to the pot.

Different SPRs favor different sorts of hands. Here's some discussion:

- Low SPRs favor hands whose strengths manifest themselves immediately, like pairs and high-card hands (which on the flop either become high pairs or miss entirely). Their immediate strength means that you can cheerfully get all-in with them quickly, which is what's likely to happen with a low SPR.

- High SPRs favor drawing hands whose strength emerges on later streets: suited cards, connectors, or suited connectors. The high SPR means that these hands can call a bet and see another card or two without getting committed to the pot. High SPRs are unfavorable for high-card hands because as a hand reaches the later streets, the chance that a single pair remains best will drop faster than the pot is getting large.

Get in the habit of quickly reviewing the SPR on the flop, and you can avoid some costly errors later in the hand.

Part Two

Playing Online

Playing Online

Introduction

Prior to the Web, poker-playing was a pretty straightforward business. You went somewhere, sat down with a group of folks face to face, and played poker. The "somewhere" might have been your kitchen table, or a more formal weekly game in a friend's basement, or a casino in a distant city. The game might have been a cash game for reasonable stakes, or a big tournament. But no matter where it was, to play poker you had to sit down with real people at a real table, and play with real cards.

This all began to change in the late 1990s as entrepreneurs discovered there was money to be made in offering poker games online. The early sites mostly featured limit poker on full ring tables and you could play for free using play money. But if you wanted an extra thrill, you could send the site some money and play in actual cash games for modest stakes, trusting that you'd be able to get your money out when the time came. After awhile, the sites spread more tables and began to offer more games at higher stakes. They ran tournaments, which proved increasingly popular, and after a few years started spreading no-limit games in addition to limit.

By the time the poker boom started in the spring of 2003, online poker was well-established with over a dozen successful sites spreading tournaments and cash games. The cash games were still mostly limit, but no-limit began to grow, especially once no-limit was featured on the early poker shows. Among the no-limit cash games, full ring games with nine or ten players were the most popular, but a new format called 6-max had been introduced, and many players were gravitating to that game which featured increased action and a heightened level of aggressiveness.

As time passed, the online landscape gradually evolved. Pokerstars and Full Tilt Poker spent generously on advertising and software development, and became the two dominant online sites. Party Poker, which had been the market leader, refused to allow American players after 2006, and gradually contracted. Many of the smaller sites merged into large networks with enough players to survive. The 6-max form of the game eventually overtook full ring play in popularity, especially at the higher-stakes, and heads-up play achieved a limited success at the highest stakes. And while in 2003 most of the online players were Americans, by the time of this writing, Internet poker has become a worldwide phenomenon.

Online Play versus Live Play

Online no-limit hold 'em and live no-limit hold 'em are technically the same game. However, they offer completely different experiences, so different that in some respects, it's worth treating them as separate games entirely, united only by the common rules of hold 'em. Let's take a look at some of the ways online games are different from live games.

Stakes

A large casino poker room might spread no-limit hold 'em with three different stakes: $1/$2 (or $1/$3 in some cases), $2/$5, and $5/$10. A very large room might spread a table of an even higher stake, perhaps $10/$20 or $25/$50. A small room might drop the $5/$10 table, and just spread a few $1/$2 tables with perhaps a single $2/$5 table.

Online, sites will spread tables with so many different stakes that we need to categorize them. In this book, we'll group the stakes as follows, according to the similarity in how the games play:

1. Micro-stakes: $0.01/$0.02, $0.02/$0.05, $0.05/$0.10, and $0.10/$0.25.

2. Small-stakes: $0.25/$0.50, $0.50/$1, and $1/$2.

3. Medium-stakes: $2/$4 and $3/$6.

4. High-stakes: $5/$10, $10/$20, and $25/$50.

(Online stakes are also sometimes categorized by the price of a 100-big blind buy-in. Thus a $0.01/$0.02 game might be called a '$2 NL game,' while a $0.50/$1 games is a '$100 NL game.' We'll use both notations in this book.)

The difficulty of the games steadily rises as you move up the scale. Micro-stakes games are weaker than small stakes games by a noticeable amount, and so on. Within a category, the higher stakes games will be tougher than the lower stakes games, but there will be enough players committing the same general sorts of errors that the games will have a similar feel.

Because of the large number of different stakes, online games are the perfect starting environment for the beginning player. Since no-limit hold 'em is a game that requires a large amount of practice to master, you can start at a very low level, and for a tiny investment you can play tens of thousands or even hundreds of thousands of hands, moving up in stake only when you feel completely confident that you've mastered your current level.

Are live games and online games roughly comparable at the same blind level? Not at all! An online $1/$2 game will be much tougher than a $1/$2 game in a casino. The reason is easy to see. In a casino, $1/$2 is the smallest game spread, so a beginner who wants to play will gravitate to that game. Online, the same beginner will usually start at much lower stakes and only move up to the $1/$2 game after acquiring a considerable amount of skill. (There are, of course, a few exceptions.) So if you're able to beat a $1/$2 online game, you should find the equivalent live game massively profitable.

Multi-Tabling

In live games you play one table and one table only. Online you can play pretty much any number you want up to a limit of 24, but the exact number is determined by the sites themselves.

How many tables should you play? That's a complicated question. If you're learning the game, I think you're best served by playing just one table and concentrating on what you're doing and what your opponents are doing. But once confident that you're a winning player at the stakes you've chosen, you can try adding more tables, but be careful. Whatever your win per table may be at one or two tables, it will drop as you add more tables and your attention becomes fragmented. If your win rate drops too much, the additional tables may be costing you money. Proceed cautiously and try to determine the number of tables that is optimal for you.

Physical Reads

The value of physical reads and tells in live play is a controversial topic. Some players feel their ability to read their opponents gives them an edge. Others feel they can't read their opponents, or at least not as well as their opponents can read them.

In online play, physical tells essentially disappear, and are replaced by the information provided by betting patterns and Heads-Up Displays, known as HUDs. Most studious players probably consider this trade-off a net plus. If you're a player who feels you have an extraordinary ability to sniff out your opponent's holdings from his mannerisms, you may consider it a minus. In any case, the absence of physical reads is a clear difference between online and live play.

Buy-Ins

In live games, allowable buy-ins vary from casino to casino. A typical policy might allow a minimum buy-in of 40 to 50 big blinds, and a maximum of 100 to 200 big blinds. Most players at such a table would be buying in for 100 big blinds. This policy creates an interesting table with a fairly wide range of stack sizes.

Some casinos, particularly Indian casinos, cap the buy-in at a very low number. A $1/$2 game might have a $100 maximum buy-in, equivalent to 50 big blinds. This limits the potential losses for any player at the cost of greatly limiting implied odds on any drawing hand and making holdings like small pairs and suited connectors less playable.

Most online tables allow a minimum buy-in of 20 big blinds and a maximum of 100 big blinds. Some sites, however, are experimenting with allowing larger buy-ins at 'deep stack' tables, up to 200 or 250 big blinds. The very low minimum buy-ins allow some players to experiment with various short stack strategies, often to the annoyance of the deeper stacks at the tables. The presence of short stacks has an effect on overall strategy; as we mentioned before, however, online sites are moving to curb small buy-ins, so short stack strategies may soon become a historical relic.

Summary

Should you play online or live? This isn't really a fair question. If you're learning no-limit hold 'em, online poker is the best training venue ever devised. You can start for incredibly small stakes, play hundreds of thousands of hands, analyze your play along the way, move up in stakes as you're ready, and emerge in a relatively short period of time as a seasoned player with a variety of options.

At that point, you might decide that you like online play, live play, or more likely both. But there's no doubt that starting online is the way to go.

Databases

As online poker became established, software entrepreneurs realized that a market existed for tools that could help players gain an edge. Within a short time, poker database managers began to appear with features that most players found essential.

Analyzing your play after a live session is a spotty and somewhat haphazard business. If you can remember a few key hands, you can write them down and review them, looking for better lines of play. If you're thorough and think you might face some of these same players again, you might even write down a few observations in a notebook. Over time, these observations might coalesce into a reasonably clear picture of an opponent's tendencies. You might also get a rough sense whether play in a particular card room is easier or tougher than in other rooms you've played in. Still, gathering information from live games is a slow business.

Online, however, some fantastic tools are available. The two most notable are PokerTracker and Hold 'Em Manager, database managers that perform similar functions for a similar price. Each program logs all the hands you play online into a database, then presents the data in a variety of ways, and using these programs allows you to easily check for systematic errors in your game.

Heads-Up Displays (HUDs)

The database managers don't just log your data; they also log the data for all your opponents at the same time. The Heads-Up Displays, or HUDs as they are commonly known, take this data and superimpose it on your screen next to your opponent. The choice of data is up to you, and you can choose from hundreds of available data points. By choosing your data carefully, the HUD can be an incredibly useful tool.

Understanding
PokerTracker Data

The two most important poker database programs are PokerTracker and Hold 'em Manager. Both are firmly established in the marketplace, and each has its loyal fans and supporters. Since both are evolving and are regularly updated, we won't recommend one over the other. In this book, when we refer to "PokerTracker," we're using the word in a generic sense to mean any fully-functional database package.

The most important feature of these programs is the HUD, or heads-up display. When you play at an online table and turn on your HUD, it superimposes a subset of your opponent's data on the table near their seat. The data is current: PokerTracker updates the display after each hand. Exactly what data is displayed is up to you. Selecting data properly is important since not all of the data in your opponent's database carries the same weight. Select properly, and you'll have clear insight into how your opponent plays. Select badly, and you'll get a collection of data that's not as helpful as it could be. So in this section, we'll show you how to build a HUD that displays the data you really want.

Basic Information

We'll begin with some information that you'll want to display:

1. Player Name
2. Hands
3. BB/100

1. **"Player Name"** is simply the player's name on this site. It might seem you could skip this since you can see the player's name displayed at his seat. Mostly that's true. However, having the name displayed in the HUD is actually important in a couple of situations.

   The first occurs when a player exits a table and a new player immediately occupies his seat and posts a blind to play the next hand. In that case, the old player's information will persist for a hand until PokerTracker recognizes that a new player is in action. Without the Player Name in the HUD, you might not notice that the displayed information describes a player who's no longer at the table.

   The second situation occurs on some of the smaller sites. If you've selected a favorite seat at a table but PokerTracker, for whatever reason, can't recognize what's happened, the HUDs may be displayed at the wrong seats. (This can also occur in tournaments when you've been moved to a new table in the middle of the tournament.) In this case, you'll need to move the HUDs manually to the correct seats, and you'll need to see the player names.

2. **"Hands"** is the count of the number of hands for this player in the database. It's an essential piece of information because different statistics converge to useful values at different rates. Knowing how many hands make up the data tells you how reliable the data might be for a given statistic.

   Note that your "Hands" count is just the number of hands you've played in this session. For your opponents, it's a total count over all the hands in the database.

3. **"BB/100"** shows the number of big bets won (or lost) by this player per 100 hands. This statistic takes a long time to converge for a player whose winning or losing rate is a small number. For players who are big winners or big losers at a particular stake, it converges more quickly. In any case, it's

a better measure of results than simple "amount won," a statistic which is also available.

There's a historical anomaly to note here. PokerTracker was the earliest database program and was originally developed for limit hold 'em tables. The "BB" in "BB/100" was intended to mean "big bet," which in limit hold 'em is twice the big blind. PokerTracker carried this definition over into no-limit, even though a bet of twice the big blind has no special significance in no-limit. Be aware that the "BB/100" number is half what it would be if actual big blinds were counted.

Statistics can be color-coded, and that's a useful feature. You might want to code a winning player with BB/100 colored green, and use red for a losing player. That way you can instantly look at a table and spot the winners and losers.

The Classics

The most-commonly referenced PokerTracker statistics are two which really define a player's preflop game:

1. Voluntarily Put Money in the Pot (VP$IP)
2. Preflop Raise (PFR)

1. **"VP$IP"** shows the percentage of time that a player enters a pot preflop, either by raising or calling. Note that you have to actually put money in the pot to qualify here. Checking in the big blind after some players have limped in doesn't count.

VP$IP numbers range from below 10 (for very tight players) to above 80 (for incredibly loose players.) In a 6-max game, good players usually show numbers ranging from lows of 15 to 18 to highs of 25 to 30. In a full ring game, the numbers will be lower. This number has more meaning, however, when combined with the PFR number.

2.   **"PFR"** shows the percentage of time that a player raises preflop. Aggressive players will have high numbers, often over 20 but almost always under 30. Passive players, who call a lot but don't like to raise, might have a PFR of 10 or lower. Also, this number will be lower in a full ring game than in a 6-max game.

Combining the two basic statistics tells us much of what we want to know about a player's preflop style, and lets us categorize opponents into a few well-defined types. Let's take a quick look at these types and their characteristic statistics.

1.   **The Nit:** Typical VP$IP and PFR statistics for the nit are 4/4, 8/6, or 10/8. Nits are super-tight players who just want to go to the flop with premium hands. For example, a 5 percent hand range consists of a set of hands like the following:

> AA through TT
> AKs through ATs
> AKo, AQo, KQs

or alternatively

> AA through 88
> AKs through ATs
> AKo, KQs.

An 8 percent range looks more like this:

> AA through 88
> AKs through ATs
> KQs through KTs
> AKo through AJo
> QJs

In either case, we're talking about a player who plays a range consisting exclusively of high pairs, suited Broadway cards, and very high unsuited aces. These hands are likely to be best preflop, and will often make hands like top pair, top kicker when they hit the flop. The nit is much more comfortable with having the best hand at the moment than with creating a disguised monster that can win his opponent's whole stack.

2. **The Tight-Aggressive:** Tight-Aggressives, or TAGs as they are commonly called, play a wider range of hands than the nits. Their preflop VP$IP and PFR statistics in a 6-max game might look like 18/16, 20/17, or 24/20. Notice that although they play a wider range, their PFR number is very close to their VP$IP number which indicates that when they enter a pot, they are usually raising and very rarely just calling. A tight-aggressive player will almost never open-limp (enter the pot before anyone else by calling the big blind). Instead, he prefers to raise or fold.

    Tight-aggressive players at 6-max tend to have VP$IP and PFR numbers that cluster around 20 percent. A 20 percent hand range looks like the following:

> All pairs
> Any two cards ten or higher
> A9s-A8s
> Q9s, J9s
> Suited connectors from T9s to 76s

This is a much wider range than the super-tight ranges of the nits, but still consists of recognizable hands and quality cards: pairs, high card combinations, and suited connectors. Playing this range requires more skill than playing the nit's range since many of these hands could hit the flop but be dominated. The TAG has to be able to maneuver post-flop to be successful with this range, and winning players at 6-max most commonly play some variation of a TAG style.

3. **The Loose-Aggressive:** Loose-Aggressives, also known as LAGs, play more hands than the tight-aggressives. Their typical statistics might look something like 30/24, 32/24, or 28/20. Notice that their PFR numbers are not as close to their VP$IP numbers as was the case with the TAGs. Although they're more willing to call and see a flop with a speculative hand than the TAGs, the difference is a matter of degree. Their style is still heavily oriented around preflop aggression.
    A 30 percent hand range looks like this:

> All pairs
> All suited aces
> AK through A7 offsuit
> All suited and unsuited Broadway cards
> Suited connectors from T9s through 54s
> Unsuited connectors from T9 through 65
> K9s, Q9s, J9s, and T8s

This is a very wide range and makes a loose-aggressive player difficult to read. A talented loose-aggressive player is a dangerous opponent since he could be holding the nuts on almost any flop.

4. **The Loose-Passive:** Loose-Passives are common in the micro-stakes games but become less common as you move up the ladder. Loose-passive players like to play lots of hands and see lots of flops. Their statistics could look like anything from 30/10 to 40/5 to 75/15. When they miss flops, (a common occurrence), they'll throw their hand away and move on. When they hit a flop, even with something like middle or bottom pair, they'll usually hang around for at least a bet or two.

Over time, loose-passives are steady losers because they're involved in too many pots with weak hands. In addition, their raises generally indicate strong hands, so they're comparatively easy to read. In a micro-stakes game, you might see two or three of these players at your table at any one time. You'll also see them in small-stakes games, but again they will be less common and their statistics will be less extreme.

Take note of an important point with loose-passive players: The guy with statistics of 40/5 is much less dangerous than the guy whose statistics are 40/0! The first player will tell you when he picks up a very good hand because he'll raise with it. You can then play accordingly. But the 40/0 player limps or calls *all* his hands preflop, including aces. He plays poker for the thrill of trapping you with a better hand, so beware! If an otherwise loose player shows absolutely no preflop raises after 40 or 50 hands, he probably fits this category. Watch out when you're in a pot with him.

5.   **The Maniac:** A maniac will have statistics like 40/30, 50/40, or 65/50. Maniacs believe that pretty much all hands are playable, and a playable hand is a raising hand! Against this guy you'll never know where you stand. When you do pick up a hand or hit a flop, you have to be prepared to go to the mat with it. Occasionally, he'll take your stack; more often, you'll take his.

Other Useful Preflop Statistics

Besides those basic two statistics, there are four other preflop statistics that belong on your HUD:

1.   3-Bet Preflop (3B)
2.   Fold to 3-Bet Preflop (F3B)
3.   Attempt to Steal (ATS)
4.   Fold Big Blind to Steal (FBS)

1.   A **"3-Bet Preflop"** is simply a reraise. Let's say in a 6-max game the first player to act raises, the second and third players fold, and on the button, you toss in a reraise. Your reraise is known as a 3-bet.

       The 3-bet preflop statistic tells you the percentage of time a player 3-bets when the pot has been raised in front of him. Since opening raises happen frequently, this statistic generates meaningful data a bit faster than you might expect; after the number of hands played passes 60 or so, I'll start to pay close attention to this number.

       A normally tight player is a little reluctant to 3-bet with hands like a pair of jacks or ace-queen; he's probably only comfortable tossing in a 3-bet with a pair of queens or better, or ace-king, suited or unsuited. A player who's that tight will have a 3-betting range of about 3 percent. A somewhat looser player will probably toss a few more hands into the mix. If he's willing to 3-bet with tens, jacks, and ace-queen, as well as the better hands, then his 3-betting range will be more like 5 percent. Throw in nines, eights, ace-jack, and king-queen, and the range gets up to 8 percent.

As you move up through the ranks, 3-betting ranges tend to get wider. In micro-stakes games, 3-bets usually mean an extremely strong hand, and typical 3-bet numbers are 3 percent or lower. Small stakes players will reraise with a wider range, and the ranges of high stakes players will typically be wider yet.

2. An equally important statistic is the **"Fold to 3-bet"** number. Obviously, it represents the percentage of time a player open-raises and then folds when someone 3-bets him. Theoretically, this number should be directly proportional to a player's PFR. A nitty player with a low PFR should also have a low Fold to 3-bet number because most, if not all, of the few hands that he's raising are strong enough to either call a 3-bet or even make a 4-bet. In contrast, a player with a high PFR is raising a lot of marginal hands, and should be willing to fold most of them to a 3-bet.

    In small stakes and high stakes games, this relationship will generally hold. But in micro-stakes games, most fold to 3-bet numbers are low, regardless of the underlying PFR. The nits don't fold because they're already playing strong hands, and the loose players don't fold because they just want to see a flop, and they mostly don't really care exactly what price they have to pay to see the flop. But as we saw in "Part One: Basic No-Limit Hold 'em Concepts," if a player's fold to 3-bet number is too high, then you may be able to 3-bet him with any two cards and show an instant profit.

3. The remaining two preflop statistics are useful but not crucial. An **"Attempt to Steal"** is just an opening raise from

the late seats, either the cutoff or button. Aggressive players will raise a wide range of hands when first to act in these positions since they will have position over the blinds after the flop if the blinds choose to play. The ATS statistic gives us some data on just how aggressive a player chooses to be in this spot.

The ATS statistic isn't crucial since the information overlaps to a large degree with the PFR statistic. A player who generally raises a lot of hands when first to act can be expected to have a high ATS number, and in fact that's usually the case. However, the converse isn't always true since there are tight players who nonetheless like to raise a lot from late position. With a large enough sample of data, the ATS number can identify them.

4. **"Fold Big Blind to Steal"** is also useful because players vary in the amount of effort they'll expend to defend the big blind from a late-position raise. But if their folding number is more than 80 percent, you should be able to show a profit by raising on the button with virtually any two cards, and by raising a wide range from the cutoff.

    There's not much point in keeping track of a player's folding rate in the small blind, although that information is available. Players will fold the small blind more often than the big blind since they have less invested in the pot, their post-flop position is worse, and the player in the big blind can put in a reraise. As a result, this number is usually high and can be ignored when you're planning a steal attempt. Focus on the folding percentage of the big blind and you'll have most of the information you need.

Post-Flop
Action Statistics

There are several useful statistics that describe how players act after the flop.

1. C-Bet Flop (CB)
2. Fold to Flop C-Bet (FC)
3. Fold to Turn C-Bet (FTC)
4. Total Aggression Factor (AF)
5. Flop Aggression Factor (FA)
6. Turn Aggression Factor (TA)
7. River Aggression Factor (RA)

1. **"C-Bet Flop"** gives the percentage of time that a player makes a continuation bet on the flop. A *continuation bet* is a bet made on the flop after a player has taken the lead in the betting preflop. This person indicated that he had a good hand preflop, and now says he still likes his hand after the flop.

    Most good players will make a continuation bet on the flop about 65 to 75 percent of the time. It's a high-percentage play since the hand that's in the lead preflop will mostly still be leading after the flop. The defender will want a good hand to continue playing, but on average a non-paired hand will only hit a pair or better on the flop about 30 percent of the time.

    A 'c-bet flop' percentage of 50 percent or less indicates a player who's pretty passive after the flop, and who doesn't like to keep putting money in the pot unless he really has a hand. You should obviously call more often preflop against such a player with the idea of picking up pots after the flop when you both miss.

A very high 'c-bet flop' percentage (over 80 percent) shows that this player makes continuation bets almost all the time. You should be prepared to raise this player's continuation bet more often when you hit the flop, and *float* (call a continuation bet with nothing) more often as well.

There is no perfect value for 'c-bet flop,' but it needs to make sense in context with the VP$IP and PFR numbers. If your VP$IP and PFR numbers are low (indicating tightness preflop), then you're only playing good hands and your continuation bet percentage should be high (75 to 80 percent at least) since those hands will often be best post-flop. On the other hand, high VP$IP/PFR numbers show that you're playing loosely preflop, trying to see a flop with a lot of weak hands. Now your continuation bet percentage should be lower (55 to 65 percent perhaps), reflecting that you can't be hitting all these hands post-flop. If your 'c-bet flop' number isn't aligned with your VP$IP and PFR numbers, a canny opponent will be able to exploit you.

2. **"Fold to Flop C-Bet"** shows how often a player gives up when his opponent makes a continuation bet. This is useful information provided it's based on enough hands. If you have one or two hundred hands of data, you'll want to think carefully about this statistic before making a continuation bet.

Assuming you have enough data, the key ranges for this statistic are: greater than 70 percent, 50 to 70 percent, and less than 50 percent.

If your opponent folds to a continuation bet more than 70 percent of the time, then he's calling or raising less than 30 percent. Since he'll hit the flop about 30 percent of the time, you can assume that he's playing fit or fold poker. If his fold to continuation bet is very high (more than 80 percent), then he's continuing only with strong hands and strong draws. If his number is more like 70 percent, then he's playing his reasonably good made hands and an assortment of draws. Players in this range are most likely never floating the flop. Your plan should be to continuation bet almost all the time, but reevaluate when you encounter resistance.

If your opponent folds to a continuation bet less than 50 percent of the time, he's playing all his made hands and draws, and floating some of the time when he misses completely. Two kinds of players fit this profile: weak calling stations and strong players who believe they can outplay you after the flop. You'll need more information to decide in which group this particular opponent fits. However, if you believe your opponent is a calling station, be prepared to value bet him strongly when you have a hand, but avoid wasting money when you don't. Against a strong player, you'll again mostly want a real hand to continue, but also be prepared to bluff occasionally as well.

A fold to continuation bet range of 50 to 70 percent is fairly average. Against this range, just play your normal game on the flop.

3. **"Fold to Turn C-Bet"** gives the percentage of time that a player folds to a bet on the turn after he has called a continuation bet on the flop. This statistic converges slowly, so don't place much confidence in the number until you have a couple of thousand hands on a player. But once you have some evidence, it tells you how often a player will fold to a double-barrel bet (a flop continuation bet followed by a turn bet).

Sometimes you'll encounter a player who has a low 'fold to c-bet' number but a high 'fold to turn c-bet' number. Such a player understands that many continuation bets are bluffs, and wants to see if you are willing to bet again on the turn before he folds his own weak hand. Double-barreling will be profitable in this situation.

4. **"Total Aggression Factor"** is a measure of how often a player takes an aggressive action after the flop, compared to a passive action. It's a ratio defined as

    Aggression Factor = (bet% + raise%) / (call%)

    A player whose 'calls after the flop' total is equal to the number of his bets and raises would have an aggression factor of 1. A player who mostly bets and raises with just a few calls, will have an aggression factor larger than 1, and players who make few post-flop calls can have aggression factors equal to 2, 3, 4, or even higher.

    The term "aggression factor" is a bit misleading. Note that folding percentage and checking percentage are not included in the definition of the term, so the aggression that's being measured is just a particular type of aggression, namely the percentage that a player takes an aggressive action *given that he does not fold or check.* To see the problem, let's consider two very different types of opponents and look at their aggression factor.

    Opponent A is a nit's nit. His preflop statistics are 6/4, so he's playing only pairs and premium high cards preflop. After the flop he'll be making a continuation bet, but folding to resistance unless he has a hand like top pair, top kicker or better. If we look at his post-flop aggression factor, it will be quite high because he's folding (or checking) when he misses, and betting strongly when he has a hand.

    Opponent B, on the other hand, is a crazy person. His VP$IP/PFR stats are 60/45. He knows only one speed, pedal to the metal. After the flop, he takes a shot at pretty much every board, but like Opponent A, he folds when he encounters resistance or doesn't have a hand (which is most of the time). His aggression factor will be similarly high, but he's much less likely to actually have a hand than Opponent A.

An aggression factor in the range of 1.5 to 2.0 is about normal for the typical tight-aggressive player. He'll bet and raise more often than he'll call, but not to an unreasonable degree.

An aggression factor under 1.0 indicates a likely calling station. He prefers to see the hand through when he has something, even if it's a small pair, and is usually suspicious that he's being bluffed. When this person raises, beware, he probably has a big hand. But when you hold a good hand, top pair, top kicker or better, you should keep betting and extracting value.

An aggression factor of 2.5 or more indicates a very aggressive player. In general, he'll be taking the lead and trying to push you out of pots if you don't show strength. However, you can frequently trap him for a couple of bets, especially if you're in position with a big hand and he was the preflop aggressor.

Aggression factor is a useful statistic because it correlates with a number of tendencies. When you look at a player's aggression factor, consider the following:

Low aggression factor indicates:

1. More likely to slowplay, less likely to bet monster hands.

2. More likely to call with a drawing hand.

3. More likely to call with a weak hand.

High aggression factor indicates:

1. More likely to bet strong hands, less likely to slowplay.

2. More likely to semi-bluff a drawing hand.

3.   More likely to fold a weak hand.

Combining your opponent's aggression factor with his preflop statistics can provide a lot of clues for playing post-flop.

5.   **"Flop Aggression / Turn Aggression / River Aggression"** show aggression broken out on a street by street basis. These are useful numbers because they help you spot certain recurring patterns of betting which can be exploited.

For example, most players now know to make a continuation bet on the flop when they led the betting preflop. But if that bet doesn't win the pot, a weaker player won't be sure how to continue on the turn. He may shut down at that point either for pot control (if he actually has something) or because he's afraid his opponent has a hand and can't be pushed off it. So a pattern of high flop aggression coupled with low turn and river aggression indicates a player who's only confident of putting more money in the pot on the turn and river with a big hand. It's worth floating this player and stealing pots with late bets or raises.

Another common pattern is the player who has low aggression on the flop and turn but high aggression on the river. This is probably a player who's playing a lot of draws and mid-pair/low-pair type hands, and who wants to see all his cards before folding. You can extract a lot of value from this player with a real hand, but a river bet from him probably means he has something good.

For most players, flop aggression will be higher than turn aggression, which in turn will be higher than river aggression. That's because they know about continuation bets on the flop, so a higher aggression number on that street is common. But after meeting resistance, they will then switch to a pot control mode and slow down without a strong hand, so the aggression numbers drop off on the later streets.

Note that these statistics require many hundreds or even thousands of hands to converge to solid numbers, so don't assign too much weight to them until you've played with a particular opponent for awhile.

Post-Flop Summary Statistics

These last three statistics are very important. They summarize the result of a player's post-flop actions and provide clues on how to proceed against them.

1. Win Money When Seeing Flop (W$WSF)
2. Went to Showdown (WtSD)
3. Win Money at Showdown (W$SD)

1. **"Win Money When Seeing Flop"** just gives the percentage of time a player wins the hand given that he saw the flop. This number tends to be lower than most people expect. Imagine, for instance, that about 70 percent of the time you see the flop heads-up and the other 30 percent you see a three-way flop. (These are reasonable numbers for a 6-max game.) If you win half of your heads-up pots and a third of your three-way pots, your W$WSF number will be about 45 percent.

$$0.45 = (0.50)(0.70) + (0.33)(0.30)$$

That number, 45 percent, is actually a good average number for this statistic which has a relatively small range.

If your W$WSF number is greater than 50 percent, you're winning a lot of pots, probably by aggressively betting on multiple streets. You're not going to see a lot of showdowns because your opponents will have folded to your aggression. But you may not win a lot of showdowns since your opponents will only be getting that far with good hands. In all likelihood, however, the pots you take down make up for your losses on the river, and overall you're a solid winning player.

If your W$WSF number is less than about 40 percent, you're playing too passively post-flop. You don't want to go deep in the hand without a strong holding, and you're probably getting pushed out of too many pots when your opponents take a strong betting line. You won't see a lot of showdowns, but when you do your winning percentage is likely to be high.

A W$WSF in the mid-40s isn't too significant in itself. Look at the other statistics in this group for exploitable tendencies.

2. **"Went to Showdown"** is just what you might expect, the percentage of time a player went to showdown given that he saw the flop. Like W$WSF, this statistic has a relatively narrow range. Average numbers for 'went to showdown' are 25 to 27 percent.

A player whose 'went to showdown' number is very low (less than 20 percent) is getting pushed off a lot of hands easily. However, if he stays in a pot past the flop, he probably has something good. You should make continuation bets against this player almost all the time, but be wary when that bet doesn't take the pot down.

A player with a high 'went to showdown' number (over 30 percent) is probably hanging around with a lot of second-best hands even though the betting indicates he is beaten. You should be betting for value frequently against this player.

3. **"Win Money at Showdown"** gives the percentage of time that a player goes to showdown and wins the hand given that he went to showdown in the first place. Mostly, this number should be inversely correlated with the 'went to showdown' number. The less a player gets to showdown, the stronger his showdown hands will tend to be, and vice versa.

    For most players, this statistic has a fairly narrow range between about 47 and 53 percent. Players with a winning percentage above 53 are only trying to get to showdown with their stronger hands. You can bet aggressively against these players and push them out of many pots. On the other hand, players with a winning percentage under 47 percent are getting to showdown too often with weaker hands. You probably can't bluff them much, but with a good hand, you can certainly bet for value.

Constructing Your HUD

Once you understand the data that's available, you're ready to start the process of actually building your HUD. So why not just throw in all the data we listed in the previous section? Well, you could do that, but there are several reasons why you might not want to. A HUD takes up screen space, and a big HUD with all the data we just listed takes up a lot of screen space. If you're just playing one 6-max table at a time, that's not going to be a problem. A big HUD can easily fit around a single table with just six players. Move up to a full ring table with nine players and things get a little more crowded. Open two tables instead of one and things get a lot busier. Put four tables on the screen at the same time and the tables get dramatically smaller, but the size of your HUD doesn't change. Now your screen is really crowded.

Just how big you want your HUD to be is a function both of how experienced you are interpreting the various statistics and how many tables you want to play at the same time. Let's take a look at how you can start small, then add information to your HUD over time.

A Minimal HUD

Here's an example of a HUD which is about as small as it can be while still being useful.

HansBeegFeesh / (60) / -4
VP 40 / PF 5 / AF 0.8

In the first line, we have our opponent's name followed by the number of hands of data that are in the database. In this case it's just 60 hands, which is enough to begin to have confidence in some of our numbers. (It's still, however, a pretty small amount of data.) The last number, -4, shows his wins (or losses) measured in big bets per 100 hands. We know that over the 60 hands we've seen, HansBeegFeesh has lost at a rate of four big bets (or eight big blinds) per 100 hands. That translates into an actual loss of 4.8 big blinds in the 60 hands.

In the second line, we start to see some more interesting information. PokerTracker allows us to attach abbreviations to each displayed piece of data to help us remember what the numbers represent. These abbreviations can be defined by the user, so you want to make them just long enough to be recognizable without taking up too much space. Two character abbreviations will usually do the job. Here we've used 'VP' to represent 'voluntarily put money in pot,' 'PF' to represent 'preflop raise, and 'AF' to represent 'aggression factor.'

Our HUD is just two lines long and won't take up much screen space at all, but it still manages to convey some useful data. If you're just starting and don't want to get bogged down with too much information, or have a very limited amount of screen real estate, it's a good place to start.

A More Useful HUD

Most players won't settle for just a two-line HUD for very long. Here's an example of a three-line HUD that conveys a lot more information, but still doesn't take up too much screen space.

> *Feebcrusher / (180) / +2*
> *VP 20 / PF 15 / AS 20 / FB 80*
> *AF 2.5 / 5 / 1 / 0.5 / CB 90 / FC 60*

Line 1 shows that we have 180 hands of data on this player, and his win rate so far is two big bets per 100 hands.

Line 2 gives us his VP$IP and PFR as before. For this player, his numbers are a more reasonable 20/15, indicating a tight-aggressive player. On this line we've also added his 'attempt to steal' percentage, abbreviated 'AS,' and his 'fold big blind to steal' percentage, abbreviated 'FB.' We're sticking to two-letter abbreviations to save screen space without losing clarity.

Line 3 shows his aggression factor, but now the aggression factor has four numbers after the abbreviation. The first number is the overall post-flop aggression factor. The next three numbers are the aggression factors for each street broken out separately; the flop aggression is 5, the turn aggression is 1, and the river aggression is just 0.5. This is a player who bets strongly on the flop, but slows down on later streets without a strong hand.

We have two more numbers on line 3: 'CB' and 'FC.' The first is 'continuation bet' percentage, while the second is 'fold to continuation bet' percentage. Together, they tell us something about his tendencies on the flop. Note that the continuation bet percentage of 90 is consistent with the flop aggression of 5. This is a player who likes to make continuation bets whether he hit the hand or not.

A Very Detailed HUD

If space is not a problem, we can extend our HUD further and include all the statistics we discussed in the previous section. A fully-implemented HUD might look like this:

```
MrAwesome / (600) / +7
VP 28 / PF 24 / AS 35 / FB 65
3B 7 / F3 65 / AF 2.2 / 3 / 2 / 1.5
CB 70 / FC 60 / FT 70
W$F 52 / WtS 28 / W$S 48
```

We've rearranged the previous HUD a bit and added six more statistics. '3B' and 'F3' signify '3-bet' percentage and 'fold to 3-bet' percentage respectively. 'FT' on line four indicates 'fold to turn c-bet.' We're now keeping track of what happens when someone faces both a continuation bet on the flop and another bet on the turn.

The last line includes the three post-flop summary statistics: 'W$F' is 'win money when seeing flop,' 'WtS' is 'went to showdown,' and 'W$S' is 'win money at showdown.' Since these are the only statistics on line 5, we've extended the abbreviations to three characters for extra clarity.

Conserving Space

The last HUD gives us all the statistics we've discussed so far, but it's bulky and takes up a lot of screen space. That's no problem if you're playing just one or two 6-max games at a time. But suppose you're playing several tables at once, or you're playing full ring instead of 6-max? In that case, you'd like to squeeze your HUD into as small a space as possible. You could just drop back down to some of the simpler HUDs we displayed earlier, but another way is to eliminate the abbreviations, showing just the statistics. In order to do this you'll need to be very familiar with the statistics you're displaying. If we eliminate the abbreviations from the previous HUD we get a display that looks like this:

> *MrAwesome / (600) / +7*
> *28 / 24 / 35 / 65*
> *7 / 65 / 2.2 / 3 / 2 / 1.5*
> *70 / 60 / 70 / 52 / 28 / 48*

By eliminating the abbreviations and combining the last two lines into one, we've created a display that has all the information and fits in a relatively small space. Losing the abbreviations makes the display less clear, but if you use the HUD for a few days you should get very familiar with the location and meaning of all the statistics.

It helps, of course, that we've grouped items together in a logical way. The second line contains all preflop statistics, starting with VP$IP and PFR, followed by the two blind stealing stats. Line 3 begins with the last two preflop statistics relating to 3-betting, followed by the post-flop aggression factors. Line 4 contains all post-flop information, starting with the three continuation bet statistics and finishing with the three summary statistics.

Exactly how you want to construct and arrange your HUD is up to you. In the examples in this book, we'll mostly use the full display with abbreviations given above for the players who are actively involved in the hand.

Drawing Inferences

The HUD statistics aren't just stand-alone numbers. In many cases, you can use combinations of statistics to draw more interesting inferences about how your opponents play and what they're likely to do. Look at the different numbers, see how they fit together, and try to build a picture of how your opponent plays and what lines might work against him. Let's look at some sample HUDs and see just what they say about our opponents.

Sample HUD No. 1

> *JeffJ / (180) / +6*
> *VP 12 / PF 8 / AS 18 / FB 85*
> *3B 3 / F3 85 / AF 4 / 5 / 1 / 0.8*
> *CB 85 / FC 60 / FT 80*
> *W$F 42 / WtS 22 / W$S 57*

We're playing in a 6-max game at $25 NL ($0.10/$0.25 blinds), so we're at the high end of the micro-stakes spectrum. "JeffJ" is doing well at our table. What can we tell about him from his HUD?

The first thing we notice is that he's an extremely tight player, with VP$IP/PFR statistics of 12 and 8. He's entering very few pots, he's mostly raising when he enters, and when in a pot, his hand will be either a pair or two high cards with just the occasional suited connector, probably of medium strength. He's also a solid winning player overall, with a win rate of 6 big bets per 100 hands.

When we look at his steal statistics, we notice that the 'attempt to steal' number (18) is distinctly on the low side. Even when the hand is folded to him on the button, he needs a much better than average hand to get involved. But we can also draw one more important conclusion: by comparing his overall preflop raise number (8) to his attempt to steal number (18), we can deduce that he's not fully aware of the value of position. If he were, he'd be raising even more often in the button and cutoff, and his attempt to steal number would be even higher.

This insight leads to a further observation. When a player understands position, he'll usually have weaker hands when he's in position and stronger hands when he's out of position because he knows that his positional advantage compensates for the weakness of his cards. That won't be the case with "JeffJ." Expect him to have pretty good hands whether he's in or out of position.

On line 3, his 3-betting statistics are about what we would expect. His very low 3-bet number (3) shows that he'll only 3-bet with his best hands, probably aces through queens and ace-king. His fold to 3-bet number (85) is similarly high. If you 3-bet him, he'll put you on a very strong hand and fold unless he has a premium pair.

His aggression factor numbers on line 3 are high but a bit misleading. A player who plays only strong hands preflop is likely to have a lot of good hands post-flop: including top pair, top kicker, or an overpair. He should be making a lot of continuation bets, and indeed he is. In fact, his flop aggression of 5 and his continuation bet percentage of 85 percent are not only high, but probably a little too high. Looking at his turn and river aggression, we see that those numbers drop off sharply: 1 and 0.8, respectively. He needs a very good hand to keep pushing after he hits resistance.

On the other side of the coin, if we look on line 4 we notice that his 'fold to continuation bet' number is 60 and his 'fold to turn continuation bet' is even higher at 80. Those are high numbers considering that he's only playing strong hands. It seems he's a little too conservative when he doesn't have the lead, and a bit too willing to surrender to aggression.

The summary statistics on line 5 complete the picture. His 'win money when seeing flop' number of 42 is too low given his strong starting hands, so JeffJ is getting pushed out of a lot of pots when he doesn't have a super-strong hand and his opponent puts up a fight. His 'went to showdown' number is 22, below average and consistent with the previous observation. His 'win money at showdown' is 57, very high and indicative that he only brings his best hands to showdown.

Our Game Plan

Our game plan against "JeffJ" is simple: relentless aggression. Although he raises only a few hands preflop (8 percent), he doesn't have confidence in his ability to play the hand unless he's very sure his hand is best. We should exploit his uncertainty by 3-betting him on a regular basis. Note that by combining his preflop raise percentage (8 percent) with his fold to 3-bet percentage (85 percent), we know that he's willing to call or raise a 3-bet with only 1.2 percent of his total hands.

$$0.012 = (0.08)(0.15)$$

That's a range of just aces and kings, a range so tight that we can literally 3-bet him with any two cards, give up on the hand if he 4-bets, and still show a solid profit. Nice work if you can get it!

After the flop our plan is also pretty simple. Since we know he makes a lot of continuation bets but doesn't want to get to showdown without a strong hand, we should plan to 'float' a lot of his continuation bets (calling his bet without a real hand) then bet the turn after he checks. Since his turn aggression number of 1 is low compared to his flop aggression of 5, we know he's rarely able to fire a second barrel without what he believes to be a strong hand. That's a dangerous tendency when carried to extremes, and one we want to exploit ruthlessly.

At this point you might well ask "How is 'JeffJ' a winner when we're able to exploit him so easily?" The answer lies in the stakes. We met Jeff at a micro-stakes table, and at micro-stakes games excessively tight play will show a solid profit. He's winning money from the players who are too loose and too passive. (We think he'll lose some of that money back to us, but even so he'll probably still show a profit.)

If Jeff plans on moving up, however, he's going to need to raise his game. At small-stakes tables he'll run into opponents who will be less loose and passive and more aggressive, and who'll be using their own HUDs and spotting the same tendencies we just spotted. At those levels, his style of play won't be enough to show a profit. At even higher levels, he'd get crushed.

Sample HUD No. 2

```
Lucious / (120) / -10
VP 40 / PF 8 / AS 10 / FB 60
3B 1 / F3 20 / AF 1.2 / 1.5 / 1 / 0.8
CB 50 / FC 53 / FT 60
W$F 38 / WtS 33 / W$S 45
```

We're in the same 6-max game at $25NL as before, but here's a player with a very different profile from "JeffJ." We've only seen 120 hands on "Lucious," so we have a bit less confidence in our numbers than before. However, Lucious has some tendencies which jump right out. His VP$IP/PFR numbers mark him as extremely loose-passive, playing a whopping 40 percent of his hands but raising with only 8 percent. He likes to see a flop with a hand that has almost any merit, but he won't raise unless he has a premium holding. His very low attempt to steal number (10 percent) indicates that even with position he won't take the lead without a good hand.

However, note that Lucious can't be pushed around preflop. His 'fold big blind to steal' number is only 60 percent, meaning that he'll call 40 percent of the time in the big blind if you try to steal. That's the same as his overall VP$IP, so he doesn't really care what your action is representing. If he has a hand he wants to play, he'll play it. His fold to 3-bet of 20 percent supports this conclusion. No matter what strength you represent, he's not getting pushed out once he indicates interest.

His aggression factor numbers (1.2, 1.5, 1, 0.8) are all on the low side and indicate a general passivity post-flop. That is he needs a pretty strong hand to take the post-flop betting lead. The continuation bet number of 50 percent is also low and gives further confirmation that he's passive post-flop.

His summary statistics also tell a clear story. His 'went to showdown' number is 33 percent, which is very high. However, both his 'win money when seeing flop' number (38 percent) and his 'win money at showdown' number (45 percent) are low, indicating that he likes to get to showdown, but he doesn't do well when he gets there. He's probably calling on the flop with any pair or any draw, and continuing to call with those hands in the hope they hold up at showdown. Also note the subtle correlation between his preflop VP$IP/PFR numbers (40/8) and his low 'win money when seeing flop' number (38). When your preflop action is almost always a call, it becomes difficult to steal random flops that are up for grabs. A lack of preflop aggression makes taking down pots post-flop much harder.

Our Game Plan

"Lucious" presents a very different problem from "JeffJ." He's a classic loose-passive calling station, a player who wants to see the hand through and find out if he won or not, without paying much attention to how much it costs to get there. These players aren't hard to beat, but they require a mixture of common-sense aggressiveness mixed with a little caution.

First, let's note that we're not going to bluff Lucious much. We won't 3-bet him preflop without a strong hand. If we raise preflop and he calls, we can put out a continuation bet when we miss the flop to see if he'll go away. If he doesn't, he has something and he probably can't be chased off the hand, so we won't be firing any more barrels. If he starts raising, our medium-strength hands aren't going to be any good; we can safely go away.

Against Lucious, we'll make our money when we hit the flop with a good hand like top pair, top kicker. In this spot, we bet and he calls. In all likelihood he'll have a lower pair, a weaker top pair, or a draw, and we can just bet for value the rest of the way and win a nice solid pot.

Playing against Lucious sounds simple, but problems can arise. If we hit a strong hand on the flop, say top and bottom two pair, and we bet and he raises, we're in a bit of a quandary. Is he raising with a genuinely strong hand which beats us, like a set or a better two pair, or does he just have a hand which he thinks is good but really isn't, like top pair, top kicker? One comforting piece of information is that Lucious won't be semi-bluffing in this situation. If he did semi-bluff, his aggression numbers would be higher.

Players like Lucious are your bread-and-butter opponents at the micro-stakes levels. There will be plenty of them and they will be steady long-term losers. You'll also find a few of these players in the small stakes games where they are usually beginners who elected to start at small stakes rather than micro-stakes.

Sample HUD No. 3

pushypete / (210) / +8
VP 25 / PF 20 / AS 45 / FB 75
3B 10 / F3 75 / AF 5 / 6 / 4 / 2
CB 90 / FC 65 / FT 75
W$F 53 / WtS 23 / W$S 48

We've moved up to a $200 NL game (blinds of $1/$2) and we encounter a new character, "pushypete," who seems to be doing well. What's his secret?

The first thing we should notice from pushypete's HUD is that he's extremely aggressive. His VP$IP/PFR numbers are 25/20, which means he's raising most of the hands he's playing preflop. His 'attempt to steal' number is 45 percent, also very high. If it's folded to him when he's sitting on the cutoff or button, he's willing to raise with almost half his hands. Also note his 3-bet number of 10 percent. That's the highest we've seen so far; if there's a raise in front of him, he's willing to test his opponents with a reraise even if he doesn't hold a particularly premium hand. (A 10 percent range includes hands like small to medium pairs and even holdings like ace-jack offsuit or queen-jack suited.)

His post-flop numbers show more of the same. His overall aggression factor is 5, which is quite high. His flop aggression of 6 and his 'continuation bet' percentage of 90 percent are consistent and very high. If he took the lead preflop (which is most of the time), he'll be continuation betting post-flop. More interesting, however, are his turn and river aggression factors of 4 and 2. Those are also high and indicate that he's not interested in playing a pot control game. He's going to keep firing and put maximum pressure on his opponents to get out of the pot.

What happens when he encounters aggression? We have some evidence here with his 'fold big blind to steal' (75 percent), his 'fold to continuation bet' (65 percent), and his 'fold to turn continuation bet' (75 percent). These are all in a normal range which indicates that he evaluates his hand more or less according to its value when his opponent takes the lead in the betting. He doesn't try to bulldoze real resistance, but he doesn't crawl in a hole either.

His summary numbers show the effect of his overall aggression. His 'win money when seeing flop' number (53 percent) is high, the result of winning a lot of pots before any showdown is reached. His 'went to showdown' number is low (23 percent), exactly what we would expect. His 'win money at showdown' number is somewhat low for an overall winning player (48 percent), but that's because his opponents are being pushed off their weaker hands on earlier streets, and carrying only their best hands to showdown.

Our Game Plan

"pushypete" is a much stronger player than either "JeffJ" or "Lucious," as shown by his ability to beat a much stronger game. When we first play him, our main weapon will be trapping with good hands. His aggression numbers post-flop shows that he mostly views checks and calls as signs of a weak hand that can be pushed out of the pot. (A completely correct assumption against straightforward players.) On the other hand, he's willing to fold at a normal rate against players who show strength. So our best approach is two-fold:

1. Slow-play our strongest hands to extract more bets (the rope-a-dope).

2. Attack with raises on the flop and turn, using a mixture of good hands and bluffs.

Since we think "pushypete" is a good player, he should adapt to our approach after awhile. But he'll have to adapt by lowering his aggression, which in turn will allow us to see more draws cheaply and get to the river with our medium-strength hands.

Monitoring Our Own HUD

Of course poker isn't just about looking at our opponent's HUDs. Some of them will be using PokerTracker as well, and they'll be watching our statistics on their own HUD. We need to be aware of what they're doing and what conclusions they might be drawing. Here are a couple of tips.

1. Remember that what you see isn't necessarily what your opponents see. You see your statistics for this session only above your icon. They see your statistics for all the hands they've played in which you've been involved. The two sets of numbers could appear very different.

    For instance, let's say you've been sitting at the table for an hour and played 70 hands. In your own HUD (above you), it shows 70 hands played and the statistics reflect just those 70 hands at this table. Now let's say you look at the HUD of Jake on your left and it also shows 70 hands. In that case, this is your first session with Jake and if he's using PokerTracker himself, his HUD for you is showing just what yours is showing. So when you play a hand with Jake, you know that his assumptions about you are either based on the data that you're seeing next to your name (if he's using PokerTracker), or based on his imprecise impression of your play (if he's not.)

    On the other hand, suppose that Harry, on your right, has a HUD that shows 460 hands played. In that case, Harry's a veteran that you've encountered before, and Harry's HUD for you is also showing 460 hands of data. If your statistics in this session are for some reason skewed from your normal style of play, Jake and Harry may have different ideas about how you're playing.

2. As you look at your own HUD, focus on the "big three" statistics: VP$IP, PFR, and overall AF. Most everyone uses and learns the meaning of those three, and many players never use any others. Since you can't be sure who's using a HUD and what statistics they're displaying, concentrate on these three. Players who don't use a HUD will still have a

general sense of how aggressively you're playing, even if they haven't picked up much else. Focus on that when you're trying to imagine how your actions appear to the rest of the table, and you'll do all right.

Other HUD Statistics

The statistics we've listed so far for our sample HUDs are the ones we consider the most useful. There are many other statistics available, some of which you might want to consider using depending on the kind of games you regularly play. Here's a quick list of a few of them which didn't make our cut, along with their pluses and minuses.

1. **"4-Bet Flop"** gives the percentage of time that a player 4-bets given that he's been 3-bet. If you're playing in a game in which 3-betting is fairly common, this statistic assumes importance. In a game in which 3-betting is rare and almost always indicates a premium hand, it's less valuable. The corollary is **"Fold to 4-Bet,"** which is just what the name implies. If you use one of these statistics, you'll probably want to use the other as well.

2. **"Call Preflop Raise"** shows the percentage of time that a player just calls given that a raise occurred in front of him. You can get a vague estimate of this number by looking at the difference between VP$IP and PFR, the times a player gets in the pot and the times he raises to get in the pot. But that difference is heavily skewed by the number of times a player limps preflop. 'Call preflop raise' focuses instead on the likelihood that a player will call once another player has indicated a strong hand, eliminating the times a player will limp with a marginal hand just to see a cheap flop.

   The usefulness of this statistic depends also on whether or not it includes calls from the blinds, so you'll need to check your software documentation. If it includes both cold-calls (a call from a player who hasn't yet put any money in the pot) and calls from the blinds, a normal range would be in the area of 5 to 7 percent. If calls from the blinds are left out and the statistic just includes cold calls, the normal range would be very low, in the 2 to 3 percent area.

3. **"Raise Flop C-Bet"** shows the percentage of time a player makes a flop raise given that his opponent took the lead preflop and then made a c-bet on the flop. Anything over 10 percent would be on the high side for this statistic. Against an opponent with a high reading, you'd want to exercise some caution when continuation betting. For instance, if you have position and your opponent, with a 16 percent 'raise flop c-bet' number, elects to check, you might decide to check behind with a drawing hand rather than semi-bluff.

    'Raise flop c-bet' can be useful, but you can get some of the same information on how your opponent will behave by comparing his 'fold to c-bet' number and his 'flop aggression' number. If 'fold to c-bet' is low and 'flop aggression' is high, he'll be more likely than most to be raising your continuation bet.

    The real value of this statistic is that it correlates well with a player's general level of trickiness. A high value here probably indicates a player who's willing to bluff more frequently and adopt more non-standard lines. It's somewhat more useful in this respect than the aggression factor where a high number may just indicate that a player will attack until he encounters resistance.

    I wouldn't bother incorporating this number in your HUD if you play micro-stakes or the lower small stakes games. At those levels players will mostly just call continuation bets whether they have a small hand or a big hand. With a small hand they want to get to showdown, and with a big hand they want to trap. But as you rise to medium stakes, players will start to raise continuation bets with some regularity, and 'raise flop c-bet' will start to yield some worthwhile information.

4, 5. **"Bet River"** and **"Call River"** are self-explanatory. There are players who are reluctant to call a good-sized river bet without a hand that is close to the nuts. There are other players who try to exploit this by betting a higher than usual frequency on the river. Average values here are 15 to 25 percent for 'bet river' and 30 to 40 percent for 'call river.' Values outside these ranges probably indicate exploitable tendencies.

The main problem with the statistics in this section is that they require even more hands to converge to reliable values than our previous group. I wouldn't really trust any of these numbers without a minimum of one to two thousand hands of data. But if you have that much data on a lot of your opponents, you might consider adding them to your HUD.

Before we leave the topic of HUD statistics, let's address two key questions: How much data do we need to collect before we really trust these statistics? And what do we do when we have only a small amount of data?

Statisticians have ways of measuring the reliability of collections of data. Let's say you had several thousand hands of data on a player and his VP$IP was 38 percent. A statistician might be able to say that he was "95 percent confident" that the player's true VP$IP was, providing that the sample size is relatively large, (and that would certainly be the case here with several thousand hands of data), within a small range, perhaps 35 to 41 percent, and he will call this range a "95 percent confidence interval."

Unfortunately, in online poker we can never attain that degree of confidence, partly because we can't get enough data, and partly because we're measuring a moving target. If we collect a lot of data on a player over a long period of time, there's a real chance that his playing style will change during that time interval, and the numbers we see will represent a mix of his old and new style.

But instead of despairing that we just can't get enough good data to be confident, we need instead to look at the data in a different way. I like to think of HUD data as simply the online equivalent of a "tell." Specifically, in live games, tells are clues. That is, you're never sure exactly how reliable a tell is, but you use them as guides for tough decisions. In the same way, look at your HUD data as a sequence of clues. Some of your clues, like VP$IP and PFR, will be more reliable because they converge more quickly. Others, like 3-betting frequency or river aggression, will be less reliable. But they all offer guidance to how your opponent may be playing. So use them in a common sense way, but be sure to use them because having some data is better than having no data, and in the long run, you'll do better using the HUD data than pretending there is no data at all.

Taking Notes

Online play offers another feature that live play lacks: the ability to record quick notes on your opponents and save them for future reference. All sites offer this feature in the form of a small 'notes' window that you can access at any time. Notes are a powerful tool when used in conjunction with your HUD. Some notes, however, are more useful than others, so let's think a bit about what kind of notes we really want to record.

The first point to notice is that we don't want to duplicate the information that's already available in the HUD. If a player's VP$IP/PFR numbers are 40/34, we don't need a note saying "This dude is super-aggro!" We already know that. Instead, we want information not given by the HUD, but which will compliment its information in some important way.

Our second goal is to focus on what really matters. We're more interested in cards a player has when he pushes all-in than in what cards he uses to limp into an unraised pot. The former involves a bet that will win or lose an entire stack; the latter risks only a single big blind.

Our third goal is to focus on hands where our opponent has to show his cards. Once we see them, we can reconstruct his actions throughout the hand. Without seeing his cards, we can't really conclude anything that's more concrete than the information already contained in his HUD.

Example: As a starting example on note-taking, consider the following scenario. We sit down at a $50 NL 6-max table and buy in for the maximum. After the HUDs appear, we see extensive information on a couple of the players, but the other three are unknowns. In the second hand of the session, two of the unknown players get all-in against each other preflop, each with a substantial stack of approximately 100 big blinds. Player A, who pushed all-in with a 4-bet, turns over the

Player B, who 3-bet and then called the all-in 4-bet, turns over the

An ace hits on the flop and Player B wins.

There are two notes we can make, one of which is much more important than the other. First, we can note Player A's action as follows:

PF: 4BAI = KK.

When we take notes we want to be succinct; no wit, no poetry, no long blather. Just the facts, ma'am. So we'll make our abbreviations as short as possible. Keystrokes matter when you're in a hurry.

"PF" means this is a preflop note. It's best to group our notes by street, so everything we learn about this opponent's preflop tendencies will be listed after the "PF" tag.

"4BAI" means an all-in 4-bet. If we later see him 4-bet all-in with ace-queen suited, we'll add that to the note like this:

PF: 4BAI = KK, AQs.

Noting that someone will push all-in with a pair of kings preflop is not an important note to take. We'd be surprised if he didn't. If you're multi-tabling and time is pressing, you'd skip this note. If you're playing a small number of tables and you have some dead time, there's no harm in starting your notes for this person.

The second note, however, is much more important. Player B 3-bet with an ace-ten offsuit, then called an all-in with the same hand. It's vital that we get that information recorded as follows:

PF: 3B = ATo. CAI = ATo.

"C" is our symbol for calling, so "CAI" means 'calls an all-in.' We make two notes because we saw two separate important decisions for Player B. He thought ace-ten offsuit was good enough for a 3-bet, and he further thought it was good enough to call an all-in.

Just from this note, we're going to conclude for now that Player B is a loose player. Of course, we may be wrong. It's possible that Player B and Player A have a long history together, and Player B knows that Player A is really loose and wild, so that ace-ten is a perfectly good calling hand against a push from Player A. Possible, but unlikely. It's much more likely that Player B is the wild one.

Luckily, our note plays a role in the very next hand. On the button, we pick up the J♥J♠. After a fold, Player B raises to $1.50. The hand is folded to us and we 3-bet to $4.50. The blinds fold and Player B puts us all-in for our remaining $44.00. What do we do?

If we had no information on our opponent, we might be in an uncomfortable situation. If we knew his range for pushing was extremely tight, say AA — QQ, plus AK, suited or unsuited, then our jacks would actually be a 64-to-36 underdog against that range, and we'd pass. (The pot is currently $54.50 and we have to put in $44 to call, so we need about a 44.5 percent winning chance.)

But in fact we know from our previous note that his calling range for a preflop all-in includes at least ace-ten offsuit. His pushing range is probably even larger although we can't be sure. However, if we assign him a reasonable range of AA - 77, plus AT or better, suited or unsuited, our chances against his range with our jacks are about 59 percent, and our call is trivial.

Structuring Our Notes

To make your notes easy to read, you want to arrange them in some sensible structured manner. I like to group mine in the following way:

1. Notes unrelated to specific hands.

2. Preflop notes.

3. Post-flop notes which apply generally to all actions after the flop.

4. Flop notes.

6. Turn notes.

7. River notes.

Let's consider each category separately.

Notes Unrelated to Specific Hands

The first group is for notes that don't depend on the play of specific hands. I put this information on the first line and three items are particularly important here:

1. The number of tables this opponent plays at once.

2. His standard buy-in amount.

3. Whether or not he auto-rebuys.

Most sites have a feature that allows you to see how many tables a player is playing at one time. The feature is usually labeled 'Find a Player' or something similar. Click on 'Find a Player' (or ctrl-F on some sites), type the player's name, and you'll get a list of all the cash and tournament tables he's playing. This is vital information and you should make a habit early in your session of getting this information for all players at your table. At micro-stakes and small stakes tables, players who play large numbers of tables tend to play robotic poker. They have tight preflop ranges, they generally raise only with pairs and premium cards, they fold without good hands, and they 3-bet only with strong hands. When they're in the blinds, they're easy to steal from in late position because they frequently make their decision as soon as they see their cards; with weak hands they just checked the 'fold' box and moved on to the next table.

None of this is necessarily bad poker at these levels. It's enough to exploit weak players, and in fact those who play this way are probably winners overall. But because their play is so robotic, they're easy to play against. They have just what they say they have; no more and no less.

At higher stakes, this relationship doesn't hold. Players who multi-table extensively at medium stakes and higher are definitely able to vary their play and put moves on their opponents at appropriate times. But at low stakes, players who play large numbers of tables can be exploited, so make a note of how many tables your opponents are playing.

A second point to notice is the size of a player's standard buy-in since very few players vary their buy-in amount. So once you see a player buy in for 100 big blinds, chances are that he'll always be buying in for 100 big blinds. For the most part, players will buy in at one of three levels:

1. A full buy-in of 100 big blinds. (Certain sites may allow buy-ins of 200 or 250 big blinds at some levels.)

2. A half buy-in of 50 big blinds.

3. A minimum buy-in of 20 big blinds.

You want to pay special attention to those who are buying in for the 20 big blind minimum. Typically, players who play only one or two tables and buy in for the minimum at low or medium stakes are weak players who are trying to control their losses. Players who make a minimum buy in but play large numbers of tables are usually playing a specific short stack strategy. You should be aware who these players are as you will need to make certain adaptations when they're at your table.

The last point is whether or not a player auto-rebuys. An auto-rebuy is a handy feature implemented by many sites. If you buy in for a full amount and your stack dips below that level after a hand, the site automatically brings your stack back to a full buy-in and deducts your cash balance before the next hand starts. If you have an edge over the field, auto-rebuying ensures that you'll have the maximum possible stack when you bust your unwitting opponents.

Players who auto-rebuy tend to be both knowledgeable and confident. They're aware of the feature and are sure that they'll make money from its use. In general, they will be among the better players at the stake they're playing. Make a note and treat them a little more cautiously than your other opponents.

Preflop Notes

I like to focus my preflop notes on three important situations:

1. How my opponent makes and responds to 3-bets.

2. How he makes and responds to 4-bets.

3. How he makes and responds to preflop all-ins.

I might make notes on his normal raises and calls if the hand is eventually shown down, but by and large that information is implied pretty well by the VP$IP and PFR numbers in his HUD, and as previously stated, I don't like to waste time making notes that duplicate what the HUD provides.

The 3-bets, 4-bets, and all-in plays, however, are a different situation. Ordinary raises and calls happen frequently, so the VP$IP and PFR numbers rapidly converge to trustworthy numbers. These bigger bets happen more rarely, so I might need to collect hundreds of hands before the 3-bet or 4-bet statistics in my HUD can be trusted. But by making notes on hands that are shown down, I can quickly get some guidelines on just how loose or tight this player is with these big bets. Remember also that each big bet decision is much more important than a normal raise or call, and it's best to focus my note-taking on the information that can make or save me a lot of money.

There's one other preflop situation worth noting. Some weak players, especially at lower levels, like to limp into a pot and then call a raise, even if they're going to be out of position. This play makes no sense on a lot of levels. If you don't like your hand well enough to raise when no one else has shown any interest in the pot, why would you want to put in a lot more money after someone else has told you they have a strong hand? Other weak players will limp and then fold to a raise, which is almost as bad. In either case, it's worth keeping track of these players, so I'll make a note on my preflop line that looks like this:

PF: LFC = 0/1.

'LFC' just stands for 'limp and then fold or call,' and the '0/1' means I've seen him limp and call once, but haven't seen him limp and fold. The 'LFC' note is a handy marker to signify a bad player. It's a slight violation of my rule to confine notes to plays that swing large amounts of money, but I can justify it because players who give away small amounts of money this way will make many such mistakes over the course of a session.

This note is really only useful when you're playing micro-stakes, and you can discard it as you move up the ladder. Higher-stakes players aren't generally limping into pots on a regular basis.

General Post-Flop Notes

This section is for observations that apply in a general way to all post-flop play. You should be particularly interested in two pieces of information:

1. How strong a hand does a player need to bet or to call a series of bets all the way to the river?

2. What do unusual bet sizes mean for this player?

Let's start with the first item. Just how strong does a player need to be to call off his whole stack?

Suppose, for example, I'm playing in a $1/$2 6-max game and have my starting stack of $200. I pick up the on the button and the under the gun player, who's new to the table and who has 50 big blinds ($100), raises to $6. Two players fold and I call the $6 with my pair of eights. The blinds also fold so the pot is $15 and the effective stack is $94.

The flop comes the

Excellent! My set came in and I'm delighted to see the ace because my hand may get a lot of action. The under the gun player bets $9 and I just call with the idea of getting at least another bet out of him on the turn. The pot is now $33 and the effective stack is $85.

The turn is the 7♠. My opponent bets $17 and I raise to $40. He calls. The pot is now $113 and the effective stack is $45. I've gotten him pot-committed on the river, although I can't be sure he knows that.

The river is the T♦. My opponent checks and I push all-in. He calls and turns over the

and I win his stack.

Since his cards were seen, I certainly want to make a note, but the only note that's worthwhile is the following:

PostF: ATW = TPGK (50bb)

'PostF' is my tag for the line that covers general post-flop notes. 'ATW=TPGK' says that he went all the way (involved his entire stack) with a hand of top pair, good kicker, and 50bb shows the size of his starting stack. For the moment, that gives me some solid information on what hands he considers strong enough to put his whole stack at risk after the flop. I know that he certainly would risk his stack with a better hand than top pair, good kicker, but he might be willing to risk it with an even worse hand. It's a critical note because it tells me I can call him with speculative hands preflop and be getting good implied odds if I hit my hand.

Other notes can be made, but they'd be a waste of time. For instance, I could note that he raised preflop with ace-queen offsuit under the gun, but that's a standard play and tells me nothing. In the same way, I don't care that he was willing to bet a good hand (a pair of aces) on the flop. Again, this tells me nothing. But the fact that he was willing to lose his whole 50 bb stack with top pair tells me a great deal that I can use in the future.

The other point I like to note in this section are any unusual bet sizes and what they mean for this player. Unlike most other situations, it won't be necessary to get to the showdown to make a comment here. For example, consider this next hand.

We're in a 6-max game with $0.50/$1 blinds. After two folds, the player in the cutoff seat limps for $1. Your VP$IP/PFR figures for this player are 65/20, so a limp isn't exactly surprising. On the button with the 8♣8♠, you raise to $4. Your preflop notes for this player include 'LFC=1/6,' so he's called six out of seven times when he limped and was raised. Once this player indicates interest in a pot, he'll stick around with all but his worst hands. The blinds fold and the cutoff calls as expected, for $3 more, making the pot $9.50. You have about 100 big blinds left in your stack while the cutoff has you covered by a small margin.

The flop comes the 7♦7♣2♥. That's a great flop for you producing an overpair to the board. Since his PFR figure is 20 percent and he didn't raise preflop, you think it's extremely unlikely that he has a better overpair than you. There's some possibility, also unlikely, that he called with a seven in his hand.

He acts first post-flop and bets $2 into a $9.50 pot. That's an unusually low bet. More often than not, small bets from weak players in lower-stakes games are feeble stabs at the pot in the hope of taking it down for a cheap price. The pot is now $11.50. Undeterred, you put in an $8 raise and he quickly folds.

Although the hand didn't make it to showdown, his actions were so clear that you make a note:

PostF: sm bet = weak.

A small bet from this player probably indicates weakness rather than a trap. You also, of course, want to augment your preflop note to read 'LFC=1/7.'

If at a later point in the session a small bet from this player was a trap, I'd have to amend the note to say something like 'sm bet = weak or trap.' That way I not only have some information that a small bet from this player has multiple meanings, but it's also clear that actions from him aren't going to be trivially easy to interpret.

Flop Notes

Most heads-up flops consist of a continuation bet from the preflop aggressor followed by a fold or call from his opponent. This information is adequately covered by the 'continuation bet' and 'fold to continuation bet' statistics in the HUD, so we're not interested in comments which duplicate that information. But if a hand is eventually shown down, there are several pieces of information that should especially interest us:

1. If an all-in occurred on the flop, what strength of hands was involved?

2.   Did either opponent slowplay a big hand?

3.   How do the players handle draws?

4.   Did the preflop non-aggressor lead out with a donk bet, and what did it mean?

As was the case preflop, we're interested in an all-in because it gives us vital information as to what strength of hand will cause a player to commit his whole stack. A typical note on a player might look as follows:

$$F: AI = S+, TPTK, 2P. CAI = S+.$$

'F:' identifies the line as the flop note. 'AI' and 'CAI' indicate 'all-in' and 'call all-in' respectively. 'S+' means a set or better. We don't really care how much better because most players will get their money in on the flop with a set, so of course we expect them to commit with any better hand as well. 'TPTK' is 'top pair, top kicker.' A player who's willing to commit with top pair, top kicker (or worse) is a player who probably doesn't understand deep-stack poker well, and will seriously overvalue weaker hands. You can expect to win a lot of money from such players over time, so you want to identify them quickly. '2P' means 'two pair.'

Occasionally you'll find players who'll get all-in with second pair or even worse. These players are free money. To avoid confusion, I use the notation '2nP' or '3rP' for second and third pair, and use 'OVP' for overpair and 'UP' for underpair.

It's also good to know if a player slowplayed a big hand or not. As with limping preflop, I like to create a ratio of slowplaying to value betting in the notes and simply augment it as information is acquired. If after the hand, I see the opponent slowplayed a strong hand, my note will look like this:

F: SP = 1/0.

As before, 'F' identifies this line as containing flop notes. 'SP' stands for 'slowplay ratio.' '1/0' shows that I've seen him slowplay a big hand once on the flop without yet seeing him bet a big hand. If some hands later he bets a big hand on the flop, I'll amend the ratio to '1/1' and so on.

Over time, this ratio should give me an idea of just how often an opponent elects to slowplay. While I have some interest in his slowplaying frequency *per se*, this ratio is best used as a proxy for a player's trickiness, his willingness to play something other than a fit or fold style. Slowplaying is particularly useful for this purpose since slowplayed hands are more likely to get to showdown than other kinds of hands. For example, compare slowplaying to bluffing. Hands where one player bluffs the flop and perhaps the turn are much less likely to reach showdown since typically either the opponent gives up and folds, or the bluffer folds on the turn or river when the opponent shows that he's just not going away.

The third note for the flop section covers how a player handles draws. Will he passively check and call, or will he semi-bluff? A simple note that describes his behavior might look like this:

F: DR = 3/1.

Here 'DR' says this is a note on drawing hands, while '3/1' indicates that I've seen him make three semi-bluffs (either bets or raises), and once saw him do something else. This is a player heavily oriented toward semi-bluffing, which in turn points to an aggressive post-flop style.

The last note I like to make on the flop regards donk bets.[2] A typical donk bet note might look like this:

$$F: DB = 2nP.$$

When the hand was shown down, we were able to see that a player donk bet on the flop with second pair. That's a typical beginner's mistake: He hit the flop, so he felt obliged to bet. In the future, we can assume that if this player bets out of position, he hit the flop in some way, and if he checks he probably missed.

Turn Notes

I won't make quite as many notes on the turn as I will on the flop. In general, there are only two situations of interest:

1. What hand did he need to make or call an all-in?

2. Does he play for pot control with medium to good hands?

The interest in all-ins is just the same as on the previous streets. You want all the information you can get about the hands that will make him involve his whole stack.

As previously stated, pot control is a concept that arises on the turn and the river. The basic idea is to keep the pot small with a hand which may be the best hand, but which is not strong enough to commit your whole stack. As an example, suppose you hit a hand like top pair, good kicker on the flop. Your opponent checks, you bet, and he calls. On the turn your hand doesn't improve and he checks again. You could bet, but if he has a worse

---

[2] In high-stakes games, the players understand the issues involved, so donk bets will be infrequent. When they occur, they'll be a mixture of well-considered bluffs and strong value bets.

hand than you, he'll likely fold, while if he raises, you'll be very uncomfortable. Instead, you could check behind for pot control. You're trying to keep a lid on the size of the pot with your good, but not great hand.

When the showdown reveals that my opponent made a pot control move, I'll make a note:

$$T: PC = 1/0.$$

Here 'T' is the tag for turn notes and 'PC' signifies a pot control move. '1/0' means I once saw him make a pot control play on the turn, but have never seen him bet out on the turn with a hand of moderate strength. Moderate strength is, of course, board dependent. On a dry board (one with few or no possible draws) moderate strength is top pair or second pair. On a wet board (one with many draws), a hand like an overpair or two pair could be considered moderate strength.

River Notes

Since river bets tend to be big bets, anything we can determine about his river tendencies is worth a note. Does an all-in mean the nuts? Is he capable of making a big river bluff? Does his bet make sense when you see his cards? Will he exercise pot control and check down a strong hand out of fear? All of these are worth a note and will help you in the future.

Some Examples of Note-Taking

Now let's take a look at some hands from start to finish and see what notes we should take in each case.

Sample Hand No. 1

$100 NL 6-max table and you've played about 40 hands. We'll ignore data for players not involved in the hand.

UTG		$152	
MP	BarryB	$65	VP$IP/PFR = 40/17 over 40 hands. Overall AF = 4.
CO		$100	
BTN		$138	
SB	Us	$118	Posts $0.50. VP$IP/PFR = 22/18. **Hand: A♠K♠**
BB	PlayerF	$60	VP$IP/PFR = 12/8.

Before the flop, there is one fold and then BarryB limps for $1. The cutoff and button fold and we raise to $5. I like making an initial raise to three or four big blinds and adding an extra big blind for each limper, so that's a good raise. The big blind is tight and any action from him will indicate a big hand, but he folds and BarryB calls for another $4. The pot is now $11 and the effective stack is $60.

The flop is the

We have the nut flush draw and two overcards, so our hand is strong. If he has a lower pair, say two eights without a spade, we're a 54-to-46 favorite. Even in the unlikely event he has a set, we're only a 3-to-1 underdog. Since he's loose and aggressive, a bet is in order.

We bet $8 into the $11 pot and BarryB calls. The pot is now $27 and the effective stack is $52

The turn is the Q♠ and we have the nut flush. If BarryB has nothing and floated on the flop, we're unlikely to make any money if we lead on the turn. We could, however, check the turn and hope he bluffs the river. Alternatively, if he has something, a smallish bet may keep him interested and let us get all-in on the river.

We bet $13 into the $27 pot. BarryB raises all-in for $52 and we call. He shows the 9♥9♦ for a set and he has 10 outs (any queen, six, deuce, or the case nine). But the river is the 8♣ and we win the pot.

There are two notes to make on this hand, one much more important than the other. BarryB pushed all-in on the turn with a set which is certainly not surprising, but it's worth noting. If we later see him pushing all-in with weaker hands, we'll at least know that some of his all-ins are also good hands. So we'll enter this note:

$$T: AI = S+.$$

But on the flop, he slowplayed a set against a continuation bet hoping to lure us into a second bet on the turn. That's pretty standard, so we won't bother with a note.

However, there is another place where we do need a preflop note. BarryB limped with a pair of nines, one of his strongest hands. His PFR number is 17 percent, so he's been raising about one hand in six to this point. So we need to know that he's also capable of limping with a good hand, as well as a lot of the trash that he's probably been playing so far. So we'll make this note:

$$PF: limp = 99.$$

That will alert us that he may be a player who limps with his very strong hands as well as lots of weak hands, but raises his more middle-strength hands. If we can get some more evidence that he routinely does this, we can be looser about attacking some of his raises with 3-bets.

Sample Hand No. 2

$50 NL 6-max table and you've played 30 hands.

UTG		$38	
MP	JoeF	$70	VP$IP/PFR = 44/3 over 30 hands. Overall AF = 2.5.
CO	Us	$58	**Hand: Q♠2♥.**
BTN	SamG	$76	VP$IP/PFR = 22/17 over 120 hands. Overall AF = 4.
SB		$42	Posts $0.25
BB		$50	Posts $0.50

Before the flop, the under the gun player folds and JoeF in middle position limps for $0.50. So far he seems to be a typical loose-passive player at these stakes, limping into many pots, but hardly ever raising. Our hand isn't good enough to play, so we fold and watch the table.

SamG on the button raises to $2.75. We've encountered SamG before and he appears to be a tough and aggressive player. His VP$IP/PFR numbers of 22/17 show that he likes to raise when he enters the pot.

We check our notes on JoeF and see that we have a preflop note for him: 'LFC=0/4.' He's already called on four occasions when he limped and was then raised. That's a high number for just 30 hands of data, so we can assume that JoeF can't be chased out of any preflop pots where he's shown some interest. We also see that SamG's raise was to $2.75, or 5.5 big blinds. That's a little on the high side, but given that we think SamG is a tough player, it's likely that he has spotted JoeF's tendency to call as well, knows his bet will be called, and is trying to build a bigger pot. We suspect Joe has a big hand.

The blinds fold and, sure enough, JoeF calls for another $2.25. Although we're not in the hand, we'll watch events play out and see if we can learn something. The pot is now $6.25.

The flop is the

Joe leads out for $6, a big donk bet. It's a flop that would be expected to favor the preflop caller with its middle cards and various straight and flush possibilities. JoeF could have a lot of different hands: two pair, a set, a straight draw, or a flush draw. No matter what he has, a check followed by a check-raise is probably a better line than just leading out since SamG can be expected to make a continuation bet. (His c-betting frequency in his HUD is 80 percent, somewhat above average even for an aggressive player. Given JoeF's general looseness and weakness, it's unlikely that he's using a HUD, so it's unlikely that he knows any of this.) The pot is now $12.25 and the effective stack is now $61.25.

SamG now raises to $22. That's almost a pot-sized bet which probably means that SamG is angling to get his whole stack involved in this hand. It's also unlikely to be a bluff. JoeF's loose statistics and his big bet on the flop most likely mean that he caught a piece of the flop and won't let go. Since SamG raised preflop expecting to get called, we're guessing he has an overpair.

Joe calls another $16. Since he didn't reraise, we'll assume he doesn't have two pair or a set, and put him on one pair or some draw. The pot is now $50.25 and the effective stack is $39.25.

The turn is the 4♥. This shouldn't help anyone's hand.

Joe now checks. SamG moves all-in for the last $39.25 and Joe calls after some thought. SamG shows the Q♥Q♣ and JoeF has the Q♦T♣. The river is a random deuce and Sam scoops the pot.

With the benefit of our HUD information and the notes we had already, the two players' hands weren't hard to read. JoeF was very loose and willing to play a huge number of hands. SamG had probably seen this, and after picking up a pair of queens in position, was willing to get his whole stack in the pot.

There are also a couple of notes to make from this hand, both concerning JoeF's play. First, we'll augment the 'LFC=0/4' note to read 'LFC=0/5'. In the future, I wouldn't bother to update this any further. Combined with the VP$IP/PFR numbers for Joe (44/3), we know all we need to know. He limps with a huge number of hands and will keep playing after a raise. We'll also note in the turn section that he'll get his stack in with top pair, good kicker.

In low stakes games, a lot of the players will play a style that's so simple and predictable that you can eventually stop taking notes on them since more notes won't add more information. We'll probably reach that point with JoeF after a couple of hundred hands.

I wouldn't make any notes on SamG's play after this hand except perhaps a general comment that he pushes hard against weak players. His decision to get all-in on the turn with his overpair was really driven by his big bet on the flop, and the whole line was likely player-dependent. He saw how JoeF played, thought his overpair was probably good, and played accordingly.

Sample Hand No. 3

$100 NL 6-max table and you're been playing for one hour, about 60 hands.

UTG		$75	
MP	Albert	$110	VP$IP/PFR = 40/10 over 60 hands
CO	Fred	$91	VP$IP/PFR = 18/13 over 110 hands
BTN		$104	
SB	Jim	$88	(Posts $0.50) VP$IP/PFR=12/8 over
			60 hands
BB	Us	$140	(Posts $1.00) **Hand: 6♣5♣**.

Before the flop, the under the gun player folds. Albert, who is loose and weak, limps for $1. Fred, who is tight and aggressive, and seems competent, only calls. In the past, we've seen him raise limpers with a variety of hands, so we suspect he has something, but probably not a pair or two high cards. The button folds. Jim in the small blind is super-tight, but he completes and we reasonably check our low suited connectors. The pot is $4.

The flop is the

A paired flop with four players is dangerous. There's a good chance that someone is holding an eight or at least a jack. We won't be putting any more money into this pot. Jim in the small blind leads out for $2.50 and we fold. Loose Albert calls and Fred folds. The pot is $9.

The turn is the Q♥. Tight Jim checks, loose Albert bets $8, and Jim calls. The pot is $25. It's hard to say who has what here. Jim most likely has a jack since he bet the flop, but stopped betting when an overcard appeared. But either player could be trapping with an eight, and any draws are unlikely.

The river is the T♥ which completes a backdoor flush. But that's an unlikely holding given this sequence of bets. Jim now bets $20 and Albert calls. Jim shows the 8♣7♦ for trip eights, and Albert shows the 9♦8♦ for a rivered straight, although he also had trips from the beginning.

The key note to make here is Albert's action on the river. Although he rivered a straight, he only called the river bet, apparently afraid that a flush or a full house might be out. Both of these hands are unlikely given the slow betting. A full house would most likely require Jim to be holding a premium pair, either tens, jacks, or queens. But Jim just called the preflop bet from the small blind after two limpers. That's a strange (but not impossible) play from a tight player with a strong hand. The backdoor flush is possible, especially if Jim holds the J♥ along with something like the K♥ or the 9♥. But it's still an unlikely holding. The fact that Albert wouldn't raise indicates that he's not comfortable raising anything but the near-nuts on the river. Let's make this note for Albert:

R: Needs nuts to raise.

There are other comments we could make, but this is the essential one. River bets are big bets, and we want to know as much as we can about a player's river tendencies.

Making
Notes after a Session

Note-taking doesn't end when your playing session is over. To track your play properly, there are some extremely useful pieces of information you'll want to record after the session. The most important items are these three:

1.   Your results in the session.

2.   The results of all the all-in moves that occurred.

3.   The names of any noticeably weak players that you spotted.

These are very important items for evaluating and improving your online play, so let's say a little about each one.

Item No. 1: Session Results. If you're serious about improving your poker, you need to know just how well you're doing at any point in time. To do that, you need to record your session results. A spreadsheet is the right tool for this (and some other purposes as we'll see). If you can't use a spreadsheet, learn! Next to your HUD, a spreadsheet will be one of your best friends as you move up the online poker ladder.

What information should you have in your results spreadsheet? At a minimum, I'd keep track of the following pieces of information: date, site, stake, hands played, money won or lost, and numbers of tables played.

1.   **Date** is useful because, among other things, it will let you find hand histories a little more easily in your PokerTracker database.

2.   You want **Site** information because sites can differ widely in the quality of players who play there. If you spread your play among several sites and keep track of your results, you'll quickly spot the sites that are most profitable for a given stake.

3.   **Stake** is obviously essential. As you move up the ladder, you'll need to compare your current results to your results at your old stake. If they're not better, you'll want to consider moving back down.

4, 5.   **Hands played** and **money won or lost** are the key pieces of information that will allow you to calculate the numbers you really want, money won per 100 hands. You can express this as either 'big bets per 100 hands,' where a big bet is equal to two big blinds (thus remaining consistent with PokerTracker's numbers) or the more intuitive 'big blinds per 100 hands,' which will be twice as large.

6. **Number of tables** played is important when you're multi-tabling but you haven't decided how many tables you want to try to play at one time. By keeping track of how many tables you play in any session, you'll be able to sort your data by number of tables played and see what number yields the highest profit in dollars per hour.

These are the basic pieces of information you need, and I'd strongly recommend keeping track of all of them. There are a couple of other items that are more esoteric but definitely useful if you're really serious about online poker. **Time of day,** for instance, lets you see how your results vary against different player pools. If you live in the eastern United States, a morning or afternoon session will match you mostly against European players; in the evening, you'll see mostly other Americans; and if you play late-night, a lot of Asian players will have checked in. You might also want to keep track of **maximum buy-in.** While a buy-in of 100 big blinds has long been the standard, some sites now allow buy-ins of 200 or 250 big blinds at some tables. Depending on your site, these tables may have a different mix of players and be more or less profitable than the regular tables. Also, how well you play a very deep stack can impact your results.

Item No. 2: All-in Results. One way of comparing different games is by a measure called *variance*. Variance is a way, given a certain difference in skill, of measuring the dispersion of results. A game with low variance, like chess, has results that cluster together quickly. You don't need to watch two chess players play many games before you can quickly tell who the better player is. (In most cases, one game is sufficient.) Backgammon has much more variance than chess; a strong player might have to play several hours against a weak player before he pulls ahead for good. But poker is a game of truly enormous variance. Before you can be sure that you're a winning player at a given stake, you might want to log several tens of thousands of hands.[3]

Needing that many hands creates some real practical problems. Let's say, for example, that you're a winning player at $25 NL. You've logged 100,000 hands, mostly playing four tables at a time, and you've averaged 8 BB per 100 hands, or about $4 per 100 hands. Assuming you're playing four tables at a time and each table is averaging 60 hands per hour, you're making about $9.60 per hour.

So far so good. Your bankroll has grown to over $4,000, and you decide that you're ready to make the jump to $50 NL. You move up, and to be on the safe side, you decide to play only two tables at a time while you're getting your feet wet.

Oops! Your start turns out to be a little rocky. After your first week, you've logged more than 4,000 hands, but you're behind almost 250 big blinds, a loss of about 3 big bets per 100 hands. Are these guys too tough? Are you getting outplayed? Or Is it just a bad swing? Just some variance? So should you drop back down to the lower stake where you're almost certain you're a steady winner?

If all you've been doing is tracking your raw results, you still can't really answer these questions. The best you can say is that you haven't played enough hands. The conservative move is to just shrug your shoulders, admit that you might not be ready for this level yet, and move back down. A more persistent player would probably choose to keep going, but the fear that he might

---

[3] You can shorten this if you see a large number of errors made by your opponents and you do not make these same mistakes. However, be sure that what you think is an error is exactly that since expert players can sometimes trick you into misjudging the quality of their play.

be in over his head could gnaw at him, making him play worse. All in all, a tough situation.

However, our hero could make his life a lot easier by tracking his all-in results in addition to his overall results. Tracking your all-ins just means noting all the hands where either you or your opponent got all the chips in the middle, looking at the situation where the all-in occurred, figuring out your expected gain or loss (using a program like PokerStove), and comparing your expected gain or loss to your actual gain or loss.

The great advantage of this method is simple: The swings on the all-in hands represent a large part of your overall wins or losses. By calculating the expectation of the hand when the all-in occurs, and comparing that number to the actual result, you can see whether you were lucky or unlucky, and exactly how much you profited from good luck or were hurt by bad luck. When you add up the expectations and results over many all-ins, the results should be close. If they're not and your results are much worse than your expectation, you can be pretty sure that your downswing was a function of bad luck and not bad play. Let's look at a couple of concrete hands and see just how this calculation would work.[4]

First All-in Hand

You sit down for a session of $50 NL with blinds of $0.25 and $0.50. About 15 minutes into the session, there's a raise to $1.50 from the under the gun player. The player in middle position, with a total stack of $30, 3-bets to $5. On the button, you have the

---

[4] Some Poker Tracking programs will keep track of this information in summary form. However, I still recommend maintaining your own information. Over a long period of time, looking at the particular hands where you went all-in can help you plug significant leaks in your game.

and 4-bet to $15. The blinds fold and the under the gun players tosses in his hand. The middle position player pushes all-in. You call. Your opponent shows the

The pot is now $62.25. (We're going to ignore the rake because it keeps the calculations simpler.) You contributed $30 as did your all-in opponent. The under the gun player put in $1.50 and then folded. The blinds accounted for $0.75. So you're either going to have a loss of $30 (the money you put in the pot) or a gain of $32.25 (the money contributed by four other players).

You can use any of several free pieces of software to calculate the equites of the hand. (I prefer PokerStove, but it's really just a matter of taste.) When the money went in, your aces were an 81.5-to-18.5 percent favorite over his queens. Your expectation on the hand was $20.73.

$$\$20.73 = (0.815)(\$32.25) + (0.185)(-\$30.00)$$

On average, you'd expect to make a profit of almost $21 in this highly favorable situation. But in fact, your opponent hit a queen on the turn and scooped the pot, so you lost $30.

Second All-in Hand

A while later you get a second preflop all-in, this time against a relatively short stack ($12). You have the A♣K♣; he shows the Q♦J♦. No one else put money in the pot except the blinds. This time you'll either lose $12 or win $12.75.

Now PokerStove makes you a much smaller favorite, only 60.4-to-39.6 percent. Your expectation for this hand is $2.95

$$\$2.95 = (0.604)(\$12.75) + (0.396)(-\$12.00)$$

In fact, your hand holds up and you win.

Conclusions

Putting the results of these two hands together gives us a small chart that looks like this:

Hand	Expectation	Actual Result
A♥A♠ v Q♣Q♠	+$20.73	-$30.00
A♣K♠ v Q♦J♦	+$2.95	+$12.75
Totals	+23.68	-$17.75

You've had two favorable hands, one of which you won and the other you lost, but your actual result is almost $41 short of your expectation! That's a big gap. A small amount of luck in the wrong place can have a big effect.

The main advantage of tracking your all-in results is that it gives you a good handle on how well you're playing and how your luck has run. If you've played a lot of hands and your all-in expectation column is solidly positive, then you're almost certainly a winning player, consistently reading the situation well and getting your money in with the best of it. If your actual result is negative at that point, don't worry. You've had a bad run of luck, and you can expect to do better in the future.

The time to be concerned is when your expectation column is seriously negative. Now you are probably getting outplayed, whether or not your actual results are good. It's time to work on analyzing your game and plugging weaknesses, and these all-in hands are the best place to start. The solution might be something simple. Perhaps you can't lay down top pair, top kicker when you hit the flop. Perhaps you've been pushing too many semi-bluffs and getting caught. In any case, you've identified a big leak and can start working on it.

Item No. 3: Listing the Weak Players. As you play, you'll start noticing some weak players at your tables, players who are just giving their money away every session. You'll find players with VP$IP/PFR numbers of 80/60, 70/2, or something equally absurd. Or maybe you'll find a player with an AF of 15, or a 3-bet percentage of 30. You need to make a list of these people and should update it virtually every time you play.

When you log in for a session, check the available tables and see if anyone from your list is playing. If they are, sit there. It will be much more profitable than picking seats at random.

Final Thoughts

Poker is a game of information, and well-chosen notes are some of the best information available. Keep them religiously. If you've been playing a session and you find yourself getting careless about watching shown-down hands, or recording notes, then you're probably getting tired and losing concentration. Time to quit; come back when you're fresh.

Multi-Tabling

When you play no-limit hold 'em, unless you're a complete maniac, you're going to fold most of the hands you're dealt. That's just the nature of the game — moments of spine-tingling excitement and danger, separated by long stretches of dead time.

In the last section, we showed how to put some of that dead time to profitable use by taking diligent notes on your opponents. But no matter how diligent you are and how many good notes you take, you'll still have long stretches where you're not doing much more than clicking the 'fold' button.

What's the solution? Add more tables! Moving from one table to two tables doubles the number of hands you'll see in an hour. Moving to four tables quadruples the number. If you can play 60 hands per hour on a single table, you'll be able to play 240 hands on four tables, or 480 hands on eight tables. That's a lot of hands. Even a super-nit who restricted himself to just opening with very premium hands, say jacks or better and ace-king and ace-queen, would still see about 18 of those hands every hour when playing eight tables.

Assuming you're a winning player at a given stake, just how many tables should you play? That, it turns out, is an extremely difficult question. Let's talk for a little while about the issues involved and see if we can get a handle on the problem.

The number of tables you should play is affected by a bunch of different considerations. Let's address them one by one.

Consideration No. 1: Computer Configuration. If you're playing multiple tables, a typical site will give you a choice of how you want the tables displayed on your screen: *cascade mode* or *tile mode*. Cascade mode stacks the tables one on top of another. The tables offset a bit so you can bring any one to the top of the stack by clicking on it. When an action is called for, that table will automatically pop to the top of the stack. Tile mode, on the other hand, shrinks the tables and arranges them on your screen like tiles on a floor. The tables are smaller, but all are visible simultaneously.

The advantage of cascade mode is that when a table pops to the top of the stack, it's almost full-sized and your HUD will be easily visible. The downside is that new tables may pop to the top before you've been able to complete an action on the previous table. This can lead to confusion.

The advantage of tile mode is that all the tables are visible, so you can clearly see where actions are required. It's my experience that you'll make fewer mistakes and time out less often. The disadvantage is that all the tables are relatively small and may be hard to read, especially if you're using a HUD with several lines of statistics.

Of the two, it's my opinion that the advantages of tile mode outweigh the disadvantages. If you're playing four tables or more, tiling is the way to go. To minimize the disadvantages, however, you'll want your computer and screen to be as state-of-the-art as possible. Splurge on the biggest monitor you can afford with the highest screen resolution. If you're playing more than eight tables, definitely add a second monitor. Every mistake you make costs money, so buy a hardware setup that will maximize your screen area and minimize mistakes.

Consideration No. 2: Stake. The lower the stake and the simpler your general approach to poker, the easier it is to multi-table. In general, a conservative, straightforward approach to no-limit hold 'em is sufficient to beat micro-stakes games. At these levels, you'll find plenty of weak opponents who will virtually give their money away playing bad starting cards and calling off a lot of chips with sub-par hands. In that environment, playing large numbers of tables doesn't present nearly the problem it does when your opponents are cagey and thoughtful.

Consideration No. 3: HUD. Large HUDs with lots of statistics aren't as useful when playing lots of tables. If you've tiled your tables, a big HUD takes up too much room on the screen. (This is even more true if you're playing full ring rather than 6-max.) You'll also have less time to sort through the data and ponder any relationships. Stick to a reduced HUD containing just two or three lines and focus on the basic statistics like VP$IP, PFR, and AF.

Consideration No. 4: Note-Taking. Once you move beyond about six tables, note-taking becomes essentially impossible. You'll have to be content with notes that you can record after the session, keeping track of notably weak players, and updating your results charts. The better a note-taker you were when playing few tables, the more your game will be affected negatively.

Consideration No. 4: Personal Style. Everyone has a different tolerance and comfort level for handling the constant barrage of decisions involved in multi-tabling. You'll need to find your own personal level and not push yourself to go beyond it. You should know when you've pushed yourself too far and your decision-making is suffering. When you reach that point, back off.

Consideration No. 4: Rakeback. Rakeback is a business arrangement whereby a site agrees to remit to you some of the rake taken from the pots you played. It's a good deal to have, and you should always try to arrange for rakeback before joining a playing site. In addition to just being a good deal, rakeback also alters the game in a significant way that makes multi-tabling a much better option. Let's see why this is so.

First, rakeback works as follows: Playing sites are always looking for new members and they're willing to pay to get them, anticipating that the steady stream of rake income they get from a new member will more than offset the cost of acquiring the member. Let's say you've started a new poker playing site, Godzilla Poker, and you're looking for new members. You find a site, Zombie Poker, that sells poker coaching. You can now offer Zombie a deal that's good for both of you. Zombie runs a banner ad for Godzilla Poker. If anyone joins Godzilla through the banner ad, Godzilla remits part of that player's rake back to Zombie as payment. The deal is good for both parties. Godzilla doesn't have to worry about overpaying for the ad since it only pays when the member joins and begins generating rake. Zombie is happy since it gets a continuing stream of income for the banner ad.

Now suppose Zombie Poker is a site that sells not coaching but rakeback. When Zombie gets a rakeback payment from Godzilla, it takes a cut and passes the remainder to the various customers that signed up for Godzilla through Zombie. The customer himself has, in essence, become a small partner in Godzilla's business, getting a weekly or a monthly payment through Zombie from Godzilla Poker.

There are many sites like Zombie on the Web, offering rakeback deals for various playing sites. Most rakeback rates range from 25 to 35 percent, and you should make a point to seek out rakeback before joining any site. Not only will it make a huge difference in your bottom line over time, but it may be difficult to get rakeback later if you make the mistake of joining the site directly.

Once you have a rakeback arrangement, the economics of multi-tabling change dramatically. Let's say you're a modest winning player at 100 NL when playing two or four tables, but if you move up to eight, twelve, or sixteen tables you lose your edge and become just a break-even player. If you have rakeback, break-even may be good enough! It's possible that the rakeback from sixteen tables could be large enough to exceed your winnings from two or four tables.

Note as well that in addition to padding your winnings and reducing your losses, rakeback has the added bonus of reducing the relative variance of your results. Your winnings have been broken into two distinct pieces, one of which (playing) has normal variance, and the other of which (rakeback) has zero variance. So while your overall variance will be the same, it becomes, relative to your win rate, a smaller amount since your win rate is now larger.

Consideration No. 6: How many tables should you play? After all this discussion, we now hit the real question: What's the right number of tables for you to play if you want to win the most money? And unfortunately, there's no easy answer. We can, however, offer some good guidelines:

1. **Keep good records.** In the previous section on note-taking, we outlined the records you should keep. The really essential notes are site, time played, number of tables, and result. Be sure you write these down after every session and keep running totals in a spreadsheet.

2. **Make sure you can beat one table.** Multi-tabling is a silly idea if you can't beat one table. Start off by picking a stake and playing a few thousand hands. If you're losing, breaking even, or just a slight winner over that time, you'll need to work on improving your game at this stake before you should consider multi-tabling.

3. **Add tables slowly.** Once you've established that you can beat one table for a decent amount (say 5 BB per 100 hands), then add a second table and start tracking your results. Your win rate per table will probably drop whenever you add more tables. You'll make more mistakes, overlook some obvious plays, and even start misclicking (hitting 'fold' when you meant 'raise,' or the reverse). While your win rate per table should drop, your overall win rate per hour should increase. If it doesn't and you've played a lot of hands, then your previous level may be your best level, at least at your current playing strength.

4. **Move forward.** Once you feel you've located a good spot where you're a winner, keep playing. The idea is to earn while you learn and after awhile, you may feel your fundamental game has improved. In that case you have two choices: try adding more tables at your current stake, or move up in stakes.

If you feel you can make good decisions more quickly than before, but don't think your real understanding or approach to the game has changed much, then you probably want to try adding more tables at your current stake and see if you can still maintain your win rate. But if you feel you've become a better player, then consider moving up in stakes.

If you do increase your stakes, it may be best to revert to playing a single table for awhile or at least less tables than what you are currently doing. You need to see how players play at this new higher stake, and how well your improved game adapts to this new level. You might smoothly become a winner at the new level, or you may find that there's a new style of play at this stake, and you're going to have trouble adapting. Playing a single table (or less tables) buys you more time to study your opponents, take good notes, and get a handle on what's really happening. As you become sure that you're a winner, start adding tables as before.

Last Thought on Multi-Tabling

You should think about multi-tabling as a tool to increase your win rate after you have become a good player. It's difficult to improve when you're playing 12 or 16 tables at once. In essence, you just have time to react to what you see, but not enough time to plan ahead and prepare moves, or to learn to read hands well. If you believe you've become a strong player and you're beating medium or high-stakes games, that's not a problem; at this point, you're just doing your job. But if you're climbing the ladder and trying to improve at every step, extreme multi-tabling can be counter-productive. You may be increasing your immediate win rate at the cost of delaying your long-run development as a player. That's not, in general, a good trade.

Selecting Sites,
Tables, and Seats

When you go to a casino or a card room to play live poker, your choice is pretty much limited to the stake. Once you've told the host what stake you want, you'll be led to a table and assigned a seat, and off you go. (Most rooms will let you move around just a bit if you want when seats open, and of course you can always get up and go to another room.)

Online play is another world entirely. Most players maintain accounts on several different sites, and on any one site you might find hundreds of tables open for a given stake. You can look at tables and watch them for awhile before you sit down. You can look at the available seats and see if any one is more appealing than the others. And switching seats is no harder than making a couple of keystrokes.

Choosing just where to play and selecting tables and seats properly can have a substantial impact on your win rate, especially at micro-stakes and small stakes. (It has less of an impact at higher stakes because the number of tables is limited.) How do we find the right place to play? Let's see.

Selecting a Site

Online sites are not all the same. They differ in a number of important respects. Some are big, some are small. Some are new, others have been around a long time. Let's take a look at the key issues.

But before we get started, let's note that we won't be naming particular sites in this discussion. The reason? Sites can come and go quickly, or make mistakes that can cause them to lose support in the poker community quickly. The two biggest sites today were just promising up-and-comers back in 2002, while the biggest sites from that era have fallen far down the list. This book will be in print a long time, and we expect the online world to continue to evolve. But the general criteria for selection should remain valid for a long time to come.

Big or Small, New or Old?

Online poker started in the late 1990s and some of the original sites are still going. New sites, however, start on a regular basis. The old sites tend to be the big sites, and big is generally good. Big sites will spread the most tables and the most limits, which means you'll have plenty of choices. Big sites are always innovating, with ideas like deep stack tables, tables with antes, and tables with larger minimum buy-ins (eliminating some short stack strategies). Big sites will have more stable software and better support. Big sites are also generally reliable about money; if you send them your money, you'll get it back when you want.

Small, new sites have two main advantages. First, they frequently offer generous bonus programs to attract new players. When you sign up and send in some money, they'll match your deposit with a 100 or even a 150 percent bonus. This is free money which gets deposited into your account over time as you play hands. Second, the players at small new sites tend to be weaker than the players at old established ones.

Which is better? Most players, myself included, would argue that the advantages of the old, established sites outweigh any disadvantages. Knowing that good support is in place, the platform is stable, and your money is generally secure eliminates some hassles that you just don't need, and lets you concentrate on your game.

Database Support?

PokerTracker and Hold 'em Manager support most but not all sites. As far as I'm concerned, lack of database support is a deal breaker. If your database manager doesn't support a site, look elsewhere.

Datamining?

Once upon a time it was possible to log onto a site, open up the maximum number of tables for viewing at your preferred stake, turn on your PokerTracker or Hold 'em Manager, and walk away. The site would send hand histories for all the tables you were watching to your database manager, which would duly log them into your database. If you did this religiously for a few weeks, you'd have a massive amount of data ready for display on your opponents when you sat down to play.

This process was known as 'datamining,' and while not forbidden at the time, it conferred a substantial edge on the players who employed it. Eventually the major sites banned the practice by making sure that your computer only received hand histories for hands in which you actually participated. Although their decision was annoying to the professionals, it was undoubtedly a good long-run business decision.

Recently third-party sites have attempted to resuscitate the practice by selling hand histories in bulk, or providing ratings for cash game players which you can access. In turn, sites have responded by barring the use of some (but not all) of these sites in real time.

The only general advice I can offer is the following: If you like playing at a site, and it's published a ban on particular third-party software, don't use the software. You're running a risk of being barred, and the ability to play freely on a good site is worth much more than the edge which the software might provide.

Honesty?

You obviously want to play on a site that's honest. Honesty was taken for granted for many years, but the online poker world was shaken in 2008 by revelations of cheating at two sites. The cheating took the form of 'superuser' accounts which were able to play while seeing the hole cards of all the other players at the table. After the scandal was revealed, the sites announced that the users were banned, the software was repaired, and various amounts of restitution were made to players who had played at the affected tables.

The cheating took place only at relatively high-stakes games, so it didn't affect the vast bulk of players playing small stakes. Your best defense against these sorts of problems is to keep your wits about you, don't be afraid to leave a game or even a site if you see players behaving strangely and consistently winning, and stay current on online issues by regularly reading sources like the Two Plus Two Forums at www.twoplustwo.com. One of the cheating scandals was actually exposed by a poster on the Forums, while news of the other scandal was posted almost immediately. Remember that the Web is still the Wild West in many ways, and proceed with prudent caution.

One problem that you shouldn't be concerned about is the idea that a site is deliberately dealing you bad cards and bad beats, while favoring other players. Developing a random number generator to deal cards fairly is easy, and there's never been any credible evidence that a site has had problems in this respect. No-limit hold 'em is a game of huge variance, and even winning players have to be prepared for long runs of bad luck. It's just part of the game.

Incidentally, if you're convinced that sites are dealing you bad cards as part of some diabolical plot, don't bore your friends with your suspicions. Go watch 'Bigfoot Uncovered' or 'Ghost Hunters,' where you'll find kindred spirits.

Player Strength?

The most important reason to favor a site, dwarfing all others, is the quality of the players who play there. The best reason to have accounts on several different sites is to see if there are significant differences among the player pools. If you can find a site where the players seem weak, then that will probably be the most profitable place to play.

Rake
and Rakeback?

Sites make their money by charging the players a percentage of each pot, up to a certain maximum amount. This charge is known as the rake. Since online poker is a competitive market, sites generally charge about the same amount, usually 5 percent of the pot up to a maximum of $3. (The maximum may be reduced if the number of players that started the hand was small.) Sites will also usually follow the 'no flop, no drop' convention: If a hand was settled before the flop occurred, no rake is charged.

Two points to keep in mind about rakes:

1. Rakes decrease as a percentage basis as the stakes increase, and

2. Loose players pay much more rake than tight players.

To see how the rake decreases as we increase the stake, imagine that at a $25 NL table two players with $30 stacks get all-in preflop. The $60 pot will generate a rake of $3.00.

$$\$3.00 = (0.05)(\$60.00)$$

which is the maximum possible rake.

Now suppose two players at a $200 NL table, each with a full $200 stack, get all-in preflop. They're also charged a $3 rake, but now the rake represents just 0.75 percent of their $400 pot. On a percentage basis, they're only paying 15 percent of the rake of the $25 NL players!

Also notice that over the course of a session, your total rake charge is severely affected by your playing style. A loose passive player with VP$IP/PFR statistics of 40/10 is paying rake on more hands dealt than a nit with statistics of 10/8.

When you play at a new site, make a point of checking their online documentation about rakes and verify that you're not being overcharged. With rakes standardized across many sites, including the largest ones, there's no need to overpay on rake.

Rakebacks
and Bonuses?

If you're a member of a player's club at a live casino, you'll get points for the number of hours you sit at a poker table. The points probably won't accumulate very fast; they'll be proportional to the rake you should pay per hour, which in turn will be small compared to what a real plunger might lose at the slots or craps tables. But they will be enough to get you a free meal here and there.

Online sites accomplish the same goal through rakebacks and bonuses. We've discussed rakeback already. Bonuses are yet another attractive inducement. Most sites, particularly new ones, will try to drive players to their site through *bonus* incentives. The typical idea is simple: deposit some amount of money at the site (say $500) and the site will match it with a $500 bonus. Every time you play a hand, some small amount of money, perhaps just a few cents, will be moved from your 'bonus account' to your 'real account' until eventually you've cleared the bonus. As with rakeback, multi-tabling will make clearing the account much easier. Established sites will sometimes offer a bonus to their regular players as well, although these tend to be not so generous, and they usually take a lot of play to clear.

Caveat emptor: Most sites are honest. Some sites (especially new sites) may not be. As in real life, the more absurdly generous the bonus plan appears, the less likely it will actually be paid. But in general, bonuses are a good deal, and usually worth the small risk.

Selecting a Table

Once you've decided on a site, your next job is to find a favorable table. Big sites are obviously good for this purpose because you may have hundreds of tables to choose from at a given stake, whereas at a small site you may just have a few. So — how do we pick a good table?

A good table is a table with bad players, so your first job is to get your list of known weak players and start looking for them. The 'Find a Player' function is very useful in this respect. If your site doesn't support that function, just move down the list of tables, clicking on them one by one, and look for anyone you recognize. When you see someone you want to play with, either sit at the table or get on the waiting list.

If you can't find any particular weak players, your next step is to look at the column marked 'Players per Flop' or something similar. If this is high (over 40 percent for a 6-max table, over 30 percent for a full ring table) then a lot of folks are hanging around for the flop, and chances are good that it's a table with more than one loose, passive player — just the sort of table you should be seeking.

Most sites will display another statistic, 'Average Pot,' and again, larger is better. But this statistic isn't so useful because it can be heavily skewed by an all-in which might represent completely correct play.

Another useful idea is to check the stack sizes at different tables. For the most part, better players buy-in for full stacks. Weaker players, on the other hand, lack confidence and tend to buy-in for half stacks (usually 50 big blinds) or the table minimum (usually 20 big blinds). When choosing a table, focus on one with several medium stacks rather than some very short stacks simply because the medium stacks are probably no better than the short stacks, but they have more money to lose when things go awry.[5]

Once you're sitting at a table, remember you're not required to stay there. If the table isn't as favorable as you thought, or the mix of players changes radically, leave and substitute another table. If you're playing several tables over the course of a long session, don't be surprised if you switch tables a few times.

---

[5] Note that in higher stakes games this relationship breaks down. Higher-stakes players who buy-in for less than 100 big blinds often have some well-considered short stack strategy in mind and will not necessarily be easier opponents.

Evaluating Your Seat

Exactly where you sit at a table has a lot to do with whether you'll be a winner and how big a winner you'll be. Unfortunately, when you get to a table there's probably only one available seat, and unless you know most of the other players, you won't know whether it's a good seat or a bad one.

What you're going to have to do is sit down and then evaluate, over the course of a few orbits of the table, whether you've got a nice seat or not. If the seat is good, stay and play. If it's bad, you should leave and open another table. With all the choices available at a big site, there's just no reason to waste time in an unfavorable seat.

So what makes a seat good? Let's start by taking a look at the layout of a 6-max table.

ACROSS
Position 3/6

TWO TO LEFT	TWO TO RIGHT
Position 2/6	Position 4/6

LEFT	RIGHT
Position 1/6	Position 5/6

YOU

The diagram shows your position relative to the five other players at the table. In poker, it's an advantage to have position on another player, which simply means that in a given hand, you act after he acts.

At a 6-max table, we can evaluate seats by looking at how often you have position on another player, and how often he has position on you. In the diagram, take a look at the player on your right. You have position on him five out of every six hands. The only hand where he will have position on you is the hand where you're in the small blind and he's on the button. Just the reverse holds true for the player on your left. You will have position on him only one hand in six. Simply put, you have a big positional advantage over the player on your right, and a big positional disadvantage against the player on your left. Relative to you, these are the most important seats at the table; whoever sits in those two seats will have the most influence on whether you win or lose money.

A slightly different relationship exists between you and the seats two to your left and two to your right. On purely positional grounds, these seats are less important than the seats directly to your left and right because you have an advantage or disadvantage less often. However, when you are on the button, the player two to your left is in the big blind. You'll often be attacking from the button, and he'll be defending from the big blind. This unique relationship gives this seat a special importance. In four out of six hands, he has a positional advantage over you. But when you have an advantage, it's a very important advantage. As a result, you need to know a lot about the exact characteristics of this player. You want to know just how aggressively he presses his positional advantage when he has it, but you also want to know how well he defends his big blind when you attack from the button. Obviously, the inverse relationship holds between you and the player two to your right.

The least important seat is the player directly opposite from you. You're evenly balanced against him, holding a distant positional advantage three times every six hands.

So we're concentrating heavily on the players to our left and right, and in a somewhat different way on the players two to our left and two to our right. So who, exactly, do we want to see in these seats?

Let's note, if it's not immediately obvious, that money flows around a poker table in a clockwise direction. Because you have a positional advantage over the players on your right, you tend to win money from them, and for the same reason, you tend to lose it to the players on your left. Keeping that in mind, here's how an ideal table would be organized:

1. You want loose players on your right and tight players on your left.

2. You want bad players on your right and good players on your left.

3. You want big stacks on your right and small stacks on your left.

These points may not all be obvious, so let's look at each one in turn.

Point No. 1: Loose on your right, tight on your left. Loose players play too many pots and dribble away money. You'd like to be able to get into those pots with position and get that money, so you want them on your right. Tight players don't play many pots, so you'd like them to act behind since they give up some of their positional advantage by folding hands they should play.

Point No. 2: Bad on your right, good on your left. Actually, of course, you want bad players everywhere. The question we're really asking here is "If you're a good player, and you have a good player and a bad player as opponents, and you have to have one each on your right and left, where would you put them?" Having the good player on your left and the bad player on your right is better than the alternative because the positional edge will let you maximize your wins from the bad player, and your skill should let you minimize the losses to the good player. Thus you'll expect to win more from the weak player than you will lose to the good player. Part of the way you do this is by loosening up when the bad player enters the pot and tightening up a little when it is your turn, no one has yet entered the pot, and the strong player acts behind you.

Point No. 3: Big on your right, small on your left. If money flows clockwise, it follows that you want to be downstream from the big money so it can flow to you. At the same time, having a small stack on your left functions as a sort of plugged drain minimizing the money that can flow from you. Hence, you want big stacks on your right and small ones on your left.

This seems counter-intuitive to some players who remember hands when they made a speculative raise of a player who acted first only to have a short stack behind them move all-in, a move which they couldn't call. While that's annoying, it shouldn't happen often enough to counteract the general principle involved. You want to have position on the big stacks, while a small stack that has position on you can't maximize his advantage.

Of course, when you first sit down at a table, you won't know how you stand. Instead, you should just plan on playing for awhile (30 to 40 hands is a good number), then looking at the VP$IP and PFR numbers around the table and reevaluating. Take a look at these sample tables and decide if you would stay or go.

Sample Table No. 1:

ACROSS
Stack: 85bb
VP 40 / PF 5 / AF 1

TWO TO LEFT
Stack: 100bb
VP 36 / PF 20 / AF 2

TWO TO RIGHT
Stack: 120bb
VP 50 / PF 10 / AF 3

LEFT
Stack: 50bb
VP 20 / PF 15 / AF 3

RIGHT
Stack: 30bb
VP 15 / PF 10 / AF 2

YOU
Stack 100bb
VP 20 / PF 15 / AF 2

Stay. A short stacked, tight player on your right is far from ideal. But look around the rest of the table. You have three loose players sitting in the three seats across from you, each with a big stack.

That's a lot of loose money ready to come your way. Even two loose players will generally make a table quite good, but here you have three, so this table is excellent.

Sample Table No. 2:

ACROSS
Stack: 50bb
VP 30 / PF 15 / AF 2

TWO TO LEFT	TWO TO RIGHT
Stack: 100bb	Stack: 60bb
VP 22 / PF 18 / AF 2	VP 50 / PF 10 / AF 3

LEFT	RIGHT
Stack: 100bb	Stack: 120bb
VP 20 / PF 15 / AF 3	VP 45 / PF 8 / AF 1

YOU
Stack 100bb
VP 20 / PF 15 / AF 2

Stay, but be cautious. You have a perfect player on your right, loose and passive with a full stack. After him you have two medium stacks, one very loose and the other more normal. Medium stacks are generally players you like to see, so that's good. However, the two players on your left could be trouble. Both seem to be tight-aggressive players with full stacks. Continue playing because of the player on your right, but if the players on your left put too much pressure on you, be prepared to leave.

Sample Table No. 3:

ACROSS
Stack: 150bb
VP 18 / PF 16 / AF 2

TWO TO LEFT
Stack: 120bb
VP 30 / PF 22 / AF 4

TWO TO RIGHT
Stack: 40bb
VP 18 / PF 12 / AF 2

LEFT
Stack: 150bb
VP 20 / PF 15 / AF 3

RIGHT
Stack: 20bb
VP 12 / PF 10 / AF 5

YOU
Stack 100bb
VP 20 / PF 15 / AF 2

Man the lifeboats! From a statistical point of view, it doesn't get much worse than this. You have small, tight-aggressive stacks on your right, so not much money is going to flow from there. On your left are the big loose-aggressive stacks, who'll be putting pressure on you throughout the session. There must be a better table elsewhere, so leave.

Sample Table No. 4:

ACROSS
Stack: 100bb
VP 20 / PF 10 / AF 1

TWO TO LEFT
Stack: 100bb
VP 12 / PF 6 / AF 4

TWO TO RIGHT
Stack: 40bb
VP 14 / PF 8 / AF 1

LEFT
Stack: 80bb
VP 6 / PF 2 / AF 2

RIGHT
Stack: 60bb
VP 10 / PF 6 / AF 2

YOU
Stack 120bb
VP 32 / PF 22 / AF 3

Stay. To a certain extent, the kind of table and seat you want depends on your own style. Unlike the first three examples, here you're not a generic tight-aggressive player with medium statistics, but a much looser and more aggressive player, with VP$IP/PFR statistics of 32/22. For you, this table of tight players and nits is good for your style. Although you won't be winning the occasional big pot where a loose passive opponent gives away his money, you'll be able to make up for that to some extent by constantly stealing blinds. When it's folded to you in the small blind, you'll be attacking the big blind of the player on your left who has statistics of 6/2. From the button, you'll have two extremely tight players in the blinds. In this crowd, you'll also be able to collect a lot of orphan post-flop pots when players miss their hands. It's a good table for you and it will be worth your time to stay.

Part Three

Ranges
and Distributions

Ranges
and Distributions

Introduction:
The Old Way of Seeing

If you've watched a lot of poker on television, you've probably seen the following scenario play out many times. Before the flop, one player bets and another player calls. Everyone else at the table folds. The flop comes and the first player bets again and after some hesitation, the second player calls again. Now the turn card comes and the first player makes a large bet. The second player, with some sort of medium-strength hand, goes into a deep think. He is, the announcer tells us, "Trying to put his opponent on a hand."

In poker parlance, "putting your opponent on a hand" simply means figuring out what two cards he holds based on his actions so far, what you know about him, and, if it's a live game, whatever tells you may have noticed. Sometimes a player will fold his hand and announce, "I put him on king-queen," "I read him for kings," or something similar, which sounds very impressive if it turns out to be correct, and somewhat less impressive when (as usually happens) it turns out to be wrong.

Putting your opponent on a specific hand is actually difficult because you almost never have enough information to narrow the choices down to a single possibility. Let's work through a simple example and see why this is so.

Suppose you're playing a live full ring $2/$5 cash game and there are nine players at the table. You're on the button and you pick up the

The first three players fold and the fourth player, who we'll call Joe, raises to $20. The next two players fold and now it's your turn. You've been playing with Joe for a couple of hours and know a little bit about him. He seems tight, but not obsessively so. He doesn't play a lot of pots, but when he does, he's usually pushing the action. You've only seen him limp into a pot once; usually he comes in for a raise. If he raises preflop, he seems to always follow through with a bet on the flop. He might have checked the flop once — you can't remember for sure. He's only shown down a couple of hands, and both times they seemed strong enough to justify the betting.

(How does Joe see you? That's an equally important question that many players forget to ask. You've been tight so far, playing few pots. In the hands you have played you've done well, winning two big pots, one with the nut flush and one with a flopped set. Joe seems to be alert, so presumably he noticed this.)

You could raise or call with your pair of eights, but since you have position, you decide to just call. The blinds fold. The pot is $47 and the effective stack is approximately $650.

The flop comes the

That's not a bad flop for you; only one overcard to your pair. Joe bets $40. You decide that he may not have hit the king and you have a pair, so you elect to call. The pot is now $127, and there is about $610 left to bet.

The turn is the 9♠. Joe thinks for a little bit and bets $80, about two-thirds of the pot. You're not happy because a second card larger than your pair has come, and Joe has bet again. What do you do?

If you believe in the idea of putting Joe on a hand, you've got some difficulty here. The problem is that we don't have enough information to narrow down his possibilities to a single hand or anything close to that. In fact, from what's happened, it's not clear that we can narrow down the possibilities at all! Let's look at what we know right now and see why this is true.

He raised preflop with three players having folded and five players left to act behind. Since we think he's a pretty solid player, he's unlikely to be raising with nothing. His hand could certainly be a premium pair or a middle pair. It might even be any of the small pairs down to deuces. He could also have a combination of two of the high cards, aces, kings, queens, jacks, and tens. He'll certainly raise with the big combinations like ace-king and ace-queen, but he might be willing to go as low as queen-ten or jack-ten, especially if they were suited.

There are a few other possibilities as well. He might be raising with some of the suited connectors, perhaps ten-nine, nine-eight, or eight-seven. (Note that since we hold two eights, there aren't as many of these combinations available. Although there are four possible nine-eight suited combinations in the original deck, the eights that we hold eliminate two of these four, leaving just the heart and diamond combinations. The same is true for eight-seven suited.)

Less likely, but still possible, are some of the suited aces. We assume he's raising with ace-king suited through ace-ten suited as part of the high-card hands above, but he might also be raising with some of the lower suited aces, say ace-nine, ace-eight, and ace-seven. Lower aces than those would be pretty speculative, and we haven't marked him as a speculative player.

That's a fairly reasonable group of opening hands for a generally tight player raising with five players left to act. We're now beating some of these hands, and losing to others. Unfortunately, when we're losing we're way behind. If he holds king-queen, for instance, he has a pair of kings and we have just two outs on the final card, one of the last two eights. If he has a pair of jacks instead, we still have the same two outs. On the bright side, he doesn't have many outs if we're ahead. If he has ace-jack, for instance, he has to hit an ace or a jack on the river to beat us, which gives him just six outs.

Having said all that, can we put him on a hand? We know he bet the flop which he would have done if he hit his king. But he would also have bet the flop if he had aces, queens, tens, or perhaps even something like sixes. He might have bet the flop even if he hit a set, although he would have been tempted to slowplay.

What if he had ace-queen instead? There again he would probably make a continuation bet on the flop, probing to see if we had something or were ready to give up. After all, unless we called with a pair, most of our hands would miss that flop as well, in which case the first person to bet will usually take down the pot.

What about his bet on the turn? How much more does that tell us about his hand?

To be sure, it tells us a little more. Our opponent might still have a pair better than ours, and be betting for value. He could also have a set, and be betting for value. But he might have nothing much, and since we only called his flop bet, he may reasonably think we will go away when he fires a second barrel.

In short, trying to put him on a hand at this stage is pretty much guesswork. We may be ahead or we may be behind. The pot is $207 and it costs us $80 to call which are odds of a bit over 2.5-to-1. While those are attractive odds when we may well have the best hand, a bet on the river will probably be for our whole stack, and we have only two cards in the deck to improve.

In short, "putting him on a hand" leads us pretty much nowhere. If we like the pot odds we're getting we can call and see what happens on the river. (If he bets, we'll probably fold; if he checks, we'll happily show the hand down and see if our eights were good all along.) Or we can "put him on" ace-king, king-queen, or any other hand that lets us fold with dignity, and go away.

Is there a better approach to hand analysis than putting him on a hand? Yes there is. Welcome to the world of ranges.

What is a Range?

As we've discussed already, a range of hands is simply the set of hands with which a player might make a given action. If we have some information about a player's preflop tendencies, we can make an educated guess about the hands that make up his range. Fortunately for us, the basic preflop statistics in our HUD, namely VP$IP and PFR, provide that information.

Once we've estimated his range for whatever action our opponent has taken, we can look at our hand and see just how we're doing *against his range*. Notice that we're not comparing our hand to some hypothetical hand that he might have; instead, we're comparing our hand to the set of all his possible hands and seeing how we're doing on average. Measuring ourselves against his range is essential to reading hands and playing good poker. It's decidedly non-trivial, but it's a skill that can be learned. So to get a clearer idea of playing against a range, let's start with a couple of simple situations, and work through them in some detail.

Playing Against a Tight Range

We're at a 6-max online table with stakes of $1/$2. We've been here about an hour and we've compiled some data on our opponents. In this hand we're on the button. JoeyZee, under the gun, raises to $7. The players in middle position and the cutoff fold.

Our HUD on JoeyZee reads as follows:

> *JoeyZee / (72) / +5*
> *VP 16 / PF 12 / AS 22 / FB 75*
> *3B 4 / F3 70 / AF 3 / 3 / 1 / 1.2*
> *CB 80 / FC 65 / FT 70*
> *W$F 42 / WtS 25 / W$S 50*

It's a pretty standard set of HUD statistics for a player who sits somewhere between tight-aggressive and nitty. His VP$IP/PFR numbers are 16 and 12, tight but not super-tight. His ATS of 22 shows that he's willing to loosen up in position. His 3-bet number of 4 shows that he'll only reraise preflop with premium hands. The continuation bet and aggression factor numbers show that he'll fire out on the flop, then tighten up and play pot control on later streets. All in all, about what we'd expect of a generally tight player.

Our hand is the

It's not an atrocious hand, and against many players we might call or even reraise. But can we play it against JoeyZee? To start, let's try to figure out Joey's opening range, the set of hands with which he'll raise under the gun.

His overall PFR number is 12 percent, but this represents an average over all positions, and we should assume that he'll raise less in early position than in late position, so we need to scale that 12 percent number back somewhat. Let's assume that he'll raise 8 percent of the time under the gun. It's a guess, but a reasonable guess.

What does an 8 percent range look like? It depends a little bit on just what sort of hands he likes to play. Will he raise with all pairs under the gun, or just medium and high pairs? Does he like to mix in some medium suited connectors for variety, or does he prefer all high cards?

There are 1,326 possible starting hands in hold 'em, so a player willing to play 8 percent of his hands under the gun would be playing something like 106 different two-card combinations when first to act. Here are a couple of hand ranges which fit that criteria:

Hand Range No. 1: (108 combintions).

Pairs from AA to 77 (48 combinations)
AK, AQ, and AJ, suited or unsuited (48 combinations)
KQ, QJ, JT suited only (12 combinations)

Hand Range No. 2: (110 combinations).

All pairs, AA through 22 (78 combinations)
AK, AQ, suited or unsuited (32 combinations)

Let's note that while both hand ranges are extremely tight, Range No. 2 has a strength that Range No. 1 lacks. By including all pairs, Joey has the possibility of hitting a monster hand on any flop. Range No. 1, by contrast, can at most represent an overpair when the board flops low cards.

Let's note something else as well. Because we hold the A♠, there aren't as many hand combinations available to Joey as he thinks. A full deck, for instance, would have six possible ace-ace combinations, but with the A♠ unavailable, only three remain. In effect, there are fewer hands available for Joey to play than he thinks.

So how is our A♠T♠ doing against these ranges? Not too well actually. Let's start by comparing it to Hand Range No. 1.

The simple way to make this comparison is to use a software tool that can compare a hand to a given range of hands. Throughout this book, we'll use *Pokerstove* for this purpose. But for the first few examples in this section, we're going to lay out the comparison so it's clear what we're doing. Here's a little chart that shows our A♠T♠ matched against Hand Range No. 1.

Our Hand: A♠T♠ versus His Range: No. 1		
His Hand	**Number of Combinations**	**Prob of Winning (%)**
AA	3	13.3
KK	6	32.8
QQ	6	32.6
JJ	6	32.4
TT	3	34.8
99	6	47.3
88	6	47.4
77	6	48.0

AKs	3	29.3
AQs	3	29.5
AJs	3	30.1
KQs	4	58.3
QJs	4	57.4
JTs	3	68.4
AKo	9	30.9
AQo	9	31.0
AJo	9	31.7
Total	**89**	

Cumulative Winning Probability: **37.7%**

Let's take a look at a couple of features of this chart that might not be obvious at first glance. The first column just lists Joey's possible hands from the range that we had already assigned to him. The pairs are listed first, followed by the suited cards, and then the offsuit combinations.

Column 2 lists the number of card combinations available for each hand. Note that these counts reflect the fact that we hold an ace and a ten. There are six ways for Joey to hold a pair of kings, queens, or jacks, but only three ways he can hold a pair of aces or tens. In the same way, the number of ace-king suited hands drops from four to three, and the number of unsuited combinations drops from twelve to nine. The total result of the card removal effect is to drop the number of hands in his range from a theoretical 108 down to an actual 89.

The third column shows our probability of winning assuming he holds the given hand. The number just assumes the hand is dealt out to showdown with no further action, and does not take position into account. In the future, we'll refer to this as our "raw" probability of winning a given pairing. Although it's not a realistic assessment of winning chances, it's a starting point for comparing this situation to others. Holding ace-ten suited, our overall raw probability against his tight Range No. 1 is 37.7 percent.

Is that good or bad? Theoretically, it's all right. Joey's bet of $7 creates a pot of $10, so right now we're getting 10-to-7 pot odds, almost 1.5-to-1. In addition, we'll be in position for the rest of the hand. In this situation, we don't generally mind playing a hand where our range analysis says we're 35 percent or better. Out of position, we'd want somewhat better chances, say 40 to 45 percent.

Ace-ten suited, however, is one of the classic "trouble hands," That is, hands which tend to be dominated by many of the hands in our opponent's range. We can see that effect clearly in the chart where almost half his hands are either better aces or the dominating pairs (aces or tens). Against an aggressive opponent who is as tight as Joey, we'd let this go.

Now suppose he plays with Hand Range No. 2 instead of Range No. 1. Does this affect our decision? Let's construct the same chart and see what happens.

Our Hand: A♠T♠ versus His Range: No. 2		
His Hand	**Number of Combinations**	**Prob of Winning (%)**
AA	3	13.3
KK	6	32.8
QQ	6	32.6
JJ	6	32.4
TT	3	34.8
99	6	47.3
88	6	47.4
77	6	48.0
66	6	48.5
55	6	49.3
44	6	49.7
33	6	50.3
22	6	51.0
AKs	3	29.3
AQs	3	29.5
AKo	9	30.9
AQo	9	31.0
Total	96	

Cumulative Winning Probability: **39.5%**

There are a couple of interesting things to notice when we switch Joey's range to one oriented around pairs rather than Broadway cards. The first point is that we're doing better, obviously, because we've eliminated many of the dominated situations and created more pairings where we're involved in a coin flip. Overall, it would appear that his exact hand range doesn't matter much, as there's only about a 2 percent difference between our results against Range No. 1 compared to our results against Range No. 2. This, however, is an illusion, as we'll see in a second.

Now let's take a look at how some other possible hands will fare against Joey's opening range. This time we'll skip the detailed charts and just look at the results from PokerStove. Here are a few examples:

Possible Calling Hand	Result versus Range No. 1 (%) (some pairs)	Result versus Range No. 2 (%) (all pairs)
QQ	65.0	67.9
JJ	57.0	62.6
TT	51.6	59.1
99	47.0	55.0
88	43.2	51.5
77	39.2	47.8
66	37.9	44.3
55	37.8	40.7
44	37.4	36.7
33	36.9	32.8
22	36.3	28.9
AQs	48.5	43.3
AJs	41.1	40.2
ATs	37.7	39.5
KQs	40.0	40.4
KJs	37.9	41.0

T9s	35.0	39.4
98s	33.6	37.6
87s	32.4	36.2
76s	31.7	34.6
65s	31.7	32.9
54s	31.9	31.2
AQo	45.7	40.3
AJo	37.9	36.9
KQo	36.6	37.2
KJo	34.5	37.8

This table yields a number of important observations.

1. Joey's exact hand range can matter a great deal. Our original ace-ten suited hand showed less than a 2 percent difference between Range No. 1 and Range No. 2. But a hand like a pair of sevens does 8.6 percent worse against Range No. 1 than against Range No. 2. The same is true of the other medium pairs which are coin flips or big underdogs against everything in Range No. 1, but are big favorites against some of the hands (the smaller pairs) in Range No. 2.

2. If we have a small pair, however, we prefer playing against Range No. 1. We're dominated by almost everything in Range No. 2, but now have a lot of coin flips against Range No. 1.

3. The weaker high card hands (ace-jack, king-queen, and our own ace-ten suited) are about equal underdogs against either range. Against Range No. 1, they're severely dominated much of the time, but they can be a big favorite against some of his weaker high card combinations. Against Range No. 2, they're never a favorite, but they're in lots of coin flips.

4. Suited connectors are crushed by Range No. 1, but do slightly better against Range No. 2.

So there's a big lesson to be drawn here. *If your opponent is tight, you want to note any information you can about his range.* Anytime you see him raise preflop and the hand goes to showdown, make a note about his starting hand. Knowing that information will make your calling, folding, or 3-betting decisions much easier.

But it's less important to know the exact details of a loose player's range. A tight player only needs to put a few combinations in his range, so it's possible for him to construct very different ranges. A loose player has to pack in a lot of hands which requires him to put in everything reasonable: all pairs, all Broadway cards, and all suited connectors. Whether or not he likes to include queen-eight suited or nine-seven offsuit won't affect your decision-making much.

So what should we do against Joey with our ace-ten suited? The pot odds of about 1.4-to-1 and our position barely justify a call. However, we still have two players to act behind us, and if either raises we'll have to fold our hand. That consideration tips the balance to a fold.

Playing Against
Looser Opening Ranges

In the last section we assigned our opponent an 8 percent opening range under the gun, and we decided our A♠T♠ wasn't quite good enough to play, even in position. Suppose our opponent had been someone looser, however, with a much wider opening range. How would our ace-ten suited do in that case?

Let's take a look at four different ranges, varying from 15 percent to 30 percent, and see how our hand fares in each case. Let's start by seeing what these ranges might actually look like. Here's a 15 percent opening range:

All pairs AA through 22
Suited aces from AKs through ATs
All suited Broadway cards: KQs, KJs, KTs, QJs, QTs, and JTs
Unsuited aces from AKo through ATo
Some unsuited Broadways: KQo, KJo, and QJo

We can get to 20 percent by taking the 15 percent range and adding these hands:

Suited aces from A9s through A7s
Unsuited aces: A9o
Suited connectors from T9s through 65s
Unsuited connectors: JTo and T9o

Adding a few more hands gets us to 25 percent:

205

> Suited aces: A6s
> Unsuited aces: A8o
> Unsuited Broadways: KTo and QTo
> Suited connectors: 54s
> Suited one-gappers: J9s through 64s

And finally, adding these hands makes a 30 percent range:

> Suited aces: A5s through A2s
> Unsuited aces: A7o, A6o
> Suited two-gappers: Q9s, J8s, T7s
> Unsuited connectors: 98o

Using PokerStove to match our ace-ten suited against these ranges leads to some interesting results:

1. Against the 15 percent range, our raw probability of winning is 47 percent, almost even money.

2. Against the 20 percent range, our raw probability of winning rises to 52 percent, and we become a favorite.

3. Against the 25 percent range, we increase slightly to 55 percent.

4. And finally, against the 30 percent range, we increase a little more to 57 percent.

So against these looser ranges, we're always at least calling with ace-ten suited, and the only question is whether we're willing to raise or not.

Estimating
Calling Ranges

Estimating a player's range when he open-raises is a fairly straightforward exercise, especially if the range is a bit loose. But estimating a range when someone calls is more difficult. Let's look at a couple of examples and see how we should proceed.

Example: Imagine you're under the gun in a 6-max online game with blinds of \$0.25/\$0.50. You pick up the

and raise to \$1.50. The next two players fold, the button calls, and the blinds fold. The button's VP\$IP/PFR statistics are 32/10 over about 100 hands. His 3-bet percentage is 4. What sort of estimate can we make for his calling range?

The first mistake many players make is to assume that their opponent's calling percentage is just the difference between his VP\$IP and PFR. "Ah, his VP\$IP is 32 and his PFR is 10, so he must be raising with the best 10 percent of his hands and calling with the next 22 percent. Easy, no?"

Well, no, it's not that easy. The problem is that a player can enter the pot without raising in one of several ways:

1. He can limp and then fold to a raise.

2. He can limp and then call a raise.

3.   He can call in position after a raise (known as cold-calling).

4.   He can call in the blinds after a raise.

5.   He can call in or out of position after a raise and a call (or two), or after a limp and a call (or two).

Assuming that a player believes in limping into pots, he should be more likely to limp into an unopened pot than to cold-call a raise since in the first case no one has indicated they have anything, while in the second case someone has already said they have a hand they like.

What about calling in the blinds versus cold-calling in position? Calling in the blinds gives the caller a discounted price since he already has money in the pot. If the opener made a small raise or a min-raise, the big blind may be getting an excellent price to call. Cold-calling doesn't get such good pot odds, but the caller gets to play the hand in position, which is worth a lot.

Calling when several players have already entered the pot is also a much easier decision. Now you're getting excellent pot odds and probably good implied odds as well, both of which imply a wide calling range.

It's easy to see at this point that estimating calling ranges will involve a lot more educated guesswork than we needed in our last section. What I'm going to do is lay down a few rules of thumb to guide you in this process. They're not meant to be precise, but they're based on a lot of experience and are meant to be a guide that you'll find useful as you go forward.

Rule No. 1: Tight-aggressive players only call with 2 to 3 percent of their hands. If your opponent has VP$IP/PFR statistics like 18/14, 20/17, or 24/20, he's a classic tight-aggressive player. Tight-aggressive players essentially never limp, and often prefer raising (3-betting) to calling since raising gives them the chance to take the pot down right now. Calling ranges for a player like this usually include just medium pairs and some medium suited connectors. Here, for instance, is a 3 percent cold-calling range:

> Pairs: 99 through 66
> Suited connectors: JTs through 87s

In small stakes games and higher, tight-aggressive players will typically have 3-betting ranges that are at least twice as wide as their calling ranges. This is consistent with their general approach to poker which relies on taking the initiative early and dictating the pace of the hand with aggression.

In micro-stakes games, tight-aggressive players aren't quite as aggressive as their brethren at higher stakes. They're less likely to 3-bet, probably have VP$IP/PFR numbers more like 22/14 or 20/13, and have wider calling ranges, more like 6 to 8 percent. A calling range in this case might look more like

> Pairs: JJ through 66
> Suited Broadways: KQs, KJs, KTs, QJs, QTs, JTs
> Suited connectors: T9s through 87s
> Offsuit Broadways: AQo, AJo, KQo

Rule No. 2: Loose players have calling ranges that are about half as wide as the difference between their 3-bet number and their VP$IP number. The idea behind this rule is that loose players, especially at low stakes, are often eager to limp but less eager to call a raise. However, they will call raises liberally with a lot of hands that a better player would either reraise or fold.

This rule is useful, but keep in mind that it's very general and there are lots of exceptions. But as we saw earlier, with loose, wide ranges it's not too important to be precise. You just need a general, ballpark idea of the kind of hands your opponent might hold.

Let's apply this rule to the example at the start of this section. There we had an opponent whose VP$IP was 32, his PFR was 10, and his 3-bet percentage was 4. The calculation looks like this:

$$32 - 4 = 28$$

$$\frac{28}{2} = 14$$

We'll estimate that he'll 3-bet with the top 4 percent of his hands and call with the next 14 percent. That estimate produces a few possible calling ranges. One looks like this:

> All pairs: TT through 22
> All suited Broadways except for AKs and AQs
> All unsuited Broadways except for AKo and AQo

We've eliminated the premium pairs down to jacks, and ace-king and ace-queen, suited or unsuited, since those are his 3-betting hands.

Another possible range looks like this:

> All pairs: TT through 55
> Suited aces: AJs through A8s
> Suited Broadways: KQs, KJs, KTs, QJs, QTs, JTs
> Suited connectors: T9s through 65s
> Suited one-gappers: J9s through 86s
> Unsuited Broadways: AJo, ATo, KQo, KJo, QJo, JTo

From the first range we eliminated the small pairs and some of the offsuit Broadways, while substituting more suited cards.

Since calling ranges are inherently hard to specify precisely, make a habit of noting a player's hands whenever he calls the flop and gets to showdown. A few real datapoints are much better than even well-informed speculation. Remember, however, that for the very loose players, precision is both difficult and somewhat unnecessary.

What is a Distribution?

What we call a *distribution* is the result of an estimated range meeting a particular flop. It's just a listing of the probability of each possible hand type that your opponent might have on that flop. Having an idea of those probabilities lets you estimate just how well your hand is doing post-flop against his range.

Let's take an easy example. In a 6-max online game, you hold the

on the button. The player under the gun raises to three big blinds. You know he's a tight player with a PFR of 10. You estimate that under the gun, he'll only be raising with the top 5 percent of his hands. The player in middle position and the cutoff fold. You elect to call with your suited connectors. (Whether that's a wise move is another question.) The blinds fold and the pot is 7.5 big blinds.

The flop comes the

You have top pair with a decent but not great kicker. Your opponent makes a bet of five big blinds. His continuation bet percentage is 90 percent, so you think he would have made this bet whether or not the flop helped him.

Here are a few quick questions to ask.

1. What's the probability that you're ahead here?

2. What's the probability he has a flush draw?

3. What's the probability he has a straight draw?

4. What's the probability he has both a flush *and* a straight draw?

You don't know? Well, that's why we study distributions. Let's solve this fairly easy distribution problem and see what the answers are.

We'll start by constructing a spreadsheet. Across the top we'll list all the hands that make up a 5 percent range which consists of just a very few hands. We'll assume he has a range including the pairs from aces to tens, ace-king (suited and unsuited), and ace-queen (suited and unsuited).

Underneath the hands in his range we'll list the number of possible hands of that type. With no extra knowledge, there are six possible ways to catch a pair and 16 possible ways to catch a non-pair, which include 12 non-suited ways and four suited ways. Note that the number of each hand type will be affected by the five cards we know can't be in his hand, namely a jack, two tens, a nine, and a four.

Here are the first few lines of our spreadsheet:

Our Hand of J♠T♠ with Flop of T♥9♣4♥								
AA	KK	QQ	JJ	TT	AKs	AKo	AQs	AQo
6	6	6	3	1	4	12	4	12

The cards in our hand and the flop have affected his hand count in two cells. Since we hold the J♠, the number of possible pairs of jacks drops from six to three. Since two tens are accounted for, only one possible pair of tens remains: T♦T♣.

Next we list the major hand types down the side. The listing is as follows:

Set
Two pair
Overpair
Top pair
Middle or lower pair
Flush draw
Straight draw
Flush draw + straight draw
Gutshot draw
Two overcards
Zip

The top holding is a set since that's the best possible hand on this board. We then list a bunch of hands in descending order, including a few that he can't have given his range. We're lumping all types of pairs below top pair into one broad category, 'middle or lower pair,' for simplicity. The 'zip' category just means a hand with nothing better than a single overcard.

The next step is to match the different hands in the range with the flop. All six 'AA' hands, for instance, become overpairs on this flop. The four hands in the 'AKs' column, on the other hand, break into two cells. One hand, A♥K♥, becomes a flush draw, while the other three drop into the 'Two overcards' cell. When we finish assigning hands to cells, the result looks like this:

Our Hand of J♠T♠ with Flop of T♥9♣4♥									
5% Range	AA	KK	QQ	JJ	TT	AKs	AKo	AQs	AQo
Hand Type	6	6	6	3	1	4	12	4	12
Set					1				
Two pair									
Overpair	6	6	6	3					
Top pair									
Middle or lower pair									
Flush draw							1		1
Straight draw									
Flush draw + straight draw									
Gutshot draw									
Two overcards							3	12	3	12
Zip									

When we summarize the results, only four hand categories actually remain: sets, overpairs, a flush draw, and two overcards. Here's the final count with the percentage breakdowns:

Our Hand of J♠T♠ with Flop of T♥9♣4♥		
Opponent's distribution from a top-5 percent range		
	Count	**Percent**
Set	1	2
Overpair	21	39
Flush draw + two overcards	2	4
Two overcards	30	55

Now we can go ahead and answer the four questions we originally asked:

Question No. 1: *What's the probability that you're ahead here?* You're actually a slight favorite right now. His biggest category of hands is the two overcard hands, and there you're 78 percent to win. You're crushed by his set (5 percent to win) and you're in bad shape against his overpairs (22 percent to win). Interestingly, you're a slight underdog (47 percent) against a flush draw since it also contains two overcards. But he only has a flush draw 4 percent of the time. On balance, you're now 51.7 percent to win against his range since we assume he's continuation betting his entire range.

Question No. 2: *What's the probability he has a flush draw?* As we just saw, this is a tiny 4 percent. As we look at more distributions, we'll note this pattern again and again. Flush draws are a much smaller threat than people assume.

Question No. 3: *What's the probability he has a straight draw?* Zero.

Question No. 4: *What's the probability he has both a flush and a straight draw?* Zero. Draws are not your problem on this board. With his small range, he either has an overpair or two overcards.

As a net favorite with position, you can't fold your top pair. However, you also shouldn't raise since raising will just fold out his overcards while keeping the hands that are beating you in the pot. If a large percentage of his hands were some sort of draw, raising would make some sense, but as we see that can't be the case. So you have to call and see what happens on the turn.

Calculating Distributions

Can you calculate these sorts of distributions during real play? Not really. What you want to do while playing is to make intelligent estimates based partly on the range you've assigned to your opponent, partly on the flop, and partly on any work you've done with distributions at home.

Calculating distributions is an ideal homework exercise, a way to use the hand histories that are available to you from either PokerTracker or Hold 'em Manager. You can use these database programs to replay a hand that caused trouble while you were playing, while at the same time they show you the HUD that you saw at the time. An excellent exercise is to take that HUD, make an estimate of your opponent's range, and then sit down with a spreadsheet program and see just what your opponent's distribution really looked like when the flop appeared. Often this exercise will help you pinpoint real flaws in your play, situations where you wouldn't bet or call because you feared certain holdings that just weren't likely given what you should have known at the time.

Repeating this exercise with hands that didn't go well will gradually improve your ability to quickly put your opponent on a distribution once the flop hits, which in turn will make you a much more dangerous player. Let's take a look at a few more ranges and flops, and see just what sort of distributions result from them.

Distributions
Against a 12 Percent Range

As we just saw, a 5 percent raising range is so tight that it's not hard to see what kind of distributions might result. Any flop containing an ace, king, or queen is likely to be extremely strong, while any flop with lower cards creates a distribution divided between high pairs and overcards, possibly with an occasional flush draw thrown in.

In this chapter, we'll take a look at what happens when a 12 percent range meets a flop. Consider this problem:

You're playing in a 6-max online game with $1/$2 blinds. On the button, you have the

The under the gun player folds and the player in middle position raises to $6. His VP$IP and PFR numbers are 20/15. You think in middle position he'll be raising a little less than his average, perhaps about 12 percent of his starting hands. The cutoff folds and you decide to call with your middle pair. The blinds fold and the pot is $15.

How does his range perform against each of these five flops?

A. A♥Q♠7♦
B. K♥7♠2♣
C. J♠T♠9♠
D. 6♠4♣2♣
E. 9♥9♦6♦

A 12 percent range is still a little tight, but contains a much wider set of hands than a 5 percent range. Here's what a typical 12 percent raising range looks like:

> All pairs
> Suited aces: AKs through ATs
> Offsuit aces: AKo through ATo
> KQ, suited or offsuit

It's a range still heavily oriented toward aces and high cards, but the inclusion of all the pairs means that it could flop a set on any board. Against that range, our middling pair of eights are about a 52-to-48 favorite preflop. We're a big favorite against his low pairs, a big underdog against his higher pairs, and a slight favorite against his unpaired hands. Now let's see how the flop might have helped or hurt us. Using the method from the last section, here's a table showing the distribution created by this range against each of these five flops:

My hand: 8♣8♦

His raising range: 12%

	Flop A: A♥Q♠7♦	Flop B: K♥7♠2	Flop C: J♠T♠9♠	Flop D: 6♠4♣2♣	Flop E: 9♥9♦6♦
Straight flush			<1%		
Quads/ Full house					<3%
Flush			<1%		
Straight			11%		
Set	7%	7%	7%	6%	
Two pair	7%				42%
Overpair		4%	4%	30%	
Top pair	30%	18%	11%		
Middle and lower pair	56%	36%	15%	8%	
Flush draw + straight draw			4%		
Pair + draw			27%		
Flush draw			4%	3%	3%
Straight draw			7%		
Gutshot + two overcards			4%		
Two overcards			2%	52%	52%
Zip		35%			

First, let's note that we've had to add a bunch of hand categories to this chart. Some of these flops allow hands as big as a straight flush to appear, so we've listed those. We've also added some combination categories like 'pair + draw,' which could be any pair and a flush or straight draw.

Now that we can see the hand distribution, let's ask the important question: Which of these flops helped our hand and which hurt it?

Flop A clearly hurt us. The two high cards hit our opponent's range right on the nose, and in fact we're now only about 29 percent to win. The best we can hope for is that our opponent was raising with one of his low pairs, in which case we're in good shape. Every other holding is now crushing us.

Flop B hurt us, but not so badly. It's a very dry flop with only one high card, and that high card is a king, not an ace. He completely missed the flop about a third of the time, and we're beating a lot of hands in the 'Middle pair and lower' category. Still, he has lots of hands better than ours, and overall we're about 45 percent to win from this point.

Flop C is a little different. It's a monotone flop with middle cards which usually favors the caller in these confrontations. (The initial raiser is expected to have high cards, while the caller more often has middle pairs and suited connectors.) In this case, however, the board cards are just high enough to interact with his range. So we're up against a lot of big hands, and there's even a straight flush in his distribution! (He has to hold exactly K♠Q♠, but that's in his range.)

Overall, this flop hurt us; we're now about a 57-to-43 underdog. In addition, it's going to be difficult to decide how we're doing post-flop because his distribution contains an extraordinarily large range of hands. He's got flushes, straights, sets, all sorts of pairs, and lots of draws and combination draws. We have a pair and a straight draw, plus position, but the straight draw could easily be a trap. If a queen arrives on the turn, we still won't know where we stand; we've made a straight, but we could easily be facing a higher straight.

Flop D, with three low cards, is a good one since our overpair raises our chances to 55 percent. Overcards now make up slightly more than half his hands. The rest are mostly sets and overpairs.

Notice that he has only a handful of flush draws (3 percent). This latter point is important and worth noting. *Tight ranges generate very few flush draws on two-tone boards.* Most of the space in a tight range is taken up by the pairs, and there's not much left over for suited cards.

Flop E, with a medium pair and an undercard, is the best flop of all for our medium pair hand. The pair is low enough to miss his range, and as we just saw the two-tone flop doesn't hurt us much at all. So if he doesn't have an over pair, we're in good shape. Overall our winning chances are now about 62 percent.

We can summarize the result of these distributions with a relatively tight 12 percent range with a few key insights.

1. Any high card on the board is strong when your opponent has a tight range. An ace is crushing, but even the random king or queen is strong, often forming a top pair hand. A medium pair still has value, but must be careful post-flop.

2. With a flop of connected cards, you need to assess the relative tightness of a player's range. A 12 percent range interacts strongly with a jack-ten-nine flop, but it would mostly miss a ten-nine-eight flop, and almost completely miss a nine-eight-seven flop. A wider range would have a few hands that hit those lower flops as well.

3. Tight ranges don't generate flushes. A flush draw is a very minor threat on a two-tone board.

4. Low cards or paired boards are mostly bad for the tight range. They tend to strongly favor the initial caller, especially in position.

Distributions
Against a 25 Percent Range

What happens if we thought our original raiser had a 25 instead of a 12 percent range? Clearly that will change his distributions, but by how much and in what ways? Again, we'll assume that we're sitting on the button with a pair of eights, but this time we'll assume our middle position raiser has VP$IP and PFR numbers of 45/35. An overall PFR of 35 percent might translate into a PFR of 25 percent in middle position, so let's take the five possible flops that we examined in the last section and recalculate them for a PFR of 25 percent.

First, let's look at just what a 25 percent raising range looks like. There are minor possible variations, of course, but here's a typical 25 percent range:

All pairs
Suited aces: AKs through A5s
Offsuit aces: AKo through A8o
Suited Broadways: KQs, KJs, KTs, QJs, QTs, JTs
Offsuit Broadways: KQo, KJo, KTo, QJo, QTo, JTo
Suited connectors: T9s through 65s
Suited one-gappers: J9s through 75s

Now let's run this range against our sample flops. Here are the results summarized in one table as before.

My hand: 8♣8♦

His raising range: 25%

	Flop A: A♥Q♠7♦	Flop B: K♥7♠2	Flop C: J♠T♠9♠	Flop D: 6♠4♣2♣	Flop E: 9♥9♦6♦
Straight flush			<1%		
Quads/ Full house					<2%
Flush			<4%		
Straight			7%		
Set/trips	4%	4%	4%	3%	5%
Two pair	4%		6%		26%
Overpair		2%	2%	19%	
Top pair	25%	19%	9%	<1%	
Middle and lower pair	41%	25%	17%	1%	
Flush draw + straight draw			29%	1%	
Pair + draw			29%	1%	
Flush draw			2%	8%	6%
Straight draw			6%	1%	
Gutshot + two overcards			4%		
Two overcards				67%	57%
Zip	27%	59%	7%		4%

So how are we doing here? Pretty well, actually. In general, a wider range creates weaker hand distributions because a wider range contains more hands that will miss any particular flop. Compared to the 12 percent range, we're now a bigger favorite against four of these five flops. There's only one where we're actually doing worse. (Do you see which one it is?) Let's look at each flop in turn and see what has happened.

Against Flop A, we're doing better, but still not very well. Our chances were 29 percent against the 12 percent range, and now they've risen, but only to 37 percent. The problem is that a wide range doesn't do badly when an ace hits the flop because you add a lot of weak aces in the process of widening a range. That can be a problem, but only when the caller is calling with a better ace. His new, wider range also contains a lot of queens as a result of adding all the Broadway cards, so even the 'middle or lower pair' category now contains a lot of hands that are beating us.

Flop B is now genuinely good for our middle pair. We were only 45 percent against the tighter range, but now we've become a favorite at 55 percent. The reason is simple: the vast majority of the hands that were added to make a 25 percent range, like the weaker aces and the various lower suited cards now miss this flop. Dry flops with a single big card are all right with tight ranges, but become rapidly weaker with wider ranges.

Flop C, the monotone connected flop, is the one board that does better with our opponent's wider range. We were 43 percent to win against the 12 percent range, but here we've slipped to just 40 percent. Now the Broadway and suited connector hands that were added to the range mesh perfectly with the flop: 22 percent of his hands are two pair or better, while another 45 percent are strong draws, and 11 percent are either an overpair or top pair. That's a total of 78 percent that have hit this flop well. Our underpair plus straight draw certainly gives us chances. However, a wide range plus a suited, connected flop is a very dangerous combination.

Against Flop D, the three low cards, we're doing well with 62 percent chance of winning. The widening of our opponent's range has just created a lot of weak overcard hands, and our overpair is strong. We should be raising any continuation bet in this position.

Flop E is even better for us; we're 65 percent to win against the low paired board, and again we can raise any continuation bet. A few of our opponent's added hands contained a nine and hit the flop, but the rest have just missed entirely.

Let's step back and summarize the results of these two distributions. We can note a few general principles that can guide us when we're looking at flops and know our opponent's approximate opening range.

1. First, let's notice that while a wider range will hit more flops, *it won't hit any particular flop very hard*. Often players panic a little when playing against loose opponents. They see a random flop and think, "Wow, this guy has a really big range, he could have hit this flop in a lot of ways. I'd better watch out, he could have a real hand here." Well, yes, he could have a real hand. But the problem of having a wide range is that while there will always be hands in your range that will hit a random flop, they will be dwarfed by the number of hands that don't hit the flop at all. The wider the range, the weaker the distribution against most flops. The one exception to this principle, as we saw above, is the connected flop of suited middle cards which a wide range can hit from all directions.

2. Wide ranges are much more likely than tight ranges to make flush draws. A tight range is dominated by pairs and offsuit high cards, which can only hit flush draws on monotone flops. Wide ranges are partly created by adding lots of suited hands, like suited aces, suited connectors, and suited one-gappers. As a result, two-tone and monotone flops are more dangerous when your opponent has a wide range.

3. Wide ranges do poorly against dry flops with a single high card which is not an ace since wide ranges contain large numbers of aces as well as suited middling cards. The large bulk of those ranges will miss these flops.

4. Flops with an ace favor the initial raiser whether he has a narrow or wide range. Here the situation is just the opposite from the last case; the wide range hasn't been hurt because the raiser added so many aces to create his range.

5. Wide ranges do especially poorly against paired flops. The wide range will contain a few hands that make trips or hit the unpaired card. However, a pair is a strong hand on a paired flop, and wide ranges contain relatively fewer pairs than tight ranges.

In general, studying ranges, flops, and distributions is a great way to sharpen your game and improve your post-flop play. After a session, select the key hands and use the hand history function in either PokerTracker or Hold 'em Manager to see if your flop play made sense in the light of what you knew about your opponent's range and the flop that came.

Studying Hands

We can use our ability to estimate post-flop distributions to solve a lot of hand problems that commonly arise, and as with the distribution calculations, these kind of problems can't really be solved at the table. Rather, they're exercises that can be done when you're analyzing a session. We'll work through one example in detail to show what can be done with a hand history plus some time and perseverance. This next hand shows what at first seems like a routine and not terribly important decision in a three-way pot. But as you will see, there is a little more to it than first apparent.

Note: This analysis is detailed and extensive. If you're not in the mood for that right now, just skip this chapter and move on to "Part Four: Beating the Micro-Stakes Games." You can always return later.

Situation: Online $200 NL 6-max table. Blinds are $1.00 and $2.00 with only 5 players.

Table layout:

UTG	Player A $85	A's HUD Player A / (40) / -4 VP 30 / PF 10 / AS 24 / FB 70 3B 4 / F3 40 / AF 2 / 2 / 1 / inf CB 65 / FC 60 / FT 80 W$F 41 / WtS 22 / W$S 60 *Note: PF: LFC=1/4.*
CO	Player B $124	

BTN	You $226	Your HUD You / (70) / +6 VP 24 / PF 18
SB	Player C $460	C's HUD Player C / (70) / +50 VP 16 / PF 10
BB	Player D $340	D's HUD Player D / (70) / +35 VP 20 / PF 15 / AS 33 / FB 85 3B 7 / F3 70 / AF 1.5 / 0.5 / inf / inf CB 50 / FC 50 / FT 100 W$F 50 / WtS 17 / W$S 100

The Preflop Play: You pick up the 8♠7♦. Player A limps for $2 and Player B folds. What do you do?

The first play to consider here is an isolation raise, designed to put you heads-up against Player A in position. While that's not a bad play, there are a couple of factors that argue against it:

1. Your hand is weak. Low unsuited connectors rank pretty far down the list of playable hands.

2. Your opponent doesn't like to give up hands once he's entered the pot. His 'fold to 3-bet' number is just 40 percent, which is quite low. Your note says you've already seen him limp and get raised five different times, and he's called four of those.

So a raise isn't likely to have much fold equity meaning that getting more money in the pot with eight-high isn't very exciting. Just calling, however, has more merit than usual. Because we don't see much fold equity in raising Player A, the blinds may have the same data and feel the same way. Thus Player A's tendencies are inadvertently providing us some cover and as a result, calling will let us see a flop somewhat more often than normal. That's not a bad result with our hand, so we can call behind.

In fact, you call the $2, the small blind folds, and the big blind checks. The pot is $7 and you will act last after the flop.

Flop: J♣T♦4♦. The big blind checks and Player A checks. What do you do?

That's not a great flop from our point of view. We end up with a gutshot straight draw and a backdoor flush draw, and one common approach to handling this situation is to check with the idea that we are guaranteeing our ability to see the turn and thus hit our gutshot draw. If we bet, we run the risk of being check-raised off our hand by either of the other two players. The other approach, of course, is just to bet and hope that both players fold. Having exactly two opponents complicates the problem. Heads-up, most players would bet, and against three opponents checking would be standard. Let's now try to use our techniques of distribution analysis to see if there's a clearly best play against two players.

Player A's Range and Distribution: Now we need to think about how this flop may have connected with our opponents. Let's start by looking at their likely ranges.

Player A seems to like to raise with about the top 10 percent of his hands and limp with another 20 percent. But he was under the gun, however, so his raising range may be a little narrower than that, but not by much since it's just a five-handed table. So being under the gun probably won't affect his willingness to limp into the pot; players who like to call in small stakes games don't pay much attention to position when they limp. Hence, let's assume he would raise with the top 8 percent of his hands and call with the next 22 percent. That assumption gives him a limping range that looks something like this:

> Small pairs: 66 through 22
> Medium and small suited aces: A9 through A2
> Suited Broadway cards: KJ, KT, QJ, QT, JT
> Suited connectors: T9 through 54
> Suited two-gappers: J9 through 64
> Medium offsuit aces: A9 through A7
> Offsuit Broadway cards: KJ, KT, QJ, QT, JT
> Offsuit connectors: T9 through 54

Note that our goal here is not perfection. As we've seen, even narrow raising ranges can have slightly different compositions depending on how much players like to raise with the small pairs. Therefore, our goal is to get a reasonable approximation to his range so we can see how it connected with the flop.

At the table, analyzing the relationship between his range and the flop requires some experience and some quick, informed guesswork. In general, his limping range includes a fair number of middle cards and this should therefore be a decent flop for him. There's also a potential flush draw on board, and there are plenty of suited cards in his range, so he might have connected in that way as well. Away from the table, we can take our time and be much more precise.

Let's apply our methods for calculating a distribution to Player A's range and this flop and see what we get:

Player A: 233 Total Hand Combinations	
A set	1.3%
Two pair	3.9%
Top pair	10.3%
Middle pair	16.3%
Low or bottom pair	18.0%
Flush draw + pair	1.3%
Flush draw + straight draw	0.0%
Flush draw	4.3%
Straight draw	5.2%
Gutshot	2.1%
Zip (no pair, no draw)	37.3%

If we ignore the gutshot draws, about 60 percent of Player A's range connected with this flop in some meaningful way. That's pretty typical of what happens when a player limps or calls preflop and the flop arrives with middle cards like jacks, tens, and nines. His range will be light in high cards because he will raise with many of those preflop, and also light in low cards because he will still fold most of those. The meat of his range will be concentrated in non-paired middle cards, often suited.

Another key fact that emerges from the table is that draws make up a smaller portion of Player A's possibilities than many players would think. Of the 60 percent of his hands that connected with the flop, only about 10 percent (of the 60 percent) are drawing combinations, while 50 percent are pairs of some sort.

We can refine Player A's range a little further by taking into account the post-flop action. Player A acted after seeing the big blind check. Would he have checked his sets or two pair hands? On this board, the answer is: probably not. He's against two opponents, and the board contains both flush and straight possibilities. Most players with a made hand of modest strength would be betting both for value and to charge the draws. So we can modify his post-flop range a little by eliminating those two categories of hands. This gives us a new post-flop chart with slightly modified probabilities:

Player A: After Elimination of Sets and Two Pair Hands	
Top pair	10.9%
Middle pair	17.2%
Low or bottom pair	19.0%
Flush draw + pair	1.4%
Flush draw + straight draw	0.0%
Flush draw	4.5%
Straight draw	5.4%
Gutshot	2.3%
Zip (no pair, no draw)	39.4%

To make these numbers a little easier to use, we'll group them a little more tightly into just three groups:

1. Hands that will call a bet by us (top pair, middle pair, and flush or straight draws).

2. Weak hands that will fold to a bet (bottom/low pair or gutshot straight draw).

3. Hands with no value that will fold to a bet.

That grouping produces a final chart that looks as follows:

Player A's Post-Flop Hand Distribution	
Calling hands	39.4%
Weak hands	21.3%
Zip hands	39.4%

The Big Blind's Range and Distribution: Now let's turn our attention to the big blind and his range. Here we know a couple of facts:

1. He's somewhat tight and aggressive preflop with VP$IP/PFR numbers of 20 and 15, and a 3-betting percentage of 7.

2. He's less aggressive post-flop with an overall aggression factor of 1.5 and a c-betting number of just 50 percent, rather low.

3. He checked after seeing a limp and a call in front of him. The limp was from Player A who can be expected to call a raise. The call from us is probably harder to interpret, as we have more aggressive preflop numbers (24/18) and should therefore be expected to usually raise a limper rather than just limp behind.

We need to use these facts to make an educated guess as to what percentage of his range he would have raised. Once we know that, we can eliminate those hands and know that he checked with everything else. Based on his preflop tendencies, we can assume that a raising range of 15 percent is too high. That might be a reasonable range for the big blind against a single opponent, but here he's out of position against two opponents who have shown interest, at least one of whom will be hard to chase away. I'd be comfortable with assigning him a raising range of about 10 percent which looks about like this:

> Pairs: AA through 77
> AK through AT, suited or offsuit
> KQs and KJs
> KQo

That's a pretty generic 10 percent range of medium to big pairs and big Broadway cards. His checking range is therefore the other 90 percent of his hands.

We can perform the same analysis that we applied to Player A although in this case there are just more hands to consider. Once we do that, the big blind's post-flop range looks like this:

Big Blind: 981 Total Hand Combinations	
A set	0.3%
Two pair	2.9%
Top pair	9.3%
Middle pair	11.3%
Low or bottom pair	14.2%
Flush draw + pair	0.8%
Flush draw + straight draw	0.2%
Flush draw	3.4%
Straight draw	2.7%
Gutshot	3.1%
Zip (no pair, no draw)	52.0%

As with Player A, if the big blind had flopped a set or two pair, it's reasonable to assume that he would have bet the flop, both for value and to charge any draws. As our last step we'll eliminate those two hands and regroup the categories as before, yielding a little chart which looks like this:

Big Blind's Post-Flop Hand Distribution	
Calling hands	28.5%
Weak hands	17.8%
Zip hands	53.7%

Combining Both Opponents' Distribution: Let's put the big blind's distribution side by side with Player A's, and see how they compare:

	Big Blind	Player A
Calling hands	28.5%	39.4%
Weak hands	17.8%	21.3%
Zip hands	53.7%	39.4%

This is the chart we've really been looking for. But before we go on and ask what we should do in the hand, let's make a few observations.

1. Since the flop contained middle cards, it connected more strongly with Player A than with the big blind. That's to be expected. Player A elected to limp, so he's less likely to have both high cards and low cards, and more likely to have middle cards. The big blind doesn't have two high card hands in his range, but he has everything else. If the flop had contained all low cards, the big blind would be more likely to have the better distribution.

2. Even with his random distribution, the big blind has still connected with this flop better than you might think. Ignoring

the few gutshots in his distribution, the big blind flopped a pair or a draw about 42 percent of the time.

Evaluating Our Actions: Now let's return to our original question. The two players have checked to us. What should we do?

Right now our hand is close to worthless. We do have a gutshot straight draw needing a nine, which we'll hit about 8.5 percent of the time. (There are four nines left in the deck out of 47 unseen cards.) We can assume those hits are winners, although there's no guarantee we'll win any additional money if we do hit the straight. Hitting an eight or a seven might be enough to win, but with two overcards that's unlikely. So checking costs us nothing but gives us some small winning chances.

What about betting? If we bet, we'll take down the existing pot some percentage of the time. If we bet and don't take down the pot, then we're probably done with the hand. How likely are we to win if we bet? Let's go back to our post-flop hand distribution chart and make some educated estimates. Here's that chart again:

	Big Blind	**Player A**
Calling hands	28.5%	39.4%
Weak hands	17.8%	21.3%
Zip hands	53.7%	39.4%

Let's start by assuming that if we bet, both players will call with their calling hands and fold their weak hands and zip hands. If these distributions were *independent* (a statistical term meaning that one player's hand would not affect the distribution of the other player's hands) then the probability that neither the big blind nor Player A had a calling hand would be equal to the probability that the big blind doesn't have a calling hand multiplied by the probability that Player A doesn't have a calling hand which in this case is 43.3 percent.

$$0.433 = (0.715)(0.606)$$

If that's true, then the probability that one player or the other (or both) has a calling hand is 56.7 percent.

$$0.567 = 1 - 0.433$$

Now in fact, the distributions aren't independent. Since both players have cards drawn from the same deck, each player's hand affects the distribution of the other. However, they affect each other in a way that turns out to be not so important. Let's say Player A has a calling hand containing a jack. While that reduces the chance that the big blind has a calling hand, it only reduces the probability that *both* players have a calling hand at the same time. However, we don't care if both players have a calling hand. We're hoping that no one has a calling hand, and whether one player or both has us clearly beaten doesn't really matter.

There's one other factor which is important. We know that both players checked instead of betting. There's at least some possibility that either player would have bet with some of the hands we've labeled 'calling hands,' which included top pair, middle pair, flush draws, straight draws, and some combinations of made hands and draws. The big blind is less likely to have bet with these hands partly because his pairs tend to be weaker — he has hands like jack-trey and ten-deuce in his huge range while Player A does not — and partly because he might want to wait and see what happens behind him, especially in the case of his draws. In addition, Player A was more likely to have put in a bet since he had already seen one check. So while we can't be precise, the knowledge of two checks does require us to downgrade the probability that a calling hand is actually out there. For argument's sake, let's say the probability that a calling hand is out against us is more like 40 percent than the 56.7 percent we calculated from the raw math.

Calculating Our Expected Value: Now we're ready to actually do some calculations to see if a bet looks like a +EV play or not. Let's say our betting strategy is as follows:

1. We'll bet a little more than half the pot ($4). If they both fold, we get the $7 pot. Fantastic.

2. If someone raises, we fold.

3. If someone calls, we're done with the hand unless our gutshot hits on the turn (probability = 4/47). In that case, we'll bet the turn after a check and we'll raise after a bet with the goal of getting our stack in.

   Let's see how this strategy works.

We bet $4: From our previous estimate, they will both fold 60 percent of the time. We win $7.

Some small percentage of the time, one of the players raises and we fold. They might have checked one of their very good hands as a trap, or they might now be semi-bluffing with one of their draws. We don't really care since we're not looking for a big pot with our 8-high hand. Let's say that scenario happens 3 percent of the time. We lose $4.

The remaining 37 percent of the time we have a caller. Of these, we hit our gutshot on the turn about 3 percent of the time, missing the other 34 percent.

When we hit our gutshot, we're going to win the original pot ($7) plus the bet that was called on the flop ($4) plus some additional money that might go in on the flop or river. We need to make some very rough estimate of what this extra money might be. Let's say our opponent checks the turn and we bet $10. (The pot became $15 after the flop betting). Keep in mind that at this point the board is the J♣T♦4♦ 9x and our opponent saw us bet the flop and then bet again on the turn. Given this board, our line looks strong, so we can't assume we'll get a lot of action from our turn bet. Let's say that, of the 3 percent overall that we get to this point, 15 percent of the time our turn bet is called and 5 percent of the time a river bet is called as well. Let's say our turn bet is $10 and our river bet is $30. In that case these 3 percent of cases break down as follows:

● 0.15%: The turn and river bets are called. We win $51.

$$\$51 = \$7 + \$4 + \$10 + \$30$$

where:
$7 is the original pot,
$4 is the flop bet, and
$10 is the turn bet.

● 0.30%: The turn bet is called and the river bet is folded. We win $21.

$$\$21 = \$7 + \$4 + \$10$$

● 2.55%: The turn bet is folded. We win $11.

$$\$11 = \$7 + \$4$$

The 34 percent of the time we miss we will fold to a turn bet, but our opponent won't always bet. Let's assume this 34 percent breaks down into 7 percent bets (and we fold) and 27 percent checks (and we check behind). In that case we can still hit our gutshot on the river in 2 percent of these hands, while we miss and either fold or lose a showdown in the last 25 percent. In all these losses we lose only our $4 flop bet. In the 2 percent where we hit our gutshot on the river, we'll guess that we make a $10 river bet and get called 20 percent (which we win). Here's that breakdown:

- 32%: We either fold to a bet or lose the showdown. We lose $4.

- 0.4%: We hit the gutshot on river, bet $10, and get called. We win $21.

$$\$21 = \$7 + 4 + \$10$$

- 1.6%: We hit the gutshot on river, bet $10, and he folds. We win $11.

$$\$11 = \$7 + \$4$$

Now we're ready to summarize what happens when we bet. The summary looks like this:

- 60%: We bet. They fold. We win $7.

- 3%: We bet. Someone raises and we fold. We lose $4.

- 2.55%: We bet and get called. We hit the gutshot, bet, and they fold. We win $11.

- 0.30%: Same but the turn bet is called and the river bet is folded. We win $21.

- 0.15%: Same but the river bet is called. We win $51.

- 32%: We miss the gutshot, fold, or lose the showdown. We lose $4.

- 0.4%: We hit the gutshot on the river, bet, and are called. We win $21.

- 1.6%: We hit the gutshot on river, bet, and no one calls. We win $11.

100%

Pulling together equivalent amounts of wins or losses, we finally get:

Percent	Result	Expectation
60.00	We win $7	$4.20
35.00	We lose $4	-$1.40
4.15	We win $11	$0.46
0.70	We win $21	$0.15
0.15	We win $51	$0.08
EV of Betting the Flop = $3.49		

So betting the flop is a solid +EV play, earning us about 85 percent of the size of the bet. We now need to compare this to what happens if we check the flop and get a free card on the turn. This requires another involved calculation which we won't lay out in detail. In brief, if we miss our draw on the turn we fold to any bet and check if no bet was made. If we hit our draw, we bet or raise. On the river, we take the same action.

Checking the flop yielded the following approximate table of results:

Percent	Result	Expectation
88.00	We win/lose $0	$0.00
3.80	We win $7	$0.26
6.80	We win $12	$0.82
0.75	We win $22	$0.16
0.40	We win $24	$0.10
0.25	We win $47	$0.12
EV of Checking the Flop = $1.46		

Hence, betting the flop completely dominates checking even though we're against two opponents and have a hand that has some real interest in seeing a free card. It's an interesting and important example, so let's briefly summarize what we can learn from this problem.

Summary

The main reason betting dominates checking is that the flop interacts poorly with our opponent's preflop ranges. This isn't obvious at a casual glance but becomes clear as we create the post-flop hand distribution. Let's look at the distributions more closely, paying attention to the number of big value hands (sets, two pair) and draws.

There are very few sets in their distributions because both players should have raised preflop with either a pair of jacks or a pair of tens. Player A's PFR is 10 percent which puts both those hands well within any reasonable raising range. The big blind wants to raise with those hands because he's against two opponents who limped, and there are too many overcards that can hit the flop that will make him uncomfortable. Eliminating jacks and tens means that only a pair of fours will yield a set on that board. But the presence of the four makes two pair hands less likely. Hence, Player A will only make two pair with a jack-ten holding while the big blind could have any two pair since he just checked preflop, but the total number of hands in his range (981 hand combinations) is so large that he's actually *less* likely to hold two pair on a percentage basis.

In the same way, there are very few draws in the distribution simply because drawing hands will, in general, be a small part of almost any distribution. Ignoring gutshots, Player A had a distribution with 11.3 percent drawing hands (flush draws, straight draws, and combination draws) while the big blind had 7.1 percent drawing hands. (The big blind had more draws in absolute terms, but the percentage was diluted by the huge number of garbage hands.)

Remember that the logic for checking after the flop on our part was to prevent being raised off our gutshot draw by a trapper. But with such a small percentage of strong made hands and draws, the probability of being check-raised is low, too low to prevent us from betting.

Finally, let's look carefully again at the EV calculations for both betting the flop and checking the flop. What we particularly need to notice is that the actual EV contribution from the variations where we hit the gutshot straight is extremely small. That shouldn't be too surprising: The chance of hitting the gutshot is less than 10 percent on the turn, and even after we hit it there's a significant chance we won't get any extra action. In addition, the EV contribution from hitting the gutshot on the river, assuming we get there, is even smaller. Consequently, all of these tiny EV contributions are dwarfed by the EV gain from just betting the flop and taking down the pot right there.

Part Four

Beating
Micro-Stakes Games

Beating Micro-Stakes Games

Introduction: How Micro-Stakes Players Play

Imagine you're driving along a normal highway in midday traffic. Although you're surrounded by different kinds of cars — sedans, coupes, SUVs — everyone obeys the rules of the road and, with small variations, everyone is driving around the speed limit. That's sort of what a high stakes poker game feels like: different players, different styles, but everyone with the same general understanding of how the game is played.

Now imagine you take the exit ramp to a slightly different kind of highway. Here most folks are driving at 15 miles per hour; those who aren't going at 15 are driving at 120 instead. Some drivers weave back and forth slowly across four lanes of traffic; others stop in the high speed lane to change a flat. This is what a micro-stakes game feels like. You ask, "What's going on here?"

The word that best describes a micro-stakes game is *excessive*. Whatever natural style the players may have is usually exaggerated almost beyond recognition. Passive players are much too passive. Aggressive players are way too aggressive. Tight players are ridiculously tight. And loose players are absurdly loose. Some players will push all-in with a pair of sevens preflop. Others will call down to the river with just a low pair.

So how do we exploit these excessive styles? Before we outline a good strategy, let's explain the difference between poker offense and poker defense.

Offense
and Defense in Poker

Like most games, poker is played in two modes: offense and defense. When you play offense, you're trying to score; when you play defense, you're trying to prevent your opponent from scoring on you.

So what exactly is the difference between offensive and defensive poker? Let's break it down.

When you play *offensive poker*, you're doing the following:

1. You're playing strong hands preflop so you'll be more likely to have the best hand post-flop.

2. You're value betting (and raising) with strong hands to get more money in the pot.

3. You're betting when you think you have the best of it and to prevent weak hands from getting a free card and drawing out on you.

4. You bet more when you have a great hand and less when you have a good hand.

5. You're bluffing when you think timid opponents will lay down weaker hands.

When you play *defensive poker*, you're doing a few different things:

1. You're mixing up your hands preflop, combining strong hands with speculative hands, so that you can't be read easily

and your opponents have to fear that any particular flop might have helped you.

2.   You're mixing bluffs in with your value bets so your opponents can't be sure that you have a good hand when you bet.

3.   You're varying your bet sizes somewhat randomly so your opponents can't be sure that a big bet means a big hand; alternatively, you're keeping your bet sizes all the same so your opponents can't draw any conclusion at all.

4.   You're checking some good hands so your opponents can't be sure that a check means weakness.

5.   You're semi-bluffing when the opportunity presents itself so your opponents can't be sure what your bets might represent.

In short, offensive poker means trying to exploit your opponents and make as much money as possible with your good hands. Defensive poker means playing in such a way that your opponents can't exploit *you*. When you play offensive poker, you are trying to earn the maximum value from your strong hands whenever possible. When you play defensive poker, you take your opponent into account and sacrifice some value from your strong hands to prevent your opponent from getting a clear picture of what you're doing.

Beating micro-stakes games is mostly a matter of playing strong offensive poker while listening to what your opponents will tell you about their hands. For the most part, your passive opponents will not be able to conceal what they have. When they have a weak hand, they will either fold, or check and call. When they have a strong hand, they will bet and raise. Once they've told you about their hand, you can value your own hand accordingly. Your aggressive opponents, on the other hand, will bet at you whether they have anything or not. Your basic strategy will be to trap when you have a good hand, allowing them to bet most of their chips on a bluff.

As you move from micro-stakes games to small stakes to higher stakes, your balance between offensive and defensive play gradually shifts. Micro-stakes are all about offense. In small stakes games, you'll meet more and more players who observe what you do and react, so you'll need to start playing a balance of offense and defense. In higher stakes games, you can assume all your opponents are watching you carefully, and defense becomes your dominant posture.

General Advice for Beating Micro-Stakes Games

Micro-stakes games are not hard to beat. You can learn to be a winning player at these stakes fairly quickly, and in this section we'll show you how. To beat these games, you need to know what sort of players play at these stakes and what their characteristic mistakes look like. Once you know what you're up against, designing strategies to win isn't difficult. But before we get started, let's step back and see what good poker looks like and see how that differs from the sort of poker we'll see at the micro-stakes.

In a very general sense, good poker is about balance, observation, and flexibility. A good player tries to play a balanced style, one that's a mixture of offense and defense. He knows he needs to make money from his good hands, but he knows his opponents are watching him as well. He'll mostly value bet his good hands, but he'll slowplay sometimes to provide cover for his weak hands which he'd like to take to showdown. He'll also bluff sometimes so his opponents can't be sure what his bets mean. At the same time, he observes his opponents, makes notes about their actions, and watches their statistics in their HUD so that he can adjust his play to counter whatever they're trying to do. The good player is completely flexible in his style and approach; it wouldn't be unusual for different players at his table to have completely different ideas about what sort of player he is.

A good poker player is different from a good chess or backgammon player. In those games, a good move is a good move. When you play a strong move in a chess game, it doesn't really matter if your opponent can divine your intention or not. If the move is strong enough, he won't be able to counter it regardless of how well he understands you as a player. But in poker, understanding style and intention is everything. An opponent who knows your approach better than you know his will beat you in the long run. He'll win more money when his hand is best, and lose less when his hand is worse. In chess and backgammon, finding good moves is the key to winning; in poker, understanding your opponent is the key to winning.

Most micro-stakes players are beginners, and as beginners they're looking for a formula that will let them win, or at least let them enjoy playing. Different players will adopt formulas that suit their style and personality. For a naturally conservative player, a good formula might be "Play only strong starting cards" or "Wait until you hit a set, then get all your money in." An outgoing, aggressive personality might like "Bet until they fold." The formulas are different, but the approach is the same.

Your key weapons for beating micro-stakes games are your HUD and your notes. Oddly enough, these tools are relatively *more* valuable in micro-stakes games than in games at higher stakes. In higher stakes, players are constantly adjusting to the table; a player might be aggressive for the first part of a session, then turn tight as the table begins to adapt, or he might play differently against you than against the other players. In micro-stakes, players do what they do; once you know what they're trying to do, you have them pegged and can play off their tendencies for the rest of the session.

Let's start by looking at some different player types and see what each is trying to do. Imagine you're sitting at a micro-stakes 6-max table. Arranged around the table is a collection of varied characters with different styles. Let's meet them one at a time.

Sitting directly on your right is Loose Lou. Lou's an amiable guy and he likes to play poker. Sitting on the sidelines watching other people play is no fun; he wants to be in the action. Lou knows that in hold 'em any two cards can win, so he's not afraid to limp into pots; gotta risk money to make money. If he hits a pair, he wants to get to showdown and see if it's good. People are always trying to bluff Lou out of pots. He knows that and doesn't like it much. He came to play, not to toss good hands in the muck. Lou doesn't just play sure things though. If he gets a flush draw, he won't let anyone bluff him off that hand. Odds? Odds are for nerds. Lou's a people person. But he's not afraid to bet if he gets something good. If he hits his straight on the turn, he'll bet it for all it's worth. But Lou is prudent. If he doesn't have anything, he won't waste his money betting. He understands the value of a buck.

On his right is Aggro Al. Like Lou, Al understands that any two cards can win. Al understands something else too. Most folks don't have the nerve to take those two cards to showdown. Fold equity, that's what hold 'em is all about. With a big enough bet, you can chase pretty much anybody off a hand. Some people think that poker is about the cards you hold. Al knows better. Poker is about the cards you're afraid the other guy is holding. The only thing Al likes better than bluffing someone off a hand is showing him the bluff afterwards. That's the royal nuts, yes sir. When Al sits down at a table, he owns the table. Still, Al's not one-dimensional. If he's running a big bluff and the other guy sticks in a raise, Al's smart enough to lay his hand down. You need to get up pretty early in the morning to put something over on Al.

On Al's right is Johnny All-In. Johnny's a one-trick pony, but it's a good trick: all-in! Johnny discovered the key to poker early on: people are willing to raise with hands that they'll fold to an all-in. Strange but true. That's free money in anybody's book, and Johnny's just the lad to vacuum it up. Let the other folks fiddle around with their post-flop theories and hand range mumbo-jumbo. That's a fool's game and a big time-waster. None of that for Johnny. He likes to make a quick score for a few pots, and then just when everyone is getting steamed and ready to play back, he's off to a new table. Hit and run, hit and run. Poker is easy.

On Johnny's right, two to your left, is Mike the multi-table grinder. Mike plays 24 tables at once. He's got a simple style: he raises his strong hands, calls with his low pairs, and folds his weak stuff. Some might find this ABC approach unduly straightforward, but Mike is never bored. With 24 tables something is always happening. He pushes with the nuts, folds weak hands to strength, and in general stays out of trouble. Mike's discovered the secret of poker: mass production on an assembly line. He doesn't make much on each table, but string 24 tables together and he's doing all right. If Mike were a businessman, he'd be running a factory making plastic widgets at a penny a pop. There's good money in widgets if you can just make enough of them.

Finally, on your immediate left is Regular Ron. Ron is playing micro-stakes now, but in reality he's just passing through. His goal is to be successful in higher games, and he's building a bankroll and honing his skills while he prepares to climb the ladder. Ron spends a good deal of time playing, but he does other things as well. He reads books, he pours over forums, and he watches training videos. He downloads his hand histories and steps through his big hands in his PokerTracker software. He looks at his winning hands as well as his losing ones. He wants to know if he could have lost less or won more. Did he use all the knowledge he had, or was there a clue that he overlooked in his opponent's HUD? Ron is curious and relentlessly self-critical; he'll have his eye on you shortly.

You'll meet these player types constantly as you work your way through the micro-stakes world. Each is vulnerable, although they're vulnerable in different ways. Let's now take a look at some different tactical approaches and see how they apply to each of our five players.

1. **Value betting:** Betting your good hands for value is the single most important key idea in micro-stakes hold 'em. Your most common opponent will be some variation of Loose Lou, whose problem is calling too much with weak hands. In order to exploit him, you have to bet your good hands and hope that he has a weaker one and that he'll come along for the ride.

You'll also value bet against Regular Ron and Multi-tabling Mike, but there you're just playing good poker, and your value betting won't earn anything special. But you can't value bet Johnny; all you can do is decide whether calling his all-in is a good play.

Aggro Al is the value-betting exception since value betting will chase him off his bad hands, whereas acting weak will encourage him to keep trying to push you off your hand. So you'll check a lot against Al.

2. **Slowplaying:** Slowplaying is just the opposite of value betting. It's a bad idea against Lou since it allows him to catch up for free when he would have cheerfully paid for the privilege. It's mandatory against Al, signaling that you have a weak hand and he should continue betting his garbage. It's an occasional strategy against Ron and Mike. Ron will be paying attention and he'll note that you may be a dangerous and tricky player. Mike won't be able to pay attention, and you may catch him when he bets his good hand, but you have a better one.

3. **Bluffing:** Bluffing plays a role in micro-stakes games, although it's a much smaller role than at the higher stakes. The big bluffing target at this table is actually Al since he likes to take a hand and attempts to push people out of the pot, but he knows enough to retreat when they fight back with a raise. Bluffing him on the turn works well.

   But a bluff against Lou is a waste of time. If he has a pair, he wants to see if it's good. Representing a big hand doesn't impress him; he knows you're bluffing.

   If you do pull off a bluff at the micro-stakes, actually showing it is tremendously strong. Players see bluffs as personal affronts, not as part of the game. Show them a bluff and their thirst for vengeance will never die.

4. **Semi-Bluffing:** Just as bluffing plays less of a role in micro-stakes, so does semi-bluffing. Semi-bluffs depend on solid fold equity to show a profit, so semi-bluffing players who are more likely to call doesn't work as well. Target Ron, Mike, and Al for your semi-bluffs; leave Lou alone.

5. **Continuation Betting:** Continuation betting is very opponent-specific. You want to understand how each opponent is likely to react to a continuation bet before you make your decision.

   Lou will fold if he completely missed the flop, but he'll call if he has any piece or a draw. He'll also call the turn in that case. If you've actually hit the flop, you're in great shape. If you've missed, you want to make a small continuation bet which will have exactly the same effect as a larger one.

   Al sees continuation bets as bluffs, not as 'real' bets. If you bet, he'll call or raise. If you bet the flop and he calls, and check the turn, your reward will frequently be a big bet. You can make money when you hit your hand, but just check if you miss the flop.

   No continuation bets against Johnny — you'll be all-in by that point.

   Continuation bets work just fine against Mike. If he missed the flop, he's already clicked the 'fold' button and moved on to another table.

   Against Ron you're playing real poker, so use the continuation bet frequently, but not always.

6. **Limping in early position:** When you pick up a hand like a low pocket pair or a suited connector in early position, beginners and even some experienced players are tempted to limp. Since the hand isn't immediately strong, they don't want to put a lot of money in the pot, but since the hand could turn into a big hand with a good flop, they don't want

to fold it either. So limping looks like a good way to see a cheap flop.

At higher stakes games this approach doesn't work because your opponents will understand what you're trying to do and counter with an isolation raise, a raise that will force you to either fold or play the hand out of position for more money than you intended.

In micro-stakes games, however, not everyone is that sophisticated. If your opponents are all variations of Lou and Mike, limping may work as you intend. If you're up against Ron or Al, your limp may provoke an attack, defeating its purpose. In that case, just raise when you want to play a hand, your opponents won't know you only have a small pair.

7. **3-Betting:** In high-stakes and medium-stakes games, 3-betting is an art form. Players will 3-bet with strong hands, but they'll also mix in some weaker ones (known as *3-betting light*). Usually they'll raise light with hands that function as semi-bluffs, like pairs and suited aces. If they get called, they can sometimes hit a big hand, and if not they can continue to represent a premium pair.

    In micro-stakes, 3-betting is unusual and generally means a big hand, like a premium pair or ace-king, both suited and unsuited. This is actually a rational strategy since most micro-stakes players will call a 3-bet once they've raised the pot. Each player type is a little different, however, so here's what your 3-bet strategy should look like against our cast of characters:

    ● Johnny: Irrelevant. His initial raise is an all-in and a 3-bet from him will also be an all-in, so your only options will be to call or fold.

- Lou: If Lou raises he'll call your 3-bet, so make sure you're reraising with a good hand. A 3-bet from Lou almost always represents a premium pair.

- Al: He'll definitely 3-bet you light. If you want to 3-bet him, expect a call, and you can 3-bet with a wide range because he's raising preflop with an even wider range.

- Mike: When a player is watching 24 tables, he's not doing anything unusual with 3-bets. Expect his 3-bets to be premium hands and react accordingly. He knows that 3-betting usually means a big hand at these stakes, and he doesn't have time to focus on you, so you can 3-bet him light all day and expect to make a profit.

- Ron: You'll be able to 3-bet him light for awhile as he'll credit you with a big hand. But after awhile, he'll adapt.

8. **Bet sizing:** At micro-stakes, players don't pay careful attention to the size of bets, so you have the liberty of raising more with strong hands and less with the weak ones. Since the small variations go unnoticed and players will react to most bets the same way, you can earn a little extra profit this way.

    Betting more with good hands will work against Mike, Al, and Lou. Al and Lou won't really care, and Mike is looking at too many tables to notice. Ron will pick up on what you're doing after awhile, so you'll need to be careful here. And Johnny will either move all-in or he won't.

9. **Raises on the later streets:** A raise from a loose-passive player on the turn or the river almost always represents a big hand. Micro-stakes players tend to play more and more straightforwardly as the hand goes on and the pot gets bigger, so beware of raises on later streets.

A raise from Lou should arouse special alarm because he really doesn't like to raise; his goal is to get to showdown. A raise from Mike is also a concern because he's playing very direct poker, and isn't looking to figure out whether a bluff on this table might be good; he's got too many other tables to manage.

Ron might bluff because he knows that's part of the game, and after a while he'll know that you're good enough to be bluffed.

A simple raise from Al is to be expected because that's what he does. However, if Al bets, you raise, and he reraises, he has the goods.

10. **Should you play tight or loose?** Tight-aggressive play is easy to learn and apply, and will win you money. Loose-aggressive play is harder, but will win much more at micro-stakes once you've learned how to extricate yourself from difficult situations.

That's a basic outline for beating micro-stakes. It's not hard once you know what your opponents are trying to do, but it's not trivially easy either. In the rest of this section we'll elaborate on all these ideas.

Starting Hand Guide for Micro-Stakes 6-Max Games

Since many of our readers will be players just getting started in online 6-max play, we're going to describe a selection of opening hands for the different positions at the table. In fact, we'll give you two separate starting hand guides: a tight one for players who intend to play a conservative style and want the security of knowing they have solid values when they get in the pot, and a looser one for players who feel confident they're the best player at the table, and who believe they can outmaneuver their opponents post-flop.

The problem with starting hand guides is that many players look to them as a set of rote rules, and that's a bad habit if your goal is to play good poker. Remember that to succeed at poker, you need to observe your opponents and adapt your play to exploit what they're doing. (Or, if you think they're very very good and you for some reason still want to play with them, you need to adapt your play so that *they* can't exploit *you*.) In general, if you discover your opponents are too tight, you want to exploit them by loosening your requirements and raising more hands. Conversely, if they seem to be loose and aggressive, tighten your standards and play fewer hands.

Strategy No. 1: Playing Tight

With that caveat in mind, let's get started. These are hands you should raise when playing a tight style if no one has entered the pot in front of you.

259

Tight Style — Under the Gun (10 percent of all hands)

> Open raise with all pairs AA-22
> AK, AQ, and AJ, suited or unsuited
> KQ suited

Tight Style — Middle Position (13 percent of all hands)

> Open raise with all pairs AA-22
> AK, AQ, AJ, AT suited or unsuited
> KQ, KJ, suited or unsuited

Tight Style — Cutoff Seat (18 percent of all hands)

> Open raise with all pairs AA-22
> AK to A6 suited
> KQ, KJ, KT, QJ, QT, JT suited
> AK to A9 offsuit
> KQ, KJ, QJ offsuit
> T9, 98 suited

Tight Style — Button (25 percent of all hands)

> Open raise with all pairs AA-22
> AK to A2 suited
> KQ, KJ, KT, QJ, QT, JT suited
> AK to A6 offsuit
> KQ, KJ, QJ, KT, QT, JT offsuit
> T9 to 65 suited

Tight Style — Small Blind

> Raise your button range

If you're playing a tight style, do not limp into a pot when no one has entered in front of you. Either raise or fold. Limping does have a place in micro-stakes games, but we'll discuss its role later in this section.

If there is a limper in front of you, just raise your normal range. In micro-stakes games, limpers tend to have weak hands, so you will mostly be raising as a favorite.

If there are two limpers in front of you, tighten your raising requirements a little bit. If you are on the button, raise with your cutoff range. You can limp behind two limpers with some low speculative hands like small suited aces, suited one-gappers, and that sort of thing.

This opening strategy represents a good conservative approach for a beginning micro-stakes player. It's designed to keep you out of trouble and to make sure than when you enter a pot, you'll be entering with a hand that's considerably stronger than the hands that your opponents can be expected to have. With these ranges, you should have a pretty easy time playing after the flop. If you play a small pair and you hit a set, you're going to try to win your opponent's whole stack. If you play a strong ace and you hit an ace on the flop, you'll usually have the best hand. Unless you're on the button or the small blind, you won't have many drawing hands or second-best hands.

We should make one additional comment here. *This is by no means an optimal opening strategy for micro-stakes play.* Your goal is to use this strategy as a base for building your bankroll while you learn the intricacies of the game. As you gain experience, you should expect to be opening more hands and making more profits by outplaying your opponents after the flop.

Strategy No. 2: Loosening Up

With that thought in mind, here's an opening strategy more appropriate for an experienced player willing to play more hands.

Looser Style — Under the Gun (15 percent of all hands)

> Open raise with all pairs AA-22
> AK to A9 suited
> KQ, KJ, KT, QJ, QT, JT suited
> AK to AT offsuit
> KQ, KJ, QJ offsuit

Looser Style — Middle Position (20 percent of all hands)

> Open raise with all pairs AA-22
> AK to A6 suited
> KQ, KJ, KT, QJ, QT, JT suited
> AK to A9 offsuit
> KQ, KJ, KT, QJ, JT offsuit
> T9, 98, 87 suited

Looser Style — Cutoff Seat (25 percent of all hands)

> Open raise with all pairs AA-22
> AK to A2 suited
> KQ, KJ, KT, QJ, QT, JT suited
> AK to A6 offsuit
> KQ, KJ, QJ, KT, QT, JT offsuit
> T9 to 65 suited

Looser Style — Button (35 percent of all hands)

> Open raise with all pairs AA-22
> All aces. suited or unsuited
> KQ, KJ, KT, K9, K8, QJ, QT, JT suited
> KQ, KJ, KT, K9, QJ, QT, JT offsuit
> T9 to 54 suited

Looser Style — Small Blind

Raise your button range

This approach will put you in a lot more hands than Strategy No. 1. You'll usually have the better hand and you'll usually be in position, but you'll need to demonstrate a little more skill to show a solid profit. Unlike Strategy No. 1, this looser approach will more often leave you out of position, and more often leave you with a hand of questionable value after the flop.

Blind-Stealing

When you open-raise from the cutoff or button, you're often just exploiting your positional advantage to steal the blinds. In micro-stakes games that's usually an extremely profitable move because your opponents frequently won't realize just how vulnerable they are to exploitation. Some won't choose to defend their blinds while others might not be able to defend on the flop, so if you open-raise from these positions preflop and get a call from one of the blinds, you'll almost always be making a continuation bet post-flop. The combination of the preflop raise in position and the post-flop continuation bet will often take down the pot and should show a substantial profit.

But under what circumstances should you tighten your play in the cutoff and the button? In general, you want to focus on the big blind, and in particular on two statistics: 'fold big blind to steal' and 'fold to continuation bet.' If 'fold big blind to steal' is less than 60 percent, or 'fold to continuation bet' is less than 50 percent, or both, you're probably up against an opponent who at least has the concept of blind defense in place, and you'll need to tighten your range when open-raising from the cutoff or button. There's no need, however, to tighten too much: Your position still gives you a solid advantage with any reasonable hand.

Example: You're on the button in a $10 NL 6-max game. The first three players fold. Your hand is the

264

What do you do?

Six-five offsuit is a pretty marginal hand. If your raising range was about 40 percent in this situation, this hand would just make the cut. Let's take a look at the big blind and decide what we want to do.

Suppose the big blind's HUD looks like this:

Player A / (80) / -2
VP 12 / PF 6 / AS 16 / FB 80
3B 0 / F3 40 / AF 0.7 / 1 / 1 / 0
CB 100 / FC 30 / FT 50
W$F 38 / WtS 25 / W$S 60

This big blind is our perfect target. His 'fold big blind to steal' number, 80 percent, is so high we can raise with any two cards and show an immediate profit. If he does call, we're in trouble, particularly since he won't give up easily to a continuation bet (his 'fold to c-bet' is only 30 percent, which makes sense because he's only calling with good hands). So if he calls and we miss the flop, we may have to give up on or at least significantly lower our continuation bet percentage.

Now take a look at this big blind:

Player B / (80) / +3
VP 30 / PF 8 / AS 35 / FB 50
3B 0 / F3 75 / AF 1.2 / 2 / 1 / 0.5
CB 50 / FC 70 / FT 80
W$F 35 / WtS 20 / W$S 50

Here we're much more likely to be called ('fold big blind to steal' is now only 50 percent), but our chances of making money after the flop are much better since his 'fold to c-bet' and 'fold to turn c-bet' are both high. Raising with the 6♣5♦ is perfectly good here, but we'll have to be prepared to fire a continuation bet and probably a second barrel if we miss.

Bet Sizing
in Micro-Stakes Games

Let's say you're under the gun in a 6-handed $10 NL game and you pick up the

That's a fine hand and you're certainly going to raise. So how much should you raise?

Since the blinds are $0.05 and $0.10, the minimum raise you can make is twice the big blind, or $0.20. For a variety of reasons, that's not a good raise size in micro-stakes play. The most common mistake that micro-stakes players make is to play too many pots with weak hands and you want to exploit that tendency, not reward it.

When you make a small raise, you give the players behind you favorable odds to get involved. For instance, if the hand is folded to the button, the pot is $0.35 and he needs to put in $0.20 to call. That's odds of 1.75-to-1, and he'll have position in the hand to boot. Those are attractive odds, and if he holds something like the a hand that a lot of micro-stakes players would happily play, he's actually getting the correct odds to call given your holding.

If the action were to get around to the big blind, his odds of 3.5-to-1 are even more favorable since he only needs to put in $0.10 to see a pot of $0.35. Although he's out of position, he's correct to play a wide range of hands under these circumstances.

The traditional bet size for an opening raise in full ring games was always something like two-and-a-half to three times the big blind. In micro-stakes games, it's best to raise more than that given the propensity of your opponents to call with weak hands. Three times the big blind should be your minimum raise size, but 3.5 or four times the big blind are even better. In general, you're trying to charge your opponents for entering the pot too often with poor holdings.

Can you go higher than four big blinds? In general, the answer is no, although it might work against a few specific opponents. Charging too much will simply cause a lot of players to stop calling with weak hands, and that's exactly the opposite of what you want. Again, the propensity of most micro-stakes players is playing too many weak hands, and this is a fatal flaw. By raising too much and chasing your opponents away, you may be forcing them to play better.

What about 3-bets and 4-bets? Let's suppose you're in the same 6-handed $10 NL game and the player in middle position, with a stack of $11.20, opens with a raise to $0.30. The cutoff folds and you are on the button with the Q♥Q♦. How big should your raise be?

Right now the pot is $0.45. A good rule of thumb for reraises is to calculate what a pot-sized raise would be, and then raise a little less. In order to make a pot-sized raise, you would first have to put in $0.30 to call the initial raise, making a pot of $0.75, then put in an additional $0.75 to raise the pot, for a total raise of $1.05. Notice that a full pot-sized reraise is usually between three and four times the previous raise. Therefore, a good reraise amount would be something like $0.90 or $1. Note that this is still far below his stack size, so you don't need to worry that your raise is so big that you're committing him to the pot if he plays.

Against players who are relatively short-stacked, you'll need to factor their stack size into your bet-sizing consideration. Let's take the previous example, but this time we'll assume that the player in middle position is short-stacked at $1.80. Again, he raises to $0.30 and you have the Q♥Q♦ on the button. If you reraise to $1, he calls, and the blinds fold, the pot becomes $2.15 and the effective stack is now $0.80. At this point, both of you are committed to the pot (although he may not know this). And with pot commitment looming, you could just go ahead and reraise to $1.80, putting him all-in. However, this isn't such a good play since a large bet is likely to scare him, making him fold all his weak hands and play on only with his premium ones. A better play is just to raise to something like $0.80, a bet which seems not so threatening and which he's likely to call. Then you can put him all-in on a good flop with a decent chance of collecting his whole stack rather than just his initial $0.30.

Before we leave the topic of bet sizing, there's one last important consideration to mention. In high-stakes poker, players mostly keep their bet sizes the same so their opponent can't read anything from different bets. A player who raises three big blinds under the gun on one occasion will probably raise three big blinds all the time, thereby preventing his opponents from gaining information. Keeping your bets the same size is a typical "defensive poker" play. But in micro-stakes games, where so many players aren't paying attention, there's no need for defensive poker. You'll make somewhat more money if you raise more with good hands and less with speculative hands.

For instance, if your betting range preflop is three to four big blinds and you pick up a pair of aces under the gun, raise your maximum. If instead you pick up a pair of treys, just raise to three big blinds. You'll be building bigger pots when you're a favorite, and less when you're speculating, which is what you want. Of course, if you get any sense that your opponents understand what you're doing, you'll need to stop and adopt a "one bet fits all" strategy. However, that shouldn't happen very often at these stakes. To recap, here's a quick summary for raising and lowering your bet size in micro-stakes games.

1. Make bigger bets or raises when

    ●   You're against a weak player.

    ●   You're in position.

    ●   You have a strong hand.

2. Make smaller bets or raises when

    ●   You're against a strong player.

    ●   You're out of position after the flop.

    ●   You have a weaker hand.

Making these small adjustments can save or gain many big blinds over the course of a session.

Attacking Limpers
with Isolation Raises

One of the most common mistakes you'll see players making in micro-stakes games is limping into the pot with weak hands. For example, suppose a loose-passive player in second position with VP$IP/PFR numbers of something like 45/7 picks up the

He decides the hand is good enough to play because the cards are suited and they're close together, so maybe he can make a flush or straight and double up. On the other hand, he knows the cards aren't good enough to raise because, well, they're just two low cards. So what's a player to do? He limps.

The best way to exploit a passive limper is to raise him assuming no one else has beaten you to the punch. You shouldn't raise with any two cards, but if you have some reasonable holding like the

or the

just stick in what is known as an *isolation raise,* and it serves three goals:

1. You may scare off every one else and get to play the hand heads-up against the limper, usually in position. Since the other players at the table, even the loose ones, will be less inclined to call a raise, there's a good chance no one will call behind you. This includes chasing out hands that are currently beating you, and which would have entered the pot had you just limped. Plus, you might even win the pot right there if the original limper folds.

2. You may secure position in the hand post-flop. Your raise represents a strong range and decreases the chance that a player who would have position on you will enter the pot.

3. You may be able to take the initiative against the limper and thereby increase your chance of taking down the pot with a continuation bet on the flop (assuming the limper calls your raise). Remember, when you raise a loose passive limper you actually create multiple ways to win the hand:

    A. You can win preflop if the limper folds.

    B. You can win on the flop if the limper checks and folds to your continuation bet.

    C. You can actually hit the flop and win even if the limper calls your continuation bet.

D. You can win with the initiative if the limper checks to you on the later streets and you eventually catch a winning card by the showdown.

Isolation raising is simply a high-percentage tool for exploiting a certain kind of weak player, one who wants to enter a lot of pots with weak hands to see what happens.

Example No. 1: You're in a $10 NL 6-max game. The middle position player with VP$IP/PFR numbers of 40/8 limps for $0.10. The cutoff folds and you're on the button with the Q♣T♥.

This is a textbook example of the situation you're looking for. You have position and a decent hand, and the limper has announced that he doesn't have much. (Note that his PFR number of 8 tells you that he will raise with a hand that he thinks is good and this makes him less dangerous than someone with numbers of 40/0.) Calling here is also reasonable, but raising is better.

You raise to $0.40 and the blinds fold. The middle position player calls $0.30 and the pot is now $0.95.

The flop is the K♥8♣4♦ and the middle position player checks. You now have a perfect spot for a continuation bet. Limping with a weak king would have been an unusual play for him. The strong hands with a king, like ace-king and king-queen, are hands he would have been expected to raise. But if he does call this bet, you're probably not going to put any more money in the pot. You bet $0.60 and the middle position player folds.

How wide a range should you have for isolation raises? That depends a bit on just how much you know about your opponent. Assuming a player limps and he's new to the table, be happy to make an isolation raise with roughly the same percentage of hands you would open-raise from the cutoff or button, and in most situations that would be 25 to 35 percent. If you have some history on the player and he's known to limp and fold, or his 'fold to continuation bet' number is high, or his post-flop aggression is low, you can raise with more hands than this.

Example No. 2: You're in a $25 NL 6-max game. The under the gun player limps for $0.25. His VP$IP/PFR numbers are 18/12. It's folded to you on the button and you have the

This situation is different. Now the limper isn't a loose-passive player. Instead, he seems to have tight-aggressive statistics. In this case, the player is probably more knowledgeable about poker, and his hand will almost always be a low pair or a suited connector. But you should raise as before.

Some players will recognize that their hand won't be getting the high implied odds they want in a raised pot out of position, and will fold to your bet. Others will still want to see a flop and stick around. In either case, your position and knowledge of what they're trying to do will give you the edge.

You raise to $0.90. The blinds fold and the under the gun player calls. The pot is $2.15.

The flop is the

and the under the gun player checks. Given the range you've put your opponent on, this flop almost certainly missed him, while it should have hit you. So represent the high cards with a continuation bet. You bet $1.40 and your opponent folds.

Limping and Calling

When you're first to act, or the action has been folded to you and your hand is playable, you have a choice: call (also known as limping) or raise. As we've seen, limping is common in micro-stakes games and a lot of micro-stakes players are playing for the fun of playing a lot of hands and seeing a lot of flops. When they pick up a hand that by their criteria isn't good enough to raise, but which they'd still like to play, they limp. As you move up the ladder to the small stakes, you still find such players, but they are fewer in number, and by the time you get to the high stakes, open-limping is almost unknown.

The best generic advice for small-stakes and high-stakes players is to never open-limp. If you have a hand that's worth playing by your standards, and the action is folded to you, raise. Not only might your raise win the pot, it gives you the initiative and makes you unreadable to your opponents. Those are sizeable advantages, so "never open-limp" is good general advice.

In micro-stakes games, however, the situation is somewhat different. Because so many players are passive and willing to limp, open-limping in early position actually has a good chance of succeeding — seeing a cheap flop without being raised. Depending on the makeup of your table, limping into the pot with a hand like a low pocket pair, a medium or low suited connector, or a suited two-gapper may be a perfectly reasonable play. If you hit the flop well, you may win many times your original bet, while if you miss, the play has only cost you a big blind.

Remember that never limping is in essence a defensive strategy. That is you refuse to limp certain hands because limping would give away information about your range to an observant opponent. But if your opponents aren't observant, you don't need to play defense.

However, even at micro-stakes, there are two real drawbacks to open-limping.

1. The presence of one or two players who have demonstrated they will attack limpers means the play may not be profitable. In that case, you'll need to return to a default strategy of raising when you enter the pot.

2. Open-limping can become a bad habit you'll need to unlearn as you move up in stakes. You could reasonably think that the small extra money you might earn isn't worth the difficulty of unlearning the habit later, and just stick to open-raising in all circumstances. But if you do experiment with open-limping at the micro-stakes, remember that if and when you do move up, you'll need to discard it from your strategy in most circumstances.

3- and 4-Betting
in Micro-Stakes Games

Online micro-stakes games play a lot like old-fashioned live games in one respect: 3-betting and 4-betting are rare moves, and almost always indicate a huge hand. That is in these games, the light 3-betting that we discussed earlier hasn't yet made more than an occasional appearance. Although most micro-stakes players are happy to make loose calls of raises with weak hands, they aren't ready to reraise without monsters. This is actually completely consistent with the micro-stakes profiles that we've been developing. Their goal is not to make a clever move to pull down the existing pot, but to play poker, which in their minds means seeing flops, catching big hands, and winning a showdown. Light 3-betting doesn't fit this scenario well, so you won't see much of it.

The typical 3-betting range for a generic micro-stakes player is about 3 percent. That range is very tight: only a pair of queens or better plus ace-king suited or unsuited, and some players will be even tighter than this. While only a few players at micro-stakes will be looser, you'll also meet players who play a 2 percent range (aces, kings, and ace-king) or even a 1 percent range (aces and kings only).

Against such a tight range, your options are limited. Let's take a look at how a selection of possible opening hands fare against each tight range in terms of raw winning percentages (assuming the hand is played to showdown in each case).

	Against a 1% Range	Against a 2% Range	Against a 3% Range
QQ	19%	40%	40%
JJ	19%	40%	36%
TT	19%	40%	36%
88	19%	39%	36%
AKs	23%	40%	42%
AKo	18%	37%	39%
AQs	25%	28%	29%
AJs	26%	28%	29%
JTs	20%	32%	29%
87s	22%	33%	31%

Tables such as this always contain a few apparently anomalous results. Note, for instance, that a pair of jacks does better against a 2 percent range than a 3 percent range, That's because the 2 percent range has a higher proportion of ace-king hands against which the jacks have the best chance. In the same way, because of card elimination, ace-king offsuit does worse against a 1 percent range than ace-queen suited. When ace-king faces the 1 percent range, it faces an equal number of pairs of aces and kings. But ace-queen faces twice as many pairs of kings as aces, and it has a better chance against kings because an ace can hit the board.

Before we try to define a good micro-stakes strategy for 3-betting and responding to 3-betting, let's make a general point: *note-taking is crucial.* Whenever a micro-stakes player makes a 3- or 4-bet and you're able to see his hand at showdown, *make a note.* It would take you many tens of thousands of hands to tell if someone has a 1, 2, or 3 percent range just from tabulating results. But a single observation that a player 3-bet with jacks or tens will answer the question. So when you see a 3-bet, sit up and take notice, even if you're not involved in the hand.

Having said that, let's outline a few simple rules for playing in 3-bet pots at the micro-stakes. To start, if you open-raise and a relatively unknown player 3-bets, remember that unless you have solid evidence to the contrary (like a 3-bet percentage of 10 percent or so), he's not bluffing. Your play needs to reflect this knowledge. So, go ahead and

● 4-bet with AA or KK, and call an all-in, or move all-in against a 5-bet.

● Fold AQ or worse and JJ or worse.

● Call with AK and QQ in position. Fold out of position.

This last piece of advice seems absurdly tight, and it would be in higher-stakes games. But as the earlier chart showed, these hands just don't do well against extremely tight 3-betting ranges. If, on the other hand, you have evidence that your particular opponent is capable of 3-betting with more hands, ace-king and a pair of queens become strong again.

Now suppose the pot is raised in front of you. When should you 3-bet? Here the situation gets more complicated, and any notes you may have made about what someone has done in the past is helpful.

If you don't have notes, pay attention to two statistics: 'preflop raise' (PFR) and 'fold to 3-bet' (F3B). Let's consider some ranges for PFR and see what they imply for our 3-betting strategy.

1. **Low PFR (0 to 9 percent):** This is a tight range. A 9 percent PFR contains premium pairs, medium pairs down to about fives, and the best Broadway cards. As the range shrinks to 5 percent, we lose the medium pairs and perhaps some of the Broadway cards. A player in this range should also have a low 'fold to 3-bet' number since many of his raising hands

are good enough to stand up to a 3-bet. If that number is low, say 40 to 50 percent, then you should just 3-bet premium hands — TT or better along with AK and AQ, suited or unsuited. But if his 'fold to 3-bet' is high, perhaps 70 percent or more, then he's only willing to keep playing with a small fraction of his range. You can exploit that by 3-betting light, perhaps with a 20 to 25 percent range. In this case, you're just trying to profit by making him lay down most of his hands. If you 3-bet light and can't make him fold, be done with the hand unless you started with a premium hand or hit the flop hard.

2. **Medium PFR (10 to 20 percent):** These are generous ranges. For instance, a 20 percent range consists roughly of all pairs, all Broadway cards, and some suited connectors. Again, we want to base our strategy on his 'fold to 3-bet' percentage. If that's about 70 percent, attack with a lot of hands. If it's lower than 40 to 50 percent, mostly 3-bet for value. A 5 percent range (pairs 99 or better, AJ suited or better, and AQ offsuit or better) is good for this last purpose.

3. **High PFR (above 20 percent):** These are loose raising ranges and you might think that players who raise this much would be worried when they get 3-bet, but in micro-stakes that's usually not the case. Since they're used to pushing players out of pots by betting a lot, they assume that you're doing the same and are more likely to call. Consequently, their 'fold to 3-bet' numbers will typically be low, and value 3-betting, rather than light 3-betting, should be your norm.

4. **You have PFR data but no reliable 'fold to 3-bet' data:** This is actually the most common situation in micro-stakes play: You have 100 hands or less of data on an opponent, have some confidence in the PFR number, but little or no

confidence in the 'fold to 3-bet' (F3B) number. So what's a good default strategy for 3-betting?

To answer this, I recommend a simple rule of thumb:

> 3-bet with a range that's 25 percent of your opponent's raising range.

For example, if your opponent is willing to raise with 20 percent of his hands from a given position, a good 3-bet (value) range for you is the top 5 percent of your hands. If he raises with 30 percent of his hands, then 3-bet for value with the top 7.5 percent of your hands, and so on. The logic of this rule is that by choosing hands in the top quarter of his range, you'll be playing hands that are on average about a 55 percent favorite against his whole range which gives you a comfortable margin of error.

Example No. 1: You're on the button in a $25 NL 6-max online game. Player Z open-raises to $0.80 from the cutoff, and his VP$IP/PFR numbers are 40/27 and his F3B, which is based on only two hands, is 50. You've also noticed that he seems positionally aware and will raise more often from late position. What should your 3-bet range look like?

With only two hands of data, the 'fold to 3-bet' number is essentially meaningless, so let's rely on the PFR number instead. If his PFR is 27 over all seats, and he has some positional awareness, let's assume it's something closer to 36 in the cutoff seat. By our rule, we can think about 3-betting the top 9 percent of our hands, and that range looks something like this:

Pairs as low as 66
AK suited through A9 suited
AK offsuit through AT offsuit

If we check the weakest hands in the range on PokerStove, we find that indeed they are solid favorites against a typical 36 percent range.

- 66 is 55%

- A9 suited is 56%

- AT offsuit is 57%

Defending against a 3-bet is a little more tricky at the micro-stakes. That's because when you are 3-bet, extreme caution is in order. Yes this runs against the grain if you're used to dominating your opponents because you'll have to lay down some decent hands.

Example No. 2: In a $10 NL 6-max online game you're in the cutoff with a $10 stack (100 big blinds). Your hand is the

and *after* the first two players fold, you raise to $0.35. The button now 3-bets to $1.35. He's only been at the table for 18 hands, his PFR is 11, you have no 3-bet data for him yet, and the blinds fold. What should you do?

You need to fold and it's not a close decision. Here's how you stand against some prospective tight ranges: Against AA, KK, and any AK, you're 27.8 percent to win. Against AA, KK, QQ, and any AK, you're 28.6 percent to win. And against AA, KK, QQ, JJ, and any AK, you're 32 percent to win.

Also, in addition to these dreadful numbers, you're out of position the rest of the hand. Now it's possible your opponent is a light 3-bettor, in which case your A♠Q♠ will be doing all right. But as already noted, light 3-bettors are a distinct minority at these stakes, so until the data shows that's what you're facing, just fold.

The Johnny All-in Move

While 3-betting and 4-betting are less common in micro-stakes games than in higher-stakes games, there is a variation which is actually much more common. It's what I like to call the "Johnny All-in Move," (with thanks to Norman Chad).

Here's the basic idea. A new player sits down at your micro-stakes table. Three hands later, you pick up the

in middle position and you raise to three big blinds. Right behind you, Johnny All-in raises — what else? — all-in! What do you do?

What you need to know is that Johnny rarely makes this move with an actual premium hand like aces, kings, or queens. Those hands he'll play normally. Instead, the move usually represents either a medium pair, a low pair, or ace-x, suited or unsuited. Johnny's reasoning goes roughly as follows:

1. He can't call me without aces or kings, so

2. I win the pot almost all the time, and

3. Even if he calls, I can hit a set or hit my ace or my flush, so

4. It's a great move!

Johnny also tends to be a hit-and-run artist, grabbing a few small pots and then vanishing into the night.

So what sort of hand do we need to call Johnny All-in? Actually, we need less of a hand than you might think, although the answer depends a little on how big the effective stack is. But before we answer this question, let's first make a couple of assumptions.

1. Johnny's range is a pair, jacks or less, or any ace.

2. After his all-in, the action is folded around to us.

3. Johnny's stack is either 50, 75, or 100 big blinds.

4. We have Johnny covered.

5. The pot is 4.5 big blinds (1.5 from the blinds plus a 3 big blind raise from us).

Johnny's initial stack has a remarkably small effect on the odds we're being offered. If he moves all-in with 50 big blinds, for instance, the pot becomes 54.5 big blinds and we need 47 big blinds to call, so we'll be getting odds of 54.5-to-47, or about 1.16-to-1.

This means we need a 46.3 percent chance of winning to call his 50 big blind raise. If he raises 75 big blinds, we need a 47.5 percent chance, and if he raises a full 100 big blinds, we need a 48.1 percent chance, not very different.

Under those circumstances, here's what we should do with some of our possible opening hands:

	Johnny raises 50 bbs	Johnny raises 75 bbs	Johnny raises 100 bbs
JJ	call	call	call
33	call	call	call
22	fold	fold	fold
A9o	call	call	call
A8s	call	call	call
A8o	fold	fold	fold
A7s	fold	fold	fold
KQs	fold	fold	fold
KQo	fold	fold	fold

This table yields a pretty simple counter-strategy to Johnny's approach. Call with these hands:

> Pairs down to treys
> Suited aces down to A8
> Unsuited aces down to A9

and fold any other hand without a pair or an ace.

In the above, we assumed that Johnny excluded the premium pairs from his all-in range and chose to play them normally. But if he lets those hands into his range, our optimal counter-strategy changes a little, but only a little. Now our calling range is:

> Pairs down to fours
> Suited aces down to A9
> Unsuited aces down to AT

(We can actually call the 50 big blind all-in with ace-eight suited and ace-nine unsuited, but not the larger all-ins.)

If Johnny decides to tighten his range by eliminating the unsuited aces from ace-seven and below, our calling range tightens a little more. Now it is:

> Pairs down to sixes
> Suited aces down to AT
> Unsuited aces down to AJ

Since you'll never know Johnny All-in's range with exact precision, here's a good general guide for a random all-in from an unknown player at the micro-stakes:

> Call with pairs sixes or better, and AT or better, suited or unsuited

Finally, be sure to make a note of what hand he shows down, as that will start to give you some idea of his true range. But for an unknown player, the range above will keep you out of trouble while giving you a solid edge in most cases.

Playing with Ace-King

Ace-king, also known as 'Big Slick,' is a strong hand in all forms of no-limit hold 'em. Its value, however, can shift depending on just how your opponents play. In micro-stakes games, ace-king is actually a bit of a chameleon: it becomes much stronger in certain situations, much weaker in others. I'll describe a couple of examples.

When you have ace-king and hit the flop, you rate to win more bets with the hand than you would in small stakes games or high-stakes games. Suppose you raise with ace-king and get a caller behind you who holds the

The flop comes the

You've hit top pair, top kicker and your opponent holds an underpair. In a micro-stakes game, you may be able to get three streets of value. That is, you might bet the flop and get called, bet the turn and get called, and finally bet the river and get called. In higher games, an opponent who called all three bets would mostly have top pair, top kicker beaten, and you, in turn, would be looking to slow down the betting using the 'small hand small pot' principle. But in micro-stakes games, against most opponents, you've hit a very profitable situation and are entitled to try and collect a few bets.

Now let's imagine you're in the same situation and miss the flop. You raise, get the same caller behind you with the 8♣8♠, but now the flop is the 9♦7♠3♦. It turns out that you're usually worse off than in a higher stakes game. That's because when many micro-stakes players try to put you on a range after you raise in early position, they tend to put you on only one hand: ace-king! This is very profitable if you in fact raised with a big pair because you'll be paid off much more than you should. But if you've raised with exactly an ace-king, you're in effect playing with your cards exposed. Your opponent won't fold his medium pair to your flop continuation bet, and most likely won't fold to any bets on the later streets as well. Therefore, your best strategy in this second case is to make one continuation bet on the flop in case he called with something other than a pair and missed the flop, and if that bet gets called, it's probably a waste of money to invest anything more in the hand unless you happen to hit the turn or the river.

At this point, the thoughtful reader might ask "If he always puts you on ace-king, why would he call in the first example?" Good question. My best guess is that his train of thought goes something like this: *"I thought he had ace-king, and now a king hit the flop, but I have a pair, and what if he didn't have ace-king, I mean, he could have raised with a lot of hands, so maybe he raised with ace-queen, or even ace-jack, yeah, that's it, I'll bet he had ace-jack, so I call..."* Or something like that.

Value Betting
at Micro-Stakes

A value bet is just a bet made under two conditions:

1. You have reason to believe that your hand is best right now even though you might be right or wrong about that; it doesn't matter. But what matters is that you have good reason to think you have the best hand.

2. There are a lot of hands in your opponent's range that you're beating but with which he'll call your bet.

When both conditions hold, you're making a value bet and they accomplish one of three purposes:

1. They get more money in the pot when your opponent has a made hand, but one that's not as good as yours.

2. They chase opponents out of the pot, preventing them from improving to the winning hand on a later street.

3. They make drawing hands pay to stick around, and if your bet is large enough, they may not be getting the right odds to play.

Value bets are your bread-and-butter money making move in micro-stakes. Unlike higher-stakes games, many micro-stakes players will call your bets on multiple streets with weak hands because they can't allow you to bluff or they just have to see how the hand turns out.

Let's look at a few common examples of value betting.

Example No. 1: You have the

under the gun in a $10 NL game and raise to $0.30 with only the cutoff calling. His VP$IP/PFR numbers are 45/8, so you believe that he could be calling with a wide range. The pot is $0.75.

The flop is the

You're first to act and make a classic value bet of $0.50.

First, you think your hand is probably best right now. Only a few hands beat you:

1. AA, KK, and QQ, which are not likely because there probably would have been a reraise preflop.

2. 88 and 44, which are possible because there would have only been a call preflop.

3. Q8, Q4, and 84, the suited versions of which are just possible for a loose player, while the unsuited versions are unlikely.

On the other hand, there are lots of hands that you can beat and with which your opponent would call this bet:

1. Any pocket pair except eights between queens and fours, and possibly the two smaller ones as well.

2. Any other queen except ace-queen (which you tie).

3. Any other eight.

4. Depending on just how loose our opponent really is, perhaps any other four as well.

5. Any hand with two diamonds.

That's a lot of calling hands and there may even be others. Some micro-stakes players will call a bet with just an ace, while others might call with something like king-jack figuring that you might have a low pair and the kings and jacks might be outs. Exactly how many, however, isn't the point. You almost always have the best hand, and many weaker hands will likely call, so you have a good value bet.

Now look at a slightly different case.

Example No. 2: As before, you raise from under the gun in a $10 NL game, this time with the A♥K♥ and are called by the button with VP$IP/PFR numbers of 28/16. The other players all fold.

The flop is the J♦T♣7♠. A bet here would be a continuation bet, and a reasonable play, but not a value bet. You have the best two overcards, but your hand is only ace-high. Most of your opponent's calls will be with a pair, and you're trailing those hands. While he will also sometimes call with a straight draw or maybe even overcards, you can no longer say that he will continue on with many weaker hands. Sometimes that will be the case, but there won't be a lot of these because our current opponent is tighter than our previous one.

Example No. 3: In a \$10 NL game, we pick up the J♥J♦ in middle position. After a fold, we raise to \$0.30 and get one call from the button. His VP\$IP/PFR numbers are 24/14.

The flop is the K♣7♣7♦. We can, and should bet for value, but it's best to also think a little about the situation. We will get called by hands that we're beating: pairs lower than our jacks and flush draws are the obvious cases, but since our opponent is somewhat tight, we don't expect to get called by a lot of worthless hands, although he might call with something like an ace-ten. However, we'll fold out most of the junk hands and take down those pots.

But there is also a downside. Some of the calls will be with hands that either contain a king or are trapping with a seven that are beating our jacks. But the hands that we're ahead of will outnumber the hands that are beating us, so it's a good bet that should make some money. However, it's not quite as good a bet as the one in our first example. Instead, it's what's called *thin value*, a bet that will average a profit over time, but not a huge profit.

One last thought on the subject of value betting. At micro-stakes, you will sometimes have to lose your stack with good hands that run into bad players and bad boards. We call these situations coolers, and you can't worry too much about them when they happen; they're just part of the process of value-betting and exploiting weak play. Here's a typical example:

Example No. 4: In a \$10 NL game we pick up the

under the gun. We raise to $0.35 and get one call from the big blind whose VP$IP/PFR numbers are 44/6. The effective stack is $8.00.

The flop is the

Our opponent checks, we make a perfectly good value bet of $0.55, and he calls. The pot is now $1.95.

The turn is the 4♦ and our opponent checks again. Since no possible draw has hit, we bet two-thirds of the pot, or $1.30, and he calls. The pot is now $4.55.

The river is the 5♠. The effective stack is $5.80 and our opponent now bets $2.00.

The arrival of the five didn't help a lot of hands. But he might have 'put us on ace-king,' called down with a pair of fives, and hit a set on the river. If he hit a straight, then he had to call the flop and the river with either ace-trey or six-trey, which even at micro-stakes is a stretch unless he also had two hearts. Did he just make two pair? That's also unlikely, but stranger things have happened in these games.

Still, small bets on the river at micro-stakes are rarely bluffs. If he has top pair, why did he check and call both the flop and turn, but then bet the river? An overpair is unlikely, especially since he didn't raise preflop.

In short, if he's betting for value, then he probably has a hand that beats us. But since we're getting better than 3-to-1 odds, and this is micro-stakes where all things are possible, we really have to call, but it's likely we're beaten. Also note that an all-in raise on the river won't be folded by any hand that beats us at these stakes. So we call and he shows the J♦5♦, and takes the pot.

Hands like this are frustrating, but they are an inevitable part of micro-stakes play. Don't let them get you down.

Semi-Bluffing
at Micro-Stakes

Semi-bluffing works a little differently in micro-stakes than in higher stakes games. Semi-bluffs come in two flavors: the normal semi-bluff where you make a normal-sized bet or raise with a drawing hand, and the all-in semi-bluff where you push all-in with a hand that could be either a drawing hand or a monster. Let's consider how each kind of semi-bluff works in a micro-stakes game.

Normal semi-bluffs mostly work well. When you bet with a drawing hand, you'll fold out some of your opponent's weaker hands (chiefly those who missed the flop entirely), and build a larger pot against the others. And when you actually hit your draw, you're much more likely to get paid than you might be in a tougher, higher-stakes game where players will read hands better and can fold top pair to obvious strength.

However, against maniacs, those players with VP$IP/PFR numbers like 50/35 or something similar, normal semi-bluffs break down. If you semi-bluff a maniac, he's very likely to raise, which in turn destroys the implied odds you need to play a drawing hand. If you see a flop against a maniac with a drawing hand, checking and simply calling the inevitable bet from him (assuming the pot odds are reasonable) is a better strategy than semi-bluffing.

All-in semi-bluffs, representing either a monster or a drawing hand, generally aren't a good idea at micro-stakes. These bets require a high probability of folding out your opponent, and while that's possible in a high-stakes game against a seasoned player, they're less likely in a game where many players are willing to get their stack in with top pair, weak kicker. Save these moves for the time when you advance to small stakes games or when you are against someone who you know is capable of more sophisticated laydowns.

Example: You're playing in a $25 NL 6-max game and are on the button with a stack of $26. The under the gun player folds and the middle position player with a stack of $18.50 limps for $0.25. His VP$IP/PFR numbers are 28/8, and his aggression factors are low. The cutoff folds, you hold the

and raise to $1.20, a reasonable play. Notice that your hand is playable and you have position. Hence your raise may win the pot, or it may get the blinds to fold and isolate the limper, which is exactly what happens. The pot is now $2.75.

The flop is the

giving you a flush draw, and your opponent checks. You should now make a continuation bet that is also a semi-bluff because your opponent may fold or you might win if he calls and another spade comes. Your fold equity is smaller than it would be in a tougher game, but your long-term potential is probably larger since your opponent can make mistakes on both the turn and the river.

You bet $1.80 and your opponent calls. The pot is now $6.35 and the effective stack is $15.50.

The turn is the 8♠ giving you a flush, and your opponent checks again. Should you check hoping your opponent will be more likely to call a bet on the river?

No. First of all, your opponent could hold a higher spade, in which case you need to charge him to draw to a better flush. (He might actually have a better flush than you right now, but in the micro-stakes you have to pay off to those hands since he's so much more likely to call with worse ones.) Second, slowplaying is generally a serious mistake when the major error your opponents make is calling with too many weak hands. You need to bet so they can continue to make that mistake.

You bet $4 and your opponent calls. The pot is now $14.35 and the effective stack is $11.50.

The river is the J♦ and your opponent pushes all-in. Should you call?

Yes. While it's certainly possible that he has a better flush, his range is still wide, and it's most likely that the jack just helped his hand in some way. So you call and he shows the J♥T♥ for a second best two pair.

He wasn't able to let go of middle pair although you showed consistent strength throughout the hand. In fact, you might have won the rest of his stack even if the jack hadn't come on the river.

Trapping

One characteristic opponent type in micro-stakes games is the loose-aggressive maniac. These players have a high VP$IP number, a high PFR number, and a high aggression factor — in fact, more or less every measure of activity is high. They understand one key idea: most of the time players don't have a hand where they're comfortable getting their whole stack involved, and if you bet enough, at some point they'll throw their hand away.

Maniacs will bet constantly, even with nothing, as long as the opponent shows weakness by checking and calling. Their goal is to win all the pots that no one wants. If you do play back at them with a raise, they'll frequently fold their tent and go away, unless they actually have a hand.

So what's the right defense against such a player? To catch a wolf, you need to look like a sheep. That is, the best approach is to trap.

Trapping simply refers to taking a strong holding and playing it as though you are weak and capable of being pushed off the hand with sufficient pressure. Instead of betting, you check. Instead of raising, you call. In essence, you imitate the style of a loose-passive player with a weak to medium strength hand. In some cases, you might play the hand like this all the way through. In other cases, you might spring the trap with a raise on the turn or the river.

Trapping is a tool at all levels used to slow down overly aggressive opponents. In micro-stakes games, it's a brutally effective tool against a loose-aggressive maniac. In fact, trapping, along with value betting, will be one of your most profitable tools at these stakes. Let's look at an example.

Example No. 1: You're in a $10 NL 6-max online game. The player two to your right is 'Terminator,' and his HUD looks like this:

> *Terminator / (98) / +16*
> *VP 50 / PF 40 / AS 86 / FB 12*
> *3B 15 / F3 na / AF 8 / inf / 3 / 2*
> *CB 100 / FC 40 / FT 50*
> *W$F 32 / WtS 20 / W$S 38*
> *Note: Post-flop: bets & raises, folds to reraise.*
> *Turn: bet/fold=2.*

This is a typical profile for a micro-stakes maniac. Preflop, he plays half his hands raising about 80 percent of the time, and 3-bets about one-sixth of the time when he has the chance. Post-flop, his aggression factor is extremely high although it tails off a bit on the turn and river. Put another way, Terminator's approach can be summed up simply: "All pots belong to me unless you tell me otherwise."

In this hand you're in the big blind with a stack of $12.50 (125 big blinds). The under the gun player folds and Terminator, with a stack of $8.60, raises to $0.35 from middle position. The cutoff, button, and small blind fold. You have the

in the big blind and call. At micro-stakes, not raising here would be a big mistake in almost all situations, but given who you're against, it's a good play. The pot is now $0.75.

The flop is the

which is a good flop for your situation. It apparently offers both straight and flush draws, which will allow your opponent to rationalize that you're on a draw if he behaves as you expect him to.

You check indicating weakness and he bets $0.60. Since his 'c-bet' percentage is 100 percent, this is no surprise and you just call $0.60. The pot is now $1.95.

The turn is the J♣. Normally you would bet here since there are many possible draws on this board. But your goal is to have Terminator think you're drawing, so you do what a loose-passive player would do with a draw and check. Terminator, as expected, bets $1.50 and you again just call. The pot is now $4.95 with an effective stack of $6.25.

The river is the 2♠. You check, representing either a missed draw or a low pair. If you were drawing, you'll probably give up to a big bet and if you actually have a low pair, you might call. At a higher stake, this is a play with considerable risk. If Terminator has a hand like the K♣J♠, he might check his pair of jacks on the end thinking that a final bet would only be called by a better hand. But that's not the way micro-stakes play normally works. Bets on the end are often called by weak hands, so players learn to bet top pair on the river after a series of checks and calls.

Terminator now pushes all-in with his last $6.25 and you call with your overpair. His hand is the and you take the pot.

Terminator never had anything at any stage and simply relied on his ability to push you out of the pot since you never showed strength. Had you check-raised on the flop or the turn, you would have won less. But as you played it, his entire stack became yours.

Let's take a look at a second example with a slightly different twist.

Example No. 2: You're in a $10 NL 6-max online game. The player two to your right is 'Pwnmaster,' and his HUD looks like this:

> *Pwnmaster / (31) / +220*
> *VP 55 / PF 39 / AS 100 / FB na*
> *3B 0 / F3 50 / AF 4 / 4 / inf / 1*
> *CB 100 / FC 0 / FT 100*
> *W$F 47 / WtS 29 / W$S 40*

In this hand, you're in the small blind with a stack of $19.50 and Pwnmaster is in middle position with $34.30. The under the gun player limps for $0.10. Pwnmaster raises to $0.40 and both the cutoff and the button fold.

You have the T♥T♣ and you elect to reraise to $1.40. Note that calling is more dangerous than in the previous hand because there's a greater risk that overcards can appear on the flop when you have tens than when you have queens. So you really don't mind winning immediately, although you recognize that with Pwnmaster already involved, that may not be easy. However, your raise will probably chase out the big blind and the under the gun player leaving you isolated against your target.

The big blind and the under the gun player do, in fact, fold and Pwnmaster calls $1. The pot is now $3.05.

The flop is the K♦7♦5♥. It has one overcard to your tens, but otherwise is pretty good. A few hands in his range contain a king, but many more don't, so you expect to be in great shape.

You act first and bet $1.50, about half the pot. Since Pwnmaster's 'fold to c-bet' number is zero, he's expected to call, but since you 3-bet preflop, a bet here should protect your hand if he has overcards to beat you (and now you would want him to call). But instead of calling, Pwnmaster raises to $6.00.

At this point, you need to decide if you're willing to get your whole stack involved. If the answer is 'yes,' it's also best to decide how to go about it. And the answer should be yes because given Pwnmaster's HUD, you're still a big favorite to have the best hand. So what's your strategy? The right way is to just call and let Pwnmaster try to push you out of the pot on later streets. Notice that while his 'fold to c-bet' number is zero, his 'fold to turn c-bet' is 100. In other words, if you reraise or perhaps lead on the turn, he might fold some of the hands you're beating, while more passive play will get him to bet the turn with all his hands.

You call another $4.50. The pot is now $15.05, and the effective stack is $12.10.

The turn is the K♠ and you check. Notice that's a good card for you. If he already had a king in his hand, you were losing anyway, and now the chance of that has been reduced by a third.

Checking is still a good move. It indicates that perhaps you just have a low pair or a diamond draw, and it encourages your opponent to bet again regardless of his hand.

Pwnmaster pushes all-in. You call and he shows the Q♠9♦. The river is the 8♣, you take the pot, and you now endure an obligatory lecture in the chat box about how badly you play. You respond that you're just trying to learn the game and welcome the chance to play the masters.

Dealing with
Strong Bets Post-Flop

The most important rule for beating micro-stakes games is to ruthlessly value bet your good hands. The second most important rule is this:

> If a loose-passive player wakes up and makes a big bet on the turn or the river, he has what he considers to be a very strong hand. Proceed with caution.

Many players fall into the trap of thinking that a weak, loose-passive player can't have a strong holding. They can and do. But when they do hit a strong hand, they'll usually tell you which enables you to get out of the way. But you must listen to what they're saying. Loose-passive players don't like to make big bluffs. Expensive moves on the later streets are the antithesis of what they're all about, which is getting to showdown and seeing if their hand is good. So when they put in a raise, or worse, a check-raise, it's because they're confident beyond a reasonable doubt that their holding is best.

In general, you want to be more afraid of moves on the turn or the river than on the flop. Even weaker players understand that bets on the flop are part of the game. Therefore, even though I would pay close attention to a raise on the flop, big bets and raises on the turn or the river are especially dangerous.

Again, note that we're talking about loose-passive players. The super-aggressive player who will bet all three streets with nothing is a completely different breed; against him you just have to take a made hand and go all the way.

Here's a prototypical example of the sort of situation we're describing.

Example No. 1: You're playing in a 6-max $10 NL game with blinds of $0.05/$0.10, are under the gun with a $10 stack (100 big blinds), and pick up the

It's a good hand and you raise to $0.30, and only the button, who also has a $10 stack, whose VP$IP and PFR numbers are 33/6, and whose aggression factors are low across the board, calls. The pot is $0.75.

The flop comes the

You have top pair, top kicker, bet $0.60, and the button calls. The pot is now $1.95.

The turn is the 9♠. You still have top pair, top kicker and now bet $1.40. But the button raises to $5. What do you do?

You fold and it's not a close decision. Loose-passive players don't do this as a bluff, and it's also not any kind of bet with a draw. He has a big hand which on this board is probably a set even though with a loose player two-pair is still possible. In any event, you're crushed with very few outs.

Being able to fold here is one of the important plays in micro-stakes games. You've already lost 23 big blinds, but if you continue, you'll lose 100. That's 77 more big blinds that most micro-stakes players in this situation would lose, but which you won't.

Now let's look at a slightly more complex hand with a raise on the flop rather than the turn.

Example No. 2: You're in the cutoff with the K♥J♥ in a 6-max $5 NL game, blinds are $0.02 and $0.05, your stack is $13.10 or more than 260 big blinds, and the first two players fold. Your hand is certainly good enough to raise from this position so you make it $0.20 to go and the button calls. He's had a good session and his stack is $20.50, a little more than 400 big blinds. His HUD looks like this:

```
Player X / (82) / +104
VP 43 / PF 14 / AS 25 / FB 50
3B 0 / F3 33 / AF 1.0 / 1 / 0 / 4
CB 100 / FC 0 / FT 33
W$F 61 / WtS 44 / W$S 75
```

The blinds fold and the pot is now $0.47.

The flop comes the K♠Q♠7♠ and you've hit top pair on a monotone board. Looking over your opponent's HUD, you see some interesting tendencies. At first glance he's your basic loose-passive player: VP$IP/PFR of 43/14, '3-bet' frequency of zero, a low 'fold to 3-bet' of 33 percent, 'fold to c-bet' frequency of zero, and 'fold to turn c-bet' of just 33 percent. Also, and this is important, he's almost impossible to get out of a pot.

His post-flop aggression factors back up this conclusion. His flop and turn numbers are 1 and zero and his 'went to showdown' number is also high, at 44 percent. Once Player X sees a flop, he wants to get to showdown and see if he's won.

But there is also an interesting anomaly. His river aggression is a very high 4. That is, if he has something on the river, he's willing to bet it.

Anyway, right now you're in good shape and certainly should bet. Since your opponent limps and calls a lot preflop, never folds to a continuation bet, and once he sees a flop he's looking to get to showdown, a bet is virtually mandatory. Put another way, top pair is a strong hand against this player.

You bet $0.35 and he raises to $1.05. What should you do?

Oops! Time to reevaluate. A big flop raise from a loose-passive player is way out of character, and we need to look at the flop with fresh eyes. This move almost certainly doesn't represent something like king-ten or queen-jack, hands that you beat. Also note that it's almost certainly not a semi-bluff with a spade. Players who are willing to semi-bluff have higher flop aggression factors than 1 because semi-bluffing means that you frequently bet or raise draws rather than just calling with them.

Instead, this bet represents a made hand which didn't raise preflop. Since his 3-betting number is zero, and since we have a fair number of hands for Player X, it's possible he didn't even raise with his big pairs: aces, kings, or queens. Since he's not bluffing or semi-bluffing, we can put him on a small number of holdings:

A set of kings, queens, or sevens
A pair of aces
King-queen
A made flush

Our top pair, good kicker is crushed against this range, so we should fold. But instead, you call another $0.75 and the pot is now $2.52.

The turn is the J♦. By calling the flop raise, this card becomes a disaster. Notice that you didn't improve enough to beat any hand in his raising range, except for a pair of aces, even though your hand did improve. For many players, a card like this will trap them into losing their whole stack, and to beat micro-stakes, these are the traps you need to avoid. You check and Player X bets $2.50.

A loose-passive player, whose turn aggression is zero, now ventures a pot-sized bet. Again, alarm bells should be ringing! Two pair won't be good enough! But you call $2.50 and the pot is $7.52.

The river is the 3♣. You check and Player X moves all-in.

You still have $9.75 left in your stack (195 big blinds), so it's worth making the right play, which is folding. Instead, you call, your opponent shows the A♠6♠, and he takes the pot with the nut flush.

You dropped 260 big blinds in this hand, most of which could have been saved. Just like everyone else, loose-passive players can flop the nuts, and you have to let them tell you when to go away.

So far we've described examples where your top pair hand was crushed. What happens if the loose-passive player makes a play but you actually have a pretty strong hand? Look at the next example.

Example No. 3: You're on the button with the K♦T♦ in a 6-max $10 NL game, blinds are $0.05 and $0.10, and the first three players fold. Your hand is easily strong enough to raise for value, so you raise to $0.30 and both blinds call. The small blind's VP$IP/PFR numbers are 35/0 while the big blind's are 60/5. You've been playing about 60 hands and the big blind is a small winner while the small blind has been a loser. The effective stack is $10.20 and the pot is now $0.90.

The flop is the T♣T♠5♣ which is obviously a great flop giving you trips with the second best kicker, plus position. At this point, you want to check the post-flop statistics for your opponents to get a clue what you're up against.

The small blind's aggression factors are zero across the board and his 'fold to c-bet' number is also zero. Combined with his 35/0 preflop numbers, he looks like the epitome of the weak loose-passive player. The big blind has a 'fold to c-bet' of 100 percent, but fairly odd aggression factors: overall 1.7, flop 1, turn 2, river 4. He seems to start out passive, but then gets more aggressive as the hand goes on; he probably likes to try to steal on the river.

The small blind checks and the big blind makes a minimum bet of $0.10. The pot is now $1.

Two plays are available: You can raise for value or could just call and mimic a weak calling hand. As we said earlier in this section, you do not, in general, want to be passive at the micro-stakes. The overwhelming weakness of micro-stakes players is that they will call with weaker hands, but to exploit that weakness you need to be betting or raising. Slowing down where you could have raised and gotten called (or perhaps reraised) by a weaker hand is a huge blunder.

Should you be concerned about the flush draw on board? No. Although we know from our work with distributions in "Part Three: Ranges and Distributions," that wide ranges generate more flush draws than narrow ranges, the chance of a flush draw on a two-tone board is only about 6 percent for either of these players, or perhaps 12 percent for both players together. The chance that either player has a flush draw and hits it on the turn is in the 2 to 3 percent range. So raising to charge the flush draws isn't necessary if you felt that calling was otherwise a good idea.

Should you be concerned about the big blind's donk bet? Also no. Donk bets are common in micro-stakes, and almost always represent a bluff or a weak hand that will fold to a raise. A sophisticated opponent could be making a play, but the HUD statistics don't indicate that we're facing a sophisticated opponent.

So how big should your raise be? The pot will now be $1.10 if you just called the bet, so a good raise size would be $0.70 or

$0.80. If anyone has a pair they should come along, and someone with a ten and a weak kicker may well reraise.

You actually raise to $0.60, the small blind now pushes all-in for $10.20, and the big blind folds. The pot is now $11.80 and it costs you $9.60 to call. What do you do?

We've already established that the small blind was the quintessential loose-passive player with a wide preflop calling and limping range, and extreme passivity post-flop based on his aggression factor numbers. So this bet isn't a bluff since big bluffs just aren't in his repertoire. He thinks he has a hand, and he's going with it.

Since we don't have the nuts and he has moved all-in, we have to consider this call a little bit. Right now only three hands are beating us: ten-five, making a full house of tens full of fives (the nuts), a pair of fives, making a full house of fives full of tens (the second nuts), and ace-ten, for the best possible trips (the third nuts). The first hand is probably not in his range, while the second and third hands certainly are.

Now let's look at the hands that we're beating but which the small blind might think were strong enough to push all-in. The candidate hands here are a ten with a weaker kicker and the pairs that don't match the board. A ten with a weaker kicker hands are probably just QT, JT, T9, and T8. Weaker hands containing a ten aren't likely to be in his preflop range. The pairs break into two groups: the pairs higher than the tens (aces through jacks) and the lower pairs (nines through deuces, except for fives). Ordinarily, we would rule out the high pairs because he didn't raise preflop, but notice that the small blind's PFR is 0 after about 60 hands. That suggests that the small blind may be one of the players who never raises preflop and who treats every good hand as a potential trap.

Also note that the PFR of zero also suggests that he's not pushing with the nuts. Players who like to trap don't move all-in the first chance they get; they want to milk the hand for more money. The all-in push suggests that the small blind would be just as happy if you quietly went away. That in turn suggests a low pair as the most likely hand.

And finally the pot right now is offering about 1.2-to-1, a small price. There are 10 ways to make one of the three hands that beat us, 16 ways to make one of the weaker tens that we listed, and 63 ways to make a smaller pair. Even though we can't be sure of the exact likelihood, the fact that he could be pushing with a hand we beat forces us to call.

So we call and he shows the 7♠7♥. Two low cards hit the turn and the river respectively, and we scoop the pot.

Looking Forward

In this section we've shown you how to beat the micro-stakes games. Actually, we've shown you two different ways: a tight way which involves opening a small number of strong hands in early position and a slightly larger number of good hands in late position, and a loose way which allows you to open with a much larger range of hands in all positions but which requires a little more skill to navigate the more difficult situations that arise.

Both methods are effective. The first is suitable for the true beginner or the naturally conservative player. It will show a significant profit while avoiding difficult and unclear situations. The second is more profitable and better for exploiting the range of opponents you'll see at the micro-stakes. It's also better preparation for the eventual jump to higher-stakes games.

Now for the caveat. When you're ready to make the move to the NL $50, NL $100, and NL $200 games, you have to leave much of the advice in this chapter behind. Here we've taught you how to beat players who play essentially mechanically, although their mechanics may be different. To beat tougher games, you'll have to think differently and play differently. Your new opponents won't be stationary targets; they're going to start to move and shoot back. In the next section we'll show you how to adapt.

The Problems

Problem 4-1

Table layout:

UTG	Player A $12.50	A's HUD Player A / (40) / +39 VP 60 / PF 3 / AS 8 / FB 0 3B 0 / F3 0 / AF 1.1 / 1 / 1 / 3 CB 0 / FC 50 / FT na W$F 33 / WtS 33 / W$S 38 *Note: R: Bluff caught.*
MP	Player B $4.80	
CO	You $16.90	Your Hud You / (42) / +105 VP 36 / PF 24 / AS 33 / FB na 3B 0 / F3 33 / AF 4.7 / 4 / inf / 3
BTN	Player C $6.25	Player C's HUD Player C / (29) / +42 VP 41 / PF 21 / AS 29 / FB 0 3B 10 / F3 100 / AF 3.8 / 8 / 3 / 2
SB	Player D $4.50	
BB	Player E $2.50	

Situation: Online $5 NL 6-max table. Blinds are $0.02/$0.05.

Your hand: A♦8♦

Action to you: Player A limps for $0.05 and Player B folds.

Question: *What do you do?*
    Answer: Player A has VP$IP/PFR numbers of 60/3, so his range is very wide, and your hand, while not a powerhouse, is certainly good enough for an isolation raise. The danger here comes from Player C who has position and is reasonably aggressive with a 10 percent 3-bet ratio. If he 3-bets, you'll need to throw your hand away.

Action: You raise to $0.20, Players C, D, and E all fold, and Player A calls for another $0.15. The pot is now $0.47.

Flop: K♣T♥3♠

Action: Player A checks.

Question: *What do you do?*
    Answer: A more difficult decision than it at first appears. Despite his wide range, the combination of the king and the ten actually hit a fairly big chunk of his starting hands. You're about a 55-to-45 underdog against his range with that flop. His 'fold to c-bet' statistic of 50 percent (based on an admittedly small sample) shows that he doesn't like to lay down to a continuation bet. Betting is reasonable, but checking is probably a slightly better choice since you don't need to bet every flop, even against a loose player.

Action: You check and the pot remains at $0.47.

Turn: A♣

Action: Player A checks.

Question: *What do you do?*

    Answer: The ace on the turn changes the situation. Now you've become a solid favorite in the hand and should start building the pot. A bet of two-thirds to three-quarters of the pot looks like the right amount.

Action: You bet $0.35 and Player A calls. The pot is now $1.17.

River: 7♣

Action: Player A bets $0.90.

Question: *What do you do?*

    Answer: The third club appears and he bets out. There are a few holdings, like J♣T♣ or Q♣J♣, that could have played the hand this way. The giveaway, however, is contained in the HUD and notes. You've already seen him bluff the river once and get called. In addition, notice the extremely odd aggression factor line: overall aggression of just 1.1, with factors for the individual streets of 1 on the flop, 1 on the turn, and 3 on the river. Normal aggression factors show a slight decline from the flop to the river, as you might expect. It looks like Player A has learned that big bluffs on the river are effective at low stakes. With that in mind, and considering that you're getting 2.3-to-1 on your call, you should call to see what he has.

Action: You call $0.90. Your opponent shows the K♦9♠ and you take the pot.

    In a higher-stakes game, the fact that this opponent had already showed a bluff on the river might make you less inclined to call the bet on the theory that he knows he was caught and knows everyone saw him get caught. Therefore he's less likely to bet without a real hand. Remember, however, that at micro-stakes, all tendencies are carried to excess. Players who bluff really like to bluff and see that as their winning style. When you see such a tendency, don't expect it to reverse; expect it to continue.

Problem 4-2

Table layout:

UTG	Player A $3.30	
MP	Player B $3.70	B's HUD Player B / (16) / -12 VP 13 / PF 6 / AS 0 / FB na 3B 0 / F3 na / AF na / na / na / na CB na / FC na / FT na W$F 0 / WtS 0 / W$S na
CO	You $12.00	Your HUD: You / (16) / +64 VP 25 / PF 19 / AS 67 / FB 0
BTN	Player C $6.00	C's HUD Player C / (14) / -75 VP 50 / PF 14 / AS 0 / FB na 3B 11 / F3 na / AF 2.3 / 1 / inf / inf CB 100 / FC 0 / FT na W$F 60 / WtS 60 / W$S 67 *Note: Postflop: overvalues weak aces.*
SB	Player D $3.00	
BB	Player E $5.00	

Situation: Online $10 NL 6-max table. Blinds are $0.05/$0.10.

Your hand: A♦K♦

Action to you: Player A folds and Player B limps for $0.10. The pot is $0.25.

Question: *What do you do?*
    Answer: You have very little information on Player B, but in any case you're going to raise. This is technically an isolation raise of someone who might be a loose passive player, but your hand is so strong you're also raising for value.

Action: You raise to $0.40 and Player C 3-bets to $0.70. The blinds fold and Player B folds. The pot is now $1.35.

Question: *What do you do?*
    Answer: The min-3-bet is an almost exclusive phenomenon of micro-stakes games. It usually doesn't have any special significance. Player C probably likes to raise and raises by hitting the 'raise' button, thereby making a minimum raise. It's safe to say he has something, but his range is wide.
    The obvious and perfectly good play is to 4-bet to about $2 giving Player C a chance to push all-in. It's an especially good play out of position with ace-king since it negates your positional disadvantage and guarantees that you will see all five cards.
    The trappy play is to note that Player C tends to overplay his weak aces and call in the hope that he has an ace, and an ace comes on the flop. Then you'll be able to get all-in as an even bigger favorite than you currently are. It's a neat idea, but he's probably raising with a lot more hands than just his middling aces, and if you miss the flop and he bets (which is almost a certainty given his stats), you'll be in a difficult spot. The best play here is just the obvious play of 4-betting.

Action: You just call for another $0.30 and the pot is now $1.65.

Flop: A♥Q♣6♣

Question: *What do you do?*

    Answer: That's a great flop for you and if Player C indeed has a weaker ace you may get all his chips.

    Since you only called his 3-bet and his levels of post-flop aggression are generally high, checking with the idea of check-raising looks like the best idea. If he has an ace he'll almost certainly bet it, and if he doesn't hold an ace, your check will encourage him to bet and represent one

Action: You check and Player C bets $0.70. The pot is now $2.35 and the effective stack is now $4.60.

Question: *What do you do?*

    Answer: Player C has bet a little less than half the pot. Coupled with his min-3-bet earlier, that probably means that small bets are his style. Since the board does have some draws available, you're probably a little better off check-raising rather than calling and betting the turn. A standard raise would be to something like $2. However, you'd really like him to come over the top and get all his chips in, so you'd like him to be able to feel that a reraise represents a real threat.

    So if you raise to $2, the pot becomes $4.35. If he then moves all-in, the pot becomes $8.95 and his reraise to you is just $2.60, a trivially easy call on your part. Hence, I like raising to about $1.70 which makes his push seem a little more threatening. (It's possible, of course, that he's not thinking about any of this, in which case your play doesn't matter much. But it's good to do this sort of planning anyway because it's good practice for when you move up in stakes.)

Action: You raise to $2. Player C pushes all-in for $4.60 and you call. The turn and river are the K♠ and the A♠, and he shows the A♣J♠. Your full house beats his trip aces.

After the hand, you should make two notes: He's willing to get all-in on the flop with top pair, good kicker, and he's willing to 3-bet preflop with ace-jack.

Problem 4-3

Table layout:

UTG	Player A $16.00	A's HUD Player A / (2) / -1 VP 50 / PF 0 / AS na / FB 0 3B na / F3 na / AF na / na / na / na CB na / FC na / FT na W$F na / WtS na / W$S na
MP	Player B $26.30	
CO	Player C $18.90	
BTN	You $25.00	
SB	Player D $17.60	
BB	Player E $32.40	

Situation: Online $25 NL 6-max table. Blinds are $0.10/$0.25.

Your hand: 9♥9♣

Action to you: Player A raises to $0.90 and the next two players fold.

Question: *What do you do?*
   Answer: Your hand is certainly good enough to call, but a 3-bet would be frisky. Your problem is that you have no information yet on your opponent, so you can't assign him a range. This is only his third hand at the table, and so far all you know is that he got involved in one pot in the blinds. If you had some solid data on him and knew he was a loose raiser then a reraise might be perfectly reasonable. But when you lack information, it's best to assume generic ranges and a basic level of competence.

Action: You call $0.90 and the blinds fold. The pot is $2.15.

Flop: 8♦7♦2♣

Action: Player A bets $1.30.

Question: *What do you do?*
   Action: With an overpair to the board against an unknown opponent, folding is out of the question. You're going to either raise or call.

   However, you don't really want to play a monster pot against an unknown with just a pair of nines, but if you call and face another big bet on the turn, you still won't know what's going on. He may have a real hand, or he may have decided that you can be pushed off the hand since you haven't shown any strength so far.

   If you knew he was the sort of super-aggressive opponent who would just keep betting until he encountered resistance, your nines are good enough to call down to the end as a trap. But you don't know that either.

   Therefore, the prudent play is to stick in a raise and see what happens. If he has nothing, this should take down the pot. If it doesn't win the pot, you're probably going to have to give up on the hand.

While I'm generally critical of "betting to see where I'm at," this is a situation where the play makes sense. When we can't evaluate our hand because we don't know anything about our opponent, we need to look for ways to cut our losses when we're in trouble. This situation qualifies.

Action: You raise to $3.50 and Player A calls. The pot is $9.15.

Turn: 4♥

Action: Player A moves all-in for $11.60.

Question: *What do you do?*
Answer: Enough is enough. If he's a maniac, there will be a better time to get your money in against him. This isn't it.

Action: You fold.

Problem 4-4

Table layout:

UTG	Player A $4.20	A's HUD Player A / (36) / -2 VP 28 / PF 8 / AS 40 / FB 66 3B 0 / F3 na / AF 1.2 / 1.5 / 0.6 / 0 CB 50 / FC 60 / FT 50 W$F 33 / WtS 20 / W$S 50 *Note: Plays 1 table. LFC=1/3.*
MP	Player B $5.05	B's HUD Player B / (22) / 0 VP 60 / PF 0 / AS 0 / FB na 3B 0 / F3 na / AF 0.8 / 1 / 0.5 / na CB na / FC 50 / FT na W$F 40 / WtS 20 / W$S 0 *Note: Plays 2 tables. LFC=0/2.*
CO	Player C $2.35	
BTN	You $11.60	
SB	Player D $4.00	
BB	Player E $7.20	

Situation: Online $5 NL 6-max table. Blinds are $0.02/$0.05. The maximum buy-in at this table is $10 or 200 big blinds.

Your hand: K♠K♣

Action to you: Player A raises to $0.10, Player B calls, and Player C folds. The pot is now $0.27.

Question: *What do you do?*
  Answer: You're going to be making a 3-bet, but first let's review the situation a little bit. Although you haven't been playing for long, and the HUD data is a bit sketchy, you still have enough information to place both Players A and B in the loose-passive category for now:

- They apparently didn't buy-in for the full amount at the table, suggesting that they're not aggressive players. And the fact that they only play a small number of tables also suggests a general lack of confidence.

- Their VP$IP and PFR numbers are 28/8 and 60/0. These are loose-passive numbers and they tend to converge much more quickly than the other statistics, so we put a lot of confidence in them.

- The other numbers in the HUD, particularly the aggression factors, don't contradict this conclusion even though they're based on little data.

- Our notes also show a pattern of limping and then calling a raise, characteristic of a loose-passive style.

  The min-raise from first position for Player A probably means that he has a hand he likes more than his normal limping hand. Since he's raised 8 percent of his hands so far, that suggests something like a middle pair or two low Broadway cards. Player B's call just says he has a hand that's better than average, which means almost nothing.
  A pot-sized raised here would be to $0.47 ($0.10 to call, creating a pot of $0.37, then an additional $0.37 to raise,

making $0.47 in total.) That's the minimum that we should raise in this situation.

Action: You raise to $0.50 and the blinds fold. Both Player A and Player B call for another $0.40. The pot is now $1.57.

Flop: 9♦4♣4♥

Action: Both Player A and Player B check.

Question: *What do you do?*
    Answer: That's a good flop for you. Player B probably has a few fours in his range, but that's not going to stop you from betting. There are no draws on board, so your bet doesn't need to be large, but even a bet of half the pot will be enough to put either player's stack in jeopardy if you get a call.

Action: You bet $0.90. Player A raises to $1.80 leaving $1.90 in his stack, and Player B folds.

Question: *What do you do?*
    Answer: A basic principle of playing loose-passive players at low stakes is to be very aware when they show strength. In general, when they bet they have a strong hand. That's especially true when they call the flop and then make a big move on the turn or the river. In that case, they're almost always holding a monster.
    Raises on the flop, however, don't have to be that strong. Often, a raise just means that they assume you have ace-king and they can beat ace-high. In this case, that could be any pair, or a hand like ace-nine. Since there are a lot of hands you beat that could account for his play and so few monsters available, you can't fold.
    If you're against a hand like a pair of tens, they have only two outs, so you don't need to worry about giving

correct odds for your opponent to draw out. The only issue is how to get Player A's last $1.90 into the pot. You can do this by reraising now, or just calling and letting him bet on the turn. In micro-stakes, you're usually better off in these situations by letting him bet the rest of his money, so call.

Against a player with a more aggressive profile, calling would have the additional advantage of allowing him to bluff again on the turn if he was bluffing now. However, given Player A's profile, this raise is essentially never a bluff. He has something, but given this board it's likely something you beat.

Action: You push all-in and Player A calls showing the J♥J♦. The turn and river are low cards and you take the pot.

Problem 4-5

Table layout:

UTG	Player A $21.90	
MP	Player B $25.00	
CO	You $42.20	
BTN	Player C $25.00	C's HUD Player C / (16) / -2 VP 25 / PF 20 / AS 20 / FB 100 3B 0 / F3 na / AF 2 / 2.5 / 1 / na CB 50 / FC 50 / FT na W$F 50 / WtS 33 / W$S 0
SB	Player D $25.45	
BB	Player E $31.15	

Situation: Online $25 NL 6-max table. Blinds are $0.10/$0.25.

Your hand: A♥Q♥

Action to you: The first two players fold.

Question: *What do you do?*
   Answer: It's a routine raise of anything from three to four big blinds, which here is $0.75 to $1.

Action: You raise to $0.75. Player C on the button 3-bets to $2 and the blinds fold.

Question: *What do you do?*

 Answer: Three-bets in micro-stakes games should raise a big red caution flag. Light 3-betting with weaker hands is commonplace in high stakes games and even somewhat common in small stakes games. But at micro-stakes, light 3-betting is rare and three bets generally mean an extremely strong hand, and here are the typical 3-betting ranges you're likely to see:

- Super-tight: AA, KK, and AK (2% of all hands).

- Tight: AA through JJ and AK (3% of all hands).

- Moderately tight: AA through 99, AK, and AQ (5% of all hands).

You don't have enough data on Player C to even hazard a guess as to what range he might be using, and even though your holding of an ace and a queen does change the distribution of his hands within each range, you're still in trouble. Using PokerStove, we can look at your current winning chances against each range:

- Against the super-tight 2% range, you're 28 percent.

- Against the tight 3% range, you're 32 percent.

- Against the merely moderately tight range, you're 39 percent.

These numbers, of course, are simply a calculation of your winning chances if the hands are dealt to showdown.

Since you're out of position throughout the hand, and your ace-queen is often dominated, your real situation is somewhat worse than these numbers imply.

If we averaged all three ranges together, we'd arrive at 33 percent chance of winning, and I don't like calling preflop out of position with less than a 40 percent chance, so I would fold here. As a general rule, ace-queen, even suited, is not a good hand for calling a 3-bet in a micro-stakes game.

Action: You call for another $1.25 and the pot is now $4.75.

Flop: A♦K♦J♦

Question: *What should you do?* You now have top pair plus a gutshot straight draw. *Was that a good flop for you?*
Answer: Actually, it's a disaster. Take a look:

- The super-tight range has now made either a set of aces, a set of kings, or top two pair. Against that range, you're a 5-to-1 underdog. (You're only doing that well because of the gutshot draw. If we substitute the 9♦ for the J♦ on the flop, you drop to a 19-to-1 underdog!)

- The merely tight range has done almost as well. The pairs of aces, kings, and jacks have all made sets, while ace-king has again made top two pair. You're only beating a pair of queens, but two of the three available queen-queen combinations contain the Q♦, so they're drawing to the nut flush. Overall, you're now a 3-to-1 underdog.

- You're doing much better against the moderately tight range. Not only are you beating the pairs of tens or nines, but there are more of those combinations because so many high cards are accounted for. Again, however, any hand with the Q♦, T♦, or 9♦ is drawing to a flush or a straight flush! Overall, you're a 5-to-4 underdog against this range.

I would check and fold to a bet.

Action: You check and Player C bets $1.

Question: *What do you do?*
    Answer: Unexpected micro-stakes action! We were ready to fold, but now Player C bets so little we're getting good odds to call. We're only a 5-to-1 underdog in the worst case, and the pot is now $5.75 so we're getting almost 6-to-1 to call, plus we have our gutshot draw.
    Most likely this is a "suck bet" from a big hand. (A suck bet is a tiny bet designed to lure more money into the pot.) But we can't be sure, and the odds are compelling. So call.

Action: You call $1 and the pot is now $6.75.

Turn: 7♦

Question: *What do you do?*
    Answer: Our situation just got worse since any hand with a diamond just made a flush. We're now a 7-to-3 underdog even against the moderately tight range (which contains several diamonds) and worse against the others. Check again and be prepared to fold.

Action: You check and Player C bets $1.

Question: *What do you do?*
    Answer: It's now hard to believe this is anything other than a suck bet. You're extremely unlikely to have the best hand

and a raise is pointless because we can't make any better hand fold. Time to go away despite the odds.

Action: You fold.

Problem 4-6

Table layout:

UTG	Player A $10.90	
MP	Player B $24.20	B's HUD Player B / (88) / -2 VP 25 / PF 10 / AS 20 / FB 60 3B 3 / F3 75 / AF 1.5 / 1.5 / 1.5 / 1 CB 50 / FC 55 / FT 60 W$F 45 / WtS 25 / W$S 48 *Notes: LFC=1/4, LC=A2s,33*
CO	Player C $27.10	
BTN	You $36.50	Your HUD VP 22 / PF 17
SB	Player D $18.00	
BB	Player E $27.30	

Situation: Online $25 NL 6-max table. Blinds are $0.10/$0.25

Your hand: Q♥Q♣

Action to you: The first player folds. Player B limps for $0.25 and Player C folds.

Question: *What do you do?*

Answer: 'Raise' is the right action but the wrong answer. Of course you're going to raise, but the first thing you want to do is mentally assign him a preflop range. Once the flop arrives, it's too tempting to give him a range based on the flop and his action, and that range may be highly biased and inaccurate. Instead, let's stop now and think about his range, then remember what we thought when the flop comes. That's a good pattern, and it will save us from a lot of mistakes later in the hand.

From his VP$IP/PFR numbers of 25 and 10, we can see that he's a loose-passive player, but not absurdly bad. He likes to limp with a lot of hands preflop, and when raised he'll mostly call and take a look at the flop. Furthermore, we were lucky enough to see a couple of his limp/call hands that actually went to showdown. They included a low suited ace and a low pair, the sort of hands we expect a loose passive player to play. He sees they have some value, and he wants to look at a flop and see if he can hit a big hand. But he doesn't realize that he's probably not getting the implied odds to play these hands after a raise, so odds in general likely aren't his strong suit.

If his limp/calling range includes low pairs and medium-to-low suited aces, it probably also includes hands like suited connectors, unsuited connectors, and suited one-gappers. Those are the kinds of hands that loose-passive players generally use to see cheap flops. So let's go ahead and assign him the following range:

Suited aces: A9s through A2s (32 hands)
Pairs: 66 through 22 (30 hands)
Suited connectors: JTs through 54s (28 hands)
Suited one-gappers: J9s through 64s (24 hands)
Offsuit connectors: JT through 54 (84 hands)

That range includes 198 hands, almost 15 percent of the deck. It's a good estimate for three reasons:

1. It's about equal to the gap between the percentage of hands he plays (25%) and the percentage of hands he raises (10%).

2. We've noted that he eventually calls most of the hands where he first limps.

3. We've seen him limp and call with a small pair. If the small pairs are in his limping range, then his preflop raising range has to include a lot of the Broadway cards to get as high as 10 percent. Therefore, those hands aren't in his limping range and need to be omitted.

So our first goal is accomplished. We've assigned him a limping/calling range and we'll stick with it until we have new evidence to the contrary. Now on to the next step. We have a premium hand and want to raise.

Question: *How much should we raise?*
Answer: A good rule of thumb is to raise three times the big blind plus one extra big blind for every limper. Depending on the player and the table, you could raise a bit more than this if you wanted. In this case, we'll raise to $1 (four big blinds.) If the blinds fold, we fully expect to get called.

Action: We raise to $1 and the blinds fold. Player B calls and the pot is now $2.35.

Flop: K♥8♠4♦

Action: Player B checks.

Question: *What's our best line?*

Answer: If our assessment of his range is accurate, we're now crushing it. Of the 198 hands we put in his range, only three are now ahead of us — the three combinations that make a pair of fours (4♠4♥, 4♠4♣, 4♥4♣) and now give him a set. We're ahead of all the others.

Note that when we made up his limping/calling range, we didn't have any kings in it. That's a reasonable assumption given his statistics. We think he'd be raising with his big kings, like ace-king, king-queen, and probably king-jack, and folding the weaker kings. Some players, when the flop comes, start second-guessing their preflop estimates. (*"Gee, maybe he does have some kings in his range. Maybe he could have called with king-ten or king-nine. My queens might not be good here, better play for pot control."*) We're going to avoid making that mistake. We're not going to revise our estimates until he gives us some concrete evidence we were wrong. Until then, it's his range and we're sticking to it.

We have two lines here. We can simply bet for value because we think we have the best hand despite the overcard on board, or we can check, hoping to either induce a bluff on a later street or hoping Player B catches up enough to put in some money that he wouldn't put in now. Which is better?

In a higher-stakes game, the idea of checking behind to induce a bluff on the turn would have some merit. Higher-stakes players are more aggressive and would be tempted by the idea of taking the pot away. Good higher-stakes players, however, would be a little suspicious that we raised preflop but didn't follow through with a continuation bet on a dry board that practically calls out for such a bet. They would also most likely be using a HUD and they'd check our c-bet number. If that was high, they'd smell a rat and decide this perhaps wasn't the best spot to bluff.

In this game, the check behind is a little too clever. Loose-passive players in micro-stakes don't lose a lot of money by being overly aggressive; they lose money by calling with hands that rate to be worse because they love seeing showdowns when they actually have something. You exploit that by betting when you have them beaten, hoping they actually have enough of the flop to justify a call.

Based on the range we assigned, we will likely get calls from small pairs, ace-eight or ace-four suited, nine-eight or eight-seven suited or unsuited, ten-eight suited, eight-six suited, five-four suited or unsuited, and six-four suited, all of which now have a made pair. That's a total of 67 hands, more than a third of his range, all of which we're crushing.

Betting has some additional value in that we're charging the suited aces to draw. While they don't have a lot of outs (only the remaining three aces), we won't be able to chase them off the hand if they hit. Most micro-stakes players simply won't fold a pair of aces even if they suspect they are behind.

Action: We bet $1.90 and Player B calls. The pot is now $6.15.

Turn: 7♥

Action: Player B checks.

Question: *What do we do?*
    Answer: Not much has changed although eight-seven is now ahead of us. Again, we should keep trying to extract value and bet.

Action: We bet $5.00 and Player B folds.

Problem 4-7

Table layout:

UTG	Player A $10.00	
MP	Player B $14.10	
CO	Player C $8.20	C's HUD Player C / (52) / -4 VP 33 / PF 8 / AS 15 / FB 50 3B 2 / F3 66 / AF 1 / 1 / 1 / 0.5 CB 50 / FC 40 / FT 55 W$F 42 / WtS 30 / W$S 43
BTN	Player D $7.60	
SB	Player E $8.40	E's HUD Player E / (30) / -12 VP 40 / PF 6 / AS 16 / FB 40 3B 0 / F3 na / AF 1.2 / 1.6 / 0.8 / 0.4 CB 33 / FC 45 / FT 45 W$F 44 / WtS 28 / W$S 40
BB	You $13.50	

Situation: Online $10 NL 6-max table. Blinds are $0.05/$0.10.

Your hand: A♥Q♠

Action: The first two players fold. Player C calls $0.10 and the button folds. Player E in the small blind calls $0.05 and the pot is $0.30.

Question: *What do you do?*

> **Answer:** Your hand is more than good enough to raise two limpers with loose-passive statistics. A pot-sized raise would be another $0.30, but against two players who tend to call a lot you should raise more than that, although not too much more. Therefore, I would raise between $0.40 and $0.50.

Action: You raise to $0.50. Player C calls and the small blind folds. The pot is $1.10.

Flop: A♣K♠7♣

Question: *What do you do?*

> **Answer:** You have top pair, good kicker, and you're ahead of most of his range. Furthermore, since his range contains lots of weak aces and kings, you're in an excellent spot to win a big pot as a player who calls as much as Player C does will have a hard time folding top pair or maybe even middle pair.
>
> Therefore, a good bet size here is about $0.60. That's small enough so that he might stick around and see another card with a low pair, but still large enough to make his call incorrect for many of the hands that you hope he will call with.

Action: You bet $0.50 and Player C calls. The pot is $2.10.

Turn: 2♣

Question: *What do you do?*

> **Answer:** Our work on ranges back in "Part Three: Ranges and Distributions" now comes in handy. We know from those examples that a loose caller playing with a relatively wide range will have a flush draw about 5 percent of the time when the flop contains a two-flush. We can also be pretty sure our

opponent would have called with a flush draw, so there's now some chance his draw hit and we're beaten, but it's a relatively small one. More likely, we were ahead on the flop and still ahead on the turn.

With that in mind, we're going to bet, and probably $1 is a good amount to keep most of the weaker pairs in the pot. Note one crucial point: if we get raised, we're going to lay our hand down. Raises on the turn and river from loose-passive players nearly always represent a big hand, certainly a hand that's beating top pair, good kicker. Understanding this simple fact is crucial to beating micro-stakes games for decisive amounts. Our opponents in these games will tell us when we're beaten, but, as previous mentioned, *we must be listening.*

Action: You bet $1 and Player C calls. The pot is $4.10 and the effective stack is $6.20.

River: 4♦

Question: *What do you do?*
Answer: Many players are tempted to exercise pot control and shut down on the river with a single pair, but you shouldn't be here. Your opponent has given no sign that you're beaten, and unless he's been playing with exactly a pair of fours or ace-four (probably suited), then you're still ahead of him. He probably has something like ace-x or a good king and you want him to call you with those hands. But a large bet might let him fold, so bet something like $2 to $3 and see what happens.

Action: You bet $2.50. He calls and shows the A♥8♥, and you take the pot.

Your river bet was a typical good value bet at micro-stakes. Your hand wasn't a powerhouse and could have been beaten, but his actions indicated you were still all right. These sorts of river bets arise frequently in micro-stakes games, and you need to be prepared to exploit them.

Problem 4-8

Table layout:

UTG	Player A $9.20	
MP	Player B $9.20	B's HUD Player B / (121) / -4 VP 38 / PF 5 / AS 15 / FB 55 3B 0 / F3 na / AF 1 / 1.3 / 0.7 / 0 CB 40 / FC 30 / FT 50 W$F 47 / WtS 30 / W$S 40
CO	Player C $9.40	C's HUD Player C / (105) / -6 VP 42 / PF 11 / AS 16 / FB 60 3B 3 / F3 50 / AF 0.5 / 0.8 / 0.4 / 0.5 CB 50 / FC 20 / FT 55 W$F 45 / WtS 32 / W$S 38
BTN	Player D $6.90	
SB	Player E $10.20	E's HUD Player E / (94) / -2 VP 52 / PF 8 / AS 20 / FB 48 3B 0 / F3 na / AF 0.8 / 1 / 0.5 / 0 CB 0 / FC 40 / FT 40 W$F 48 / WtS 28 / W$S 44
BB	You $16.30	

Situation: Online $10 NL 6-max table. Blinds are $0.05/$0.10.

Your hand: A♥A♣

Action to you: The first player folds. Player B limps for $0.10 and Player C calls. Player D folds but the small blind calls another $0.05. The pot is $0.40.

Question: *What do you do?*
    Answer: Obviously, you'll raise. If you have any thought of trying to trap three players with aces in a low stakes game, forget about it. With a premium pair, your ideal scenario is to be heads-up against one player on the flop. The issue here is exactly how much to raise to get that one opponent.
    The standard guideline for raising when players have limped into the pot is to raise three or four big blinds, plus one extra big blind for each limper. In this case you have three limpers, so that rule would have you raising to $0.60 or $0.70. In this situation with three opponents that fit the loose-passive category, you can even raise a bit more than this and expect to get a caller. A raise to about $1.00 is completely reasonable.

Action: You raise to $1.10. Player B folds. Player C calls. And Player E folds. The pot is now $2.40 and the effective stack is now $8.30.

Flop: T♦8♣2♣

Question: *What do you do?*
    Answer: First we evaluate the board and see that it allows a flush draw in clubs as well as a few straight draws. With VP$IP and PFR numbers of 42/11, our opponent has an extremely wide calling range. Remembering our work on distributions in "Part Three: Ranges and Distributions," we can make a good estimate that about 10 percent of his hands are now draws. In addition, he has a 3 to 4 percent possibility

of a set or two-pair. (Only ten-eight is in his calling range; we can safely exclude ten-deuce and eight-deuce.)

So the right play is to bet. Right now we're a big favorite, and given his post-flop statistics, especially the low 'fold to c-bet' number, there's an excellent chance that we'll get called if he has a pair. Even if he doesn't have a pair or a draw, there's also a good chance we can get called if he has two overcards to the board.

In addition, our bet should be big enough to give us a chance to get his stack in by the river, but that shouldn't be hard given his low stack size. Therefore, I'd bet between one-half and two-thirds of the pot, somewhere between $1.20 and $1.60.

Action: You bet $1.20 and Player C calls. The pot is now $4.80 and the effective stack is $7.10.

Turn: Q♠

Question: *What do you do?*

Answer: Since he didn't raise preflop, it's very unlikely this card gave him a set of queens. If he holds exactly jack-nine, he made a straight, but that's also unlikely. Therefore, we should continue betting for value and a bet of $2.40 will, if he calls, create a pot of $9.60, and leave him with a stack of $4.70. If he has something, he should feel the need to call a river all-in getting about 3-to-1 odds.

Action: You bet $2.40 and Player C calls $2.40. The pot is now $9.60.

River: 2♠

That's a good river card as it's not likely our opponent has a deuce in his hand, and the pair on the board allows us to move ahead of hands like QT and T8. We don't think he has those hands since loose-passive players will typically raise on the flop or turn with a hand that strong. Still, it was a possibility, and one we now don't have to worry about. Hence, it's time to move all-in and see what's going on.

Action: We move all-in and Player C calls with his last $4.70 and shows the Q♥J♥. We take the pot.

He limped and then called us preflop with a suited queen-jack, called on the flop with overcards and a gutshot straight draw, and then called off his whole stack with top pair, good kicker, all pretty standard for a wide class of micro-stakes players. This hand is a textbook example of value-betting at these stakes. We should also make a note that he was willing to call off his stack with top pair, good kicker.

Problem 4-9

Table layout:

UTG	Player A $7.00	A's HUD Player A / (26) / +1 VP 54 / PF 31 / AS 63 / FB 33 3B 0 / F3 na / AF 4.5 / inf / 2 / inf CB 50 / FC 100 / FT na W$F 30 / WtS 20 / W$S 0 *Note: Flop: bets, will fold to raise (2).* *Turn: bet/fold=1.*
MP	Player B $8.90	B's HUD Player B / (94) / +9 VP 39 / PF 0 / AS 0 / FB 75 3B 0 / F3 0 / AF 1.7 / 1 / 2 / 8 CB na / FC 50 / FT 67 W$F 41 / WtS 29 / W$S 58 *Note: PF: limp=KK,JJ.*
CO	Player C $5.80	C's HUD Player C / (3) / -33 VP 33 / PF 0 / AS na / FB 100 3B 0 / F3 na / AF na / na / na / na
BTN	You $19.10	Your HUD You / (91) / +45 VP 18 / PF 14 / AS 25 / FB 100 3B 0 / F3 100 / AF 2.3 / 5 / 2 / 1
SB	Player D $10.80	

		E's HUD
BB	Player E $4.20	Player E / (26) / +5 VP 35 / PF 23 / AS 42 / FB 100 3B 0 / F3 na / AF 7 / inf / 2 / inf CB 50 / FC na / FT na W$F 50 / WtS 13 / W$S 100

Situation: Online $10 NL 6-max table. Blinds are $0.05/$0.10.

Your hand: J♥T♠

Action to you: Player A raises to $0.30 and the next two players call. The pot is $1.05.

Question: *What do you do?*

>**Question:** You have position and you're getting nice odds, so it's worth taking a cheap flop and seeing what happens.

>You're also up against a nice mix of opponents with obvious and exploitable flaws. Player A is relentlessly aggressive and keeps betting as long as he encounters calls rather than raises. He thinks every call represents weakness and assumes the pot is still winnable. He's had mixed results this session but hasn't slowed down yet.

>Player B calls frequently preflop but absolutely never raises. So far you've seen him limp with a pair of kings and a pair of jacks. His post-flop aggression pattern is very unusual, with minimal aggression on the flop increasing to high aggression on the river.

>As for Player C, we don't yet have enough information to make a judgment.

Action: You call. The small blind folds and the big blind calls $0.20. The pot is now $1.55.

The big blind, another very aggressive player, is now also in the mix.

Flop: J♦8♥6♠

Action: The big blind checks. Player A bets $0.50 and the next two players fold. The pot is now $2.05.

Question: *What do you do?*

Answer: Player A's range, even under the gun, is wide, and his flop aggression is infinite so far meaning if he plays the flop he's always betting, never calling. It's possible the presence of four other players in the hand would slow him down, but it might not. You have top pair with middling kicker, a holding which beats the large majority of his range, so it's certainly worth a call.

Question: *Should you raise?*

Answer: You don't really have a raising hand, and you certainly don't have a raising hand against this player. So far you've twice seen him bet the flop and fold to a raise, and the same on the turn. If he's betting with nothing, it's likely he'll fold again to a raise, but bet again on the turn and perhaps the river if you just call.

The other argument for just calling is to wait and see what the big blind will do. He's aggressive as well and from his statistics, his aggression seems similar to Player A, so he'll likely go away at this point unless he has a real hand. Let's wait and see what he does.

Action: You call the $0.50 and the big blind folds. The pot is now $3.05.

Turn: 2♥

Action: Player A bets $0.80.

Question: *What do you do?*
   Answer: The turn didn't change anything. Once again, a call may keep him betting with nothing while a raise will chase away the hands you beat. Call and be prepared to call pretty much anything on the river.

Action: You call $0.80. The pot is now $4.65.

River: 2♣

Action: Player A bets $2.10.

Question: *What do you do?*
   Answer: Any overcard to the jack would have been worrisome, but the 2♣ is a great card. From what you know of your opponent, he could have bet this way with a few hands that beat you, and a lot of hands that don't. Call and see what happens.
   Again, raising makes no sense. He's unlikely to call your raise with any hand that you beat, and he won't fold any hand that beats you.

Action: You call. He shows the A♠9♠ for ace-high, and you take the pot.

   This hand is a textbook example of how to exploit a large class of micro-stakes players who believe they can push anyone out of a pot who isn't willing to raise somewhere along the way. Be prepared to go all the way against them with any hand as good as top pair, medium kicker.

Problem 4-10

Table layout:

UTG	Player A $14.60	
MP	Player B $22.10	B's HUD Player B / (56) / -3 VP 48 / PF 10 / AS 16 / FB 60 3B 0 / F3 na / AF 1.3 / 1.5 / 1 / 0.5 CB 33 / FC 50 / FT 66 W$F 40 / WtS 25 / W$S 33
CO	Player C $33.40	
BTN	Player D $28.20	D's HUD Player D / (94) / +6 VP 22 / PF 16 / AS 38 / FB 60 3B 6 / F3 70 / AF 2 / 3 / 1 / 1 CB 75 / FC 70 / FT 60 W$F 45 / WtS 22 / W$S 53
SB	Player E $12.00	
BB	You $34.90	

Situation: Online $25 NL 6-max table. Blinds are $0.10/$0.25.

Your hand: K♠9♠

Action to you: The first player folds. Player B limps for $0.25 and Player C folds. Player D raises to $1 and the small blind folds. The pot is $1.60.

Question: *What do you do?*

    Answer: From his numbers, Player B seems to be a typical loose-passive player. He limps and then gets raised by Player D who looks like a competent player at these stakes and who may have a real hand or is he just making an isolation raise?

    We can't know for sure, but there's a large possibility that he's simply making a move with a wide range, in which case we should 3-bet with a wide range (but not as wide as his) and show an immediate profit. His 'attempt to steal' number is 38 percent, so our best guess for his current range is probably a little less than that. Therefore, I like 3-betting with a range of between 15 and 20 percent depending on what I know about this player, and king-nine suited easily fits this criterion.

Action: You 3-bet to $3. Player B folds and after some hesitation, Player D folds as well.

    You should make a note that Mr. D will make an isolation raise in position with a wide range of hands.

Problem 4-11

Table layout:

UTG	Player A $12.30	
MP	Player B $9.20	
CO	You $14.40	Your HUD VP 20 / PF 17
BTN	Player C $4.70	
SB	Player D $5.40	
BB	Player E $13.50	E's HUD Player E / (36) / +6 VP 23 / PF 4 / AS 8 / FB 65 3B 0 / F3 na / AF 1.2 / 1 / 0.7 / 0.3 CB 40 / FC 60 / FT 50 W$F 43 / WtS 30 / W$S 44 *Notes: PF: Raise UTG=TT.*

Situation: Online $10 NL 6-max table. Blinds are $0.05/$0.10.

Your hand: 9♠9♦

Action to you: The first two players fold.

Question: *What do you do?*

Answer: Your hand is certainly good enough to raise from the cutoff, and you have no reason to do anything else.

Action: You raise to $0.35 and the button and small blind fold. The big blind calls and the pot is $0.75.

Flop: 7♥5♠2♣

Action: The big blind checks.

Question: *What do you do?*
   Answer: You took the lead preflop and now have an overpair to the board. There's no reason to think you're not best at this point, and a lot of overcards to your nines could come on the turn, so you should just fire out a value bet.

Action: You bet $0.55 and the big blind raises to $1.60.

Question: *What do you do?*
   Answer: Check-raises at micro-stakes are rare and usually indicate a big hand. At this point you should go back and take a fresh look at the big blind's statistics. As we do, a number of points should pop out:

1.   Only 36 hands so far, not enough data to be confident, but enough to be suggestive.

2.   The VP$IP-to-PFR ratio is pretty high, almost 6-to-1. Player E doesn't like to raise preflop, but he does like to play pots.

3.   His 3-bet number is zero. With only 36 hands, that could just mean he hasn't seen a good 3-betting situation yet. Combined with his PFR number, however, it starts to indicate that Player E likes calling with a big hand more that raising with it.

4. His aggression factor numbers are low across the board, pointing to a player who doesn't spend a lot of time trying to steal pots with weak hands.

All these points suggest that he has the hand he is representing, either a set, a better overpair than ours, or perhaps two-pair. A point worth noting is that players in micro-stakes games with low preflop-raise numbers won't always have a range that represents the best hands available. You might assume, for instance, that a 4 percent raising range looks like this:

AA through TT, AKs, AKo, AQs

Instead, however, it might well look like this:

QQ through 88, AQs, AQo, AJs

Both ranges represent 3.8 percent of the possible hands, but the second range will appeal to a somewhat cagier super-tight player because it's trickier. By holding his best hands in reserve, he's ready to spring some traps after the flop.

Therefore, in micro-stakes play, our most reliable rule of thumb is that unexpected post-flop aggression from otherwise passive players usually means a big hand. None of Player E's numbers contradict this idea, so just let this hand go. His range here most likely consists of just five hands:

AA, KK, 77, 55, and 22

and against that range you're about a 9-to-1 underdog, so no pot odds can save you. Fold.

Action: You call the $1.60. The pot is now $3.95 and the effective stack is $11.55.

Turn: 9♥

Action: The big blind bets $3.

Question: *What do you do?*

    Answer: That very lucky turn card has given you top set, and now the only question is how to get the rest of your stack in the center. (Note that eight-six is the nuts, but given how this hand has been played, it's a very unlikely holding.) The pot is now $6.95 and the big blind has $8.55 left in his stack, and if our assumptions about his range are correct, we can assume that he will call an all-in at this point, so that's what we should do. Just calling allows the possibility that a river card could come that would allow him to lay his hand down. For example, if he's been playing with a pair of kings, an ace on the river might scare him off the hand. That's a long shot, but we might as well play accurately and eliminate the possibility.

Action: You move all-in and Player E calls. The river card is the Q♣. Player E shows the A♦A♠ and you take the pot.

    You should make two notes: Player E only called with a pair of aces preflop, and he check-raised the flop with an overpair. We now have some solid evidence that Player E plays a wide range but slow-plays the top of that range, and we need to get that information down.

Problem 4-12

Table layout:

UTG	Player A $14.00	
MP	Player B $18.70	B's HUD Player B / (40) / -6 VP 70 / PF 6 / AS 18 / FB 50 3B 0 / F3 na / AF 0.7 / 1 / 0.5 / 0.3 CB 33 / FC 50 / FT 50 W$F 44 / WtS 30 / W$S 41
CO	Player C $4.40	C's HUD Player C / (22) / -20 VP 52 / PF 10 / AS 22 / FB 33 3B 0 / F3 50 / AF 1.4 / 1.8 / 1 / 0.2 CB 40 / FC 60 / FT 50 W$F 38 / WtS 27 / W$S 33
BTN	You $12.30	
SB	Player D $7.90	
BB	Player E $10.10	

Situation: Online $10 NL 6-max table. Blinds are $0.05/$0.10.

Your hand: A♠K♠

Action to you: The first player folds. Player B and the cutoff both call $0.10. The pot is now $0.35.

Question: *What do you do?*

  Answer: You have a strong hand so of course you want to raise. Our normal rule for raising limpers is to raise to three to four big blinds plus one big blind for each limper, which would indicate a raise of $0.50 to $0.60. But you're against two loose passive players and when against players who like to call this much, I'd raise the higher amount.

Action: You raise to $0.60. The blinds fold and both Player B and Player C call. The pot is now $1.95.

Flop: A♣7♦2♣

Action: Both players check to you.

Question: *What do you do?*

  Answer: You have top pair top kicker on a two-tone board which is a fine hand against these two. Go ahead and bet a little over half the pot. With very loose players, it's likely at least one will stay with you.

Action: You bet $1.20. Player B calls and Player C folds. The pot is now $4.35 and the effective stack is $10.50.

Turn: 8♥

Action: Player B checks.

Question: *What do you do?*

  Answer: Again, there is no reason to believe you are beaten, so bet again for value, and around half the pot is the right amount. Making a large bet (say about the size of the pot) is a serious mistake against opponents such as Player B. They will fold a lot of the hands you are beating to a big bet, but will call a more modest bet with those same hands. Of course, if he has a hand that beats you, he's not folding to any bet.

Question: *Is there a case to be made here for pot control?*

Answer: The 'big hand, big pot; small hand, small pot' principle indicates that perhaps by betting we're building too big a pot with just top pair. Should we check behind instead?

The answer is no: We should continue to bet. Against the sort of weak loose passive players we encounter in micro-stakes games, top pair, top kicker isn't a small hand. These players are willing to call to the river with weaker pairs, and we want that money. In a high-stakes game or even many small-stakes games, checking and playing for one more small bet on the river would be a reasonable line, but here it's too conservative and leaves too much money on the table.

Action: You bet $2.20 and Player B check-raises you to $4.40.

Question: *What do you do?*

Answer: You fold. Loose-passive players will tell you when you're beaten, and this is what "I have you beaten" sounds like: the min-check-raise. Player B has a set or two pair, and you're toast. Being able to fold top pair here will save you a huge amount of money over the long run in micro-stakes games and ensure that your overall expectation is quite positive.

Action: You fold.

Problem 4-13

Table layout:

UTG	Player A $17.30	
MP	Player B $25.00	
CO	Player C Sitting out	
BTN	Player D $23.85	
SB	Player E $47.05	E's HUD Player E / (9) / +630 VP 62 / PF 0 / AS 0 / FB 100 3B 0 / F3 0 / AF 0.8 / 1 / 0.5 / na CB na / FC 50 / FT na W$F 33 / WtS 33 / W$S 100 *Note: PF: C 3B, AI=65s.*
BB	You $23.50	

Situation: Online $25 NL 6-max table. Blinds are $0.10/$0.25.

Your hand: A♠T♠

Action to you: It's folded to Player E in the small blind who calls $0.15.

Question: *What do you do?*

Answer: We're going to play the hand, but first we see what we know about our opponent. In only nine hands he's already way ahead as a result of just calling a 3-bet and a subsequent all-in against two players with six-five suited. He won the hand (the other two players had aces and kings) and hence his big stack. So we're up against a weak player who's been lucky so far.

Player E's range is extremely wide, and your hand is ahead of most of that range. Against a 60 percent range, for instance, your hand is a 62-to-38 favorite. In addition, you'll have position after the flop. So you should raise.

Question: *How much should you raise?*

Answer: A pot-sized raise would be $0.50. Your hand is pretty good for the situation, so at micro-stakes I would normally raise a little more than that, perhaps to $0.75. The weaker fields in micro-stakes games enable you to bet a little more when you stand well, a little less when you stand poorly. And against a player who will call a 3-bet with six-five suited, you're entitled to raise even more with a good hand, but not so much that you actually chase him away. The optimal raise size is probably about $1.00.

Action: You raise to $0.75 and Player E calls. The pot is now $1.50.

Flop: Q♥Q♣8♣

Action: Player E checks.

Question: *What do you do?*

Answer: In a higher-stakes game against a better opponent, I would recommend checking for pot control. Relative to the preflop situation, your hand is now weaker. It's still only ace-high and your chance at a spade draw has gone away. You have a small hand, so you should want to play a small pot.

However, against this opponent, you're probably still best, and it's not likely that he knows how to pressure you or that he'll bluff with nothing. Since Player E checked, it's reasonable to keep building the pot.

Action: You bet $0.75 and Player E calls. The pot is now $3.00.

Turn: 6♥

Action: Player E checks.

Question: *What do you do?*
   Answer: The situation hasn't changed except you're now less of a favorite since he might have a six in his hand. Therefore, I would still bet a small amount, but the argument for checking is a little stronger.

Action: You bet $1.00 and Player E calls. The pot is now $5.00.

River: K♣

Action: Player E mucks his hand and you win the pot.

This is a hand you might have lost at a stronger table, but in the micro-stakes world you were still able to play it for profit.

Problem 4-14

Table layout:

UTG	Player A $2.35	A's HUD Player A / (22) / -230 VP 18 / PF 9 / AS 29 / FB na 3B 0 / F3 100 / AF 1.0 / 1 / 1 / inf CB 100 / FC na / FT na W$F 0 / WtS 67 / W$S 0
MP	Player B $5.70	B's HUD Player B / (20) / +33 VP 20 / PF 15 / AS 33 / FB 100 3B 14 / F3 100 / AF inf / inf / inf / na CB 100 / FC na / FT na W$F 0 / WtS 0 / W$S na
CO	Player C $8.75	
BTN	You $13.30	Your HUD Player C / (49) / +32 VP 27 / PF 20 / AS 75 / FB 67 3B 13 / F3 100 / AF 1.8 / 1 / 5 / 1
SB	Player D $5.15	
BB	Player E $7.50	

Situation: Online $5 NL 6-max table. Blinds are $0.02/$0.05.

Your hand: Q♣Q♠

Action: Player A raises to $0.20. Player B calls and Player C folds. The pot is $0.47.

Question: *What do you do?*
    Answer: A pair of queens is a hand that in micro-stakes play you'll get all your money in preflop. The only exception occurs if your opponent is a super-nit, in which case you just might be able to get away from it. However, that's not the case here: both your opponents are tight but not super-tight.
    A normal 3-bet here would be to something like $0.80. If Player A then calls, the pot becomes $1.87 and his stack shrinks to $1.55, so he's more or less committing himself to the pot (although he may not know this.)
    Therefore, a better play is to raise to $2.50 right away, putting Player A all-in (if he calls). Micro-stakes players are used to seeing these 'Johnny All-In' moves, and they're aware that these plays are often semi-bluffs made with a relatively weak hand. Here it's likely that Player A has a hand good enough to call what might look to him like a bluff. As for Player B, his preflop call indicates a less than premium hand, and if he sees an all-in and a call in front of him, he'll figure that someone has a real hand and go away.

Action: You raise to $2.50. The blinds fold, Player A calls for his last $2.15, and Player B folds. Player A shows the Q♥9♠, the board comes the J♣8♠4♣A♥8♦, and you take the pot.

    Why did Player A call with queen-nine offsuit? It's micro-stakes and these things happen.

Part Five

Beating
Small Stakes Games

Beating
Small Stakes Games

Introduction: Moving Up

Most players who become steady winners in the micro-stakes games will, at some point, want to move up and try their luck in the small stakes games. In this book, we're defining "small stakes" as three specific levels of 6-max play: $50 NL ($0.25 and $0.50 blinds), $100 NL ($0.50 and $1 blinds), and $200 NL ($1 and $2 blinds). These divisions are arbitrary to some extent, but are based on our play at these levels and the surrounding ones. The gap between $25 NL and $50 NL, and the gap between $200 NL and $400 NL, seemed noticeably larger than the gaps between $50 NL, $100 NL, and $200 NL. It makes sense, then, to separate these middle three levels and refer to them as "small stakes" play.

Moving from micro-stakes to small stakes isn't an easy task for most players. At the beginning of our micro-stakes chapter, we talked about the difference between offensive and defensive poker. Offensive poker is what makes you a winner at micro-stakes, and it's a very straightforward style of play, easy to learn and master. You play good hands, you bet good hands, and you bet them strongly. The better your hand, the more you bet. If you're just starting out, you can win playing tight offensive poker, and with more experience, you can play looser offensive poker and win even more.

Small stakes is different. Many of your opponents have traveled the same road you did, and they're capable of playing a tight, intelligent game as well. They'll use a HUD, they'll watch you play, and they'll think about what you're doing. You won't be able to bet every street with top pair, top kicker and expect them to call you down to the river with third pair "just to see what happens." To win at this level, you're going to have to start incorporating some defensive ideas into your repertoire. Your opponents won't be world-class players, but they will be thinking players. To beat them, you'll have to outthink them and play good poker.

The happy times when sound but mechanical play won the money are behind you. A new world awaits.

Adapting
to Small Stakes

We'll start our adaptation process by looking at some features of micro-stakes play and seeing how they change as we move into small stakes games. Some aspects will change a little, some will change a lot, and changes in some areas will greatly affect other areas.

Regard this section as an outline of the types of adjustments you'll need to make. Most topics will be covered thoroughly with examples later in the chapter. So let's start with the most general change, the mix of player types that you're likely to see, and move on from there.

Player Types

In our micro-stakes chapter we defined several player types that dominated the action. Let's meet them again and see how they change as we move up.

- **Johnny All-In.** Johnny was one of our all-time favorites, but unfortunately, we won't be seeing him any longer at these stakes. R.I.P.

- **Loose Lou.** Lou and his cousins, with their 40/2 or 65/5 VP$IP/PFR numbers, were our most profitable customers down below. We'll still see Lou because some players skip the micro-stakes altogether and just start playing where the stakes seem interesting. However, the hunters are out in force and the herd has been thinned. Whereas at micro-stakes you might sometimes see three or four Lous at a table, now a single sighting makes a good table, and two is cause for celebration. At this level, good players keep track of folks like Lou, so expect to see long waiting lists at Lou's table.

- *Aggro Al.* Like Lou, he still exists but in smaller numbers. He's also a bit harder to spot at first since many of the good aggressive players will push aggressively at pots when they smell weakness. After awhile, however, his 60/40 VP\$IP/PFR numbers will give him away. In addition, the other players will spot his tricks quickly, so he may not last long enough for you to bag his carcass.

- *Multi-Tabling Mike.* Mike is still here playing his 16 to 24 tables, and his mechanical 'ABC' style was easy to play against at lower stakes. But now you can expect the upgraded Mike to be more dangerous, able to vary his play, and even have a sense of what you're trying to do. Plus he's willing to work bluffs into his game, and he can even trap you on occasion. You're still happy to see Mike, but you'll need to be a little more cautious as you try to exploit him.

- *Regular Ron.* Ron has continued his education and morphed into Tight-Aggressive Ron. You'll see two or three versions of him at every table, and Ron will be a tough opponent. He'll be running a HUD, be thinking about what he's doing, and have acquired a lot of experience since his micro-stakes days. You'll have to work as hard to beat him as he'll work to beat you. Identify him by his VP\$IP/PFR statistics, which will converge pretty quickly to numbers in the 18/14 to 25/20 range. If you see three or four Rons at a table, you can be pretty sure that easy money will be hard to make. Prepare to move on to greener pastures.

In contrast to micro-stakes, the range of skills that you'll see at a small stakes table will be somewhat greater. Lou, Al, and their ilk won't be much different from their micro brethren, but Ron and players like him will be much better. When you're trying to exploit Lou and Al in a straightforward way, you'll now find that others players will see what you're doing, recognize it, and try to exploit you. When Lou limps and you raise for isolation, don't be surprised if you're 3-bet by someone behind you who knows what Lou is doing and also knows what you're doing.

HUD Statistics

The HUD statistics that we previously developed will serve you well at the small stakes. However, there are a couple of changes that will affect the statistics you'll want to collect:

1. In small stakes games, you'll see more aggression than you saw in micro-stakes games.

2. You have a smaller player pool, so you'll meet the same players more often. In addition, players will play longer sessions so you'll be collecting data faster and getting more meaningful data on actions that were too rare to matter at the micro-stakes.

In light of these developments, here are a few statistics you might consider adding to your HUD at these levels:

*   **4-bet:** We noted before that 3-bets were rare at micro-stakes and generally meant a strong range like queens or better or ace-king, while 4-bets were almost always aces or kings. At small stakes you'll start to see some light 3-betting, which in turn means you'll see some light 4-betting. So keeping 4-bet statistics will now start to be useful.

*   **Call preflop raise.** In micro-stakes games we generally inferred a calling range from a comparison of the VP$IP and PFR numbers. It would, however, be useful to collect the

number directly and now the data will accumulate fast enough to make the number meaningful.

- **Raise flop bet**. Continuation bets don't get raised much at micro-stakes. When they do get raised, it's almost always a big hand. At small stakes you'll start to see players raise continuation bets just as they might 3-bet an opening raise with a combination of value raises and bluffs. Collecting some data on the response to a continuation bet beyond the simple 'fold to c-bet' number is useful.

Let's note one other point about HUD statistics at higher stakes: While they show how your opponent plays, *on average*, they won't necessarily show how your opponent plays *against you*. Micro-stakes players will generally play a constant, mechanical game against anyone who happens to be in the hand with them. Higher-level players will adapt to specific opponents. For example, a player who, on average, 3-bets an 8 percent range might have concluded that, against you, that range should shrink to 3 percent. HUD statistics at small stakes are theoretically more useful because you have more information against each player, but practically a little less useful because you can't be sure how your opponent is reacting to you.

Table Selection

At micro-stakes, table selection wasn't really crucial. There were so many weak players and so many tables to choose from that even selecting tables purely at random would only have a small effect on your bottom line.

At small stakes, table selection starts to matter. At these levels, there are more tight, competent players than genuinely weak players, and fewer tables to choose among, so you're going to need to pay attention to the table composition as you decide where you'll sit.

We outlined the basics of table selection in "Part Two: Playing Online," and now would be a good time to review that section. Remember that you're looking for known weak players, a high number of players per flop, and a larger than usual pot size. At this level, you should also check for the absence of short stacks. At micro-stakes, short stacks were generally bad players and hence good for the table. At small stakes, too many short stack opponents playing an intelligent short stack strategy makes for a bad table.

Preflop Ranges and Actions

Our general advice for preflop opening raises is the set of 'Loose-Aggressive' ranges in the last section. One exception needs to be noted. Players at small stakes are more aware of position, and therefore seats where the player to your left is guaranteed absolute position after the flop are more dangerous. These seats are the cutoff and the small blind; if the action has been folded to you and you raise, the players who follow you will have absolute position in the hand if they choose to reraise. In these games, you'll get reraised more, and thus your cutoff and small blind ranges need to be a bit tighter.

In addition, isolation raises against limpers are more likely to be 3-bet by someone behind you who sees what you're doing. You still need to be on the attack, but tighten your range a bit and be ready to handle a loose 3-bet from behind.

Consistent with this, 3-bets and 4-bets are much more common. So you need to think out your raising ranges carefully so that you're prepared to respond in a balanced fashion.

Betting ranges will also need to be narrower because the very weak players with wide and easily exploitable ranges won't be able to advance to these levels. So be prepared to check for pot control more often and some of the automatic calls will become folds.

Your blind stealing range from the button doesn't need to change much. Players will, in fact, defend their blinds more often, but you won't need to tighten a lot because you still have the advantage of position. After the flop your opponents will still frequently hold weak hands, plus be out of position, so you can still make money even when they choose to defend.

Squeeze plays will start to appear. A squeeze play is a 3-bet after an opening raise and one or two calls. It's more effective than a straight 3-bet because the callers have announced some weakness (they didn't raise), while the initial raiser is squeezed because he can't be sure that the players behind him won't reraise. It's a rare play at micro-stakes where players will tend to call rather than 3-bet thinking they're getting good pot odds just to see the flop.

'Trouble hands' now require more caution. The classic trouble hands are Broadway hands that don't contain an ace, or ace-high hands lower than ace-queen. These are strong hands in the micros because they can get action from weaker hands which they dominate. At small stakes, the trouble hands are likely to be dominated if the betting action gets heavy.

Preflop implied odds are less at these stakes. Players are less likely to pay off with weak hands since they have some awareness of the 'big hand, big pot; small hand, small pot' concept.

General Post-Flop Tendencies

At these levels, the better players start to think seriously about the relationship between hand strength, pot size, and stack sizes. They recognize that hands like top pair or an overpair are good hands on the flop but not likely to be the best hand if play goes to the river and there has been serious action. The concept of 'small hand small pot' is well understood by many of the players at the table. They will grasp the idea of pot control and will try to check hands like medium pair and top pair, weak kicker after the flop hoping to see a cheap showdown.

At micro-stakes, players often checked post-flop because they only felt confident enough to bet monsters. (Hence when they did bet, you could put them on a big hand.) Here players are confident enough to bet non-monster hands, but they're also acutely aware of the dangers of being raised off hands, as well as the possibility of being trapped.

Flop Play

At small stakes, statistics will start to become more logically correlated. A player with a nitty preflop style, for instance, will now show a high continuation bet percentage. Since he only plays good hands preflop, he should continuation bet more. While at the micro-stakes, 'nitty' often meant 'afraid to get involved;' now it means 'selectively aggressive.'

In addition, continuation bets won't generally work as well as they did at micro-stakes. Everyone at the table now understands what a continuation bet represents. Thus they will not only call more often, they'll begin to raise or check-raise continuation bets, a move which would have hardly ever been seen at micro-stakes. You still need to be aggressive, but it will be necessary to dial back your continuation bet percentage a bit.

Floating (calling a bet without any hand) now has a purpose beyond a simple desire to see the next card. Floating becomes a strategy to take the hand away from the aggressor on the turn (or occasionally the river) by representing a monster that called the flop as a trap. Cheaper than a bluff-raise, it's often more effective.

Turn Play

A key area of correct strategy at micro-stakes was the insight that a big turn bet from a loose-passive opponent almost always meant a big hand, and armed with this knowledge, a good player with a top pair-type hand could save a big bet or two on the later streets. At small stakes this relationship doesn't hold as well. Players are now capable of bluffing, and a flop call followed by a big turn bet or raise could just be an elaborate bluff.

Pot control now becomes a driving concept here and on the river. Checking the turn no longer reliably means weakness. It could just be a pot control play with a good hand but not one that wants all the chips in by the river. Don't assume that a check is a missed draw or bottom pair.

Double-barreling increases in importance because your opponents are better. They're capable of floating, and they understand that a continuation bet followed by a check on the turn signals either a failed bluff or a pot control play; in either case the pot may be winnable.

River Play

At micro-stakes it was sufficient to bet the river only when it was pretty clear that we had the best hand — what's known as extracting "fat value." And since there was plenty of fat value to be had, there wasn't much need to try to profit from more marginal situations.

At higher stakes, however, we're going to need the profit that can come from analyzing these more marginal situations correctly — what's called betting for "thin value." Therefore, good hand-reading skills become more important since they help to identify those additional situations where your expectation is positive even if only by a little bit.

The river bluff will also need to become part of our repertoire. We need to know when to bluff, and how to defend against the bluff. At micro-stakes, only Aggro Al bothered to bluff the river, and because he overdid it, he was easy to pick off. Here we'll start to see good players who can bluff the river as part of a balanced strategy, and we'll need to counter them. We'll also need to develop the courage to spot good bluffing opportunities and take them.

Fancy Plays Start to Matter

Let's imagine that you're playing in a micro-stakes game. A straightforward, unimaginative player bets preflop and you call in the big blind with your suited connectors. The flop misses you and your opponent bets. You call, hoping to put a move on your opponent later. A king comes on the turn. "Perfect," you think. "I'll bet now representing a hand like king-queen and take down the pot." You bet and your opponent calls. Another king comes on the river and you bet again, hoping to represent a monster. Your opponent calls again and shows a pair of fours, a lowly underpair. "How could you call the river???" you type into the chat box. "I had two pair, kings and fours. I had to call," he types back.

You just fell victim to Fancy Play Syndrome, a dread disease often fatal at micro-stakes. You thought you had cleverly represented a big hand, big enough to chase your opponent away. Your opponent saw things a little differently: *I've got a pair, and pairs are hard to come by. Just think of all the times I've seen a flop and didn't even catch a pair! My hand might be best, and the only way to find out is to see the hand through. Who cares what your bet was supposed to represent? Most bets are bluffs anyway. Everybody knows that.*

You win at micro-stakes by value betting loose players, trapping super-aggressive players, and getting out of the way when a passive opponent says he has a big hand. But your small stakes opponents are also graduates of Micro-Stakes U. To beat them, you're going to have to enlarge your bag of tricks. You'll need to 3-bet light, set up the occasional multi-street bluff, and represent a scare card on the turn, among other things. Your opponents will usually understand what you're representing, and sometimes they'll have to get out of the way.

Defense
Starts to Matter

As we emphasized in "Part Four: Beating Micro-Stakes Games," micro-stakes no-limit hold 'em is usually a game of pure offense. Since your opponents mostly aren't paying attention, it's not necessary to be tricky or deceptive. For the most part, deceptive ideas like slowplaying simply cost you money that you might have won had you gone ahead and bet. Instead, you make the most money by just betting your good hands and folding your bad ones.

In small stakes games, many (but not all) of your opponents will be paying attention. As a result, you have to start playing defensive poker. At the start of Part Four, we outlined what defensive poker looks like: playing a wider selection of hands preflop, starting to bluff, starting to slowplay good hands, and semi-bluffing with strong draws.

But even as you start to do these things, be aware that you'll be facing a player mix that will be even wider than in the micro-stakes games. You'll still be facing some weak players, just not as many of them as you were used to and against those players, offensive play is still optimal. But if both weak and strong players are still alive in the hand, you're going to have to perform some tricky balancing acts, trying to exploit the weak players in a direct manner while being aware that a better player may see through what you're doing and react to it.

Good Hand
Reading is Now Important

Hand reading is just the art of reducing your opponent's hand range from a large number of hands to a small number of hands by making logical deductions from his actions. What hands would he have called preflop? Which of those hands would have called a bet on the flop given what he knows about my preflop tendencies? Which of those hands would then have raised my bet on the turn? Do I have positive equity betting the river given what I now know, or is checking better? Answering these questions well is part of the art and skill of being a good hand reader.

Good hand reading doesn't matter much at micro-stakes because your opponent's hand ranges are wide and their actions are unpredictable. Here's an example.

Example: Against a loose, passive player you raise preflop and get a call. On the flop you hit top pair, top kicker and bet; you get another call. The turn is an innocuous small card; you bet and get called again. The river is another middling card which might make a straight, although your opponent would have had to call two streets with a gutshot. Should you bet?

From what you've seen so far, you could be facing anything from a made straight to bottom pair. It's not out of the question that your opponent could have had you beaten the whole way and just called you down. At micro-stakes, all you can say is that against a player like this, top pair, top kicker is good much more often than it's not, and betting will get calls from enough worse hands to make it profitable.

Although at micro-stakes you're forced to play your own hand to a large extent, at small stakes that won't be enough. You'll have to put yourself inside your opponent's head, examine his actions, and deduce your opponent's possible hands from the available evidence. Succeed at hand-reading and you'll do well in the small stakes games.

Playing Against Short Stacks

A "short stack" is simply a stack of 20 to 30 big blinds, as contrasted with a full stack of 100 big blinds or more. A player might get a short stack by starting with a big stack and losing money. More often, a player just buys in for less and plays the session with a small number of chips.

At micro-stakes, a short stack player is usually just playing to reduce his risk of losing money. Having a short stack changes your theoretically proper strategy: You should play high cards and big pairs. If you play the hand, you'll often be all-in on the flop and a top pair-type hand might be best at that point. Small pairs and suited connectors don't work because your short stack isn't giving you the implied odds to call a raise with these hands. But micro-stakes players with short stacks tend to play these hands anyway, losing more money in the long run.

There is, however, a separate strategy for playing a short stack which is perfectly viable. You play a tight game waiting for premium hands, then play those hands strongly trying to get all the money in the pot by the flop, if not preflop. This strategy works because your full-stacked or deep-stacked opponents are doing something different, playing more speculative hands that rely on the high implied odds in deep-stack play.

At small stakes, you need to analyze the short stacks at the table and see if they're playing a genuine short stack strategy or just trying to splash around with a few chips. If it's the latter, they don't really have any independent significance. If it's the former and they have position on you, take them into account and tighten up your preflop play a bit.

Preflop Starting Hands

In "Part Four: Beating Micro-Stakes Games," we discussed opening hand ranges for micro-stakes play and described two different ranges: a tight range suitable for a beginning player looking to stay out of trouble, and a looser range suitable for a more experienced player looking to get involved more often and confident of outplaying his opponents after the flop.

Now we'll outline an opening range for small stakes play. It will be based on the loose opening range for micro-stakes, but we're going to make a few modifications for two main reasons:

1. **Your opponents will exhibit a much wider array of skills.** Some will be as weak as any micro-stakes player and exploitable in the same way. Others will play quite well and you'll have to be careful against them, especially out of position. Still others will fit somewhere in the middle. Your preflop play will need to take more account of who's involved in the hand than was ever necessary at micro-stakes.

2. **Position matters more.** Your micro-stakes opponents often couldn't exploit their positional advantages. Some of your small stakes opponents, however, will be skilled enough to put uncomfortable pressure on you when you're the one out of position. Accordingly, your ranges need to tighten when you're more likely to be first to act on the flop.

Let's get started.

Small stakes: Under the gun.

> Open raise with all pairs: AA-22
> AK to AT suited
> KQ, KJ, QJ, QT, JT suited
> AK to AJ offsuit
> KQ, KJ, QJ offsuit (14% of all hands)

Compared to our loose micro-stakes range, we've tightened this a bit by dropping three marginal hands: A9 suited, AT offsuit, and KT suited. The non-premium aces were stronger under the gun at micro-stakes because you could often be called by weaker aces. That's less likely to happen now so we'll let those hands go. In the same spirit, king-ten suited is more likely to be dominated, so we'll drop it as well. But we're still left raising with 14 percent of all hands, a moderately active number.

Small stakes: Middle position.

> Open raise with all pairs: AA-22
> AK to A8 suited
> KQ, KJ, QJ, QT, JT suited
> AK to AT offsuit
> KQ, KJ, KT, QJ, JT offsuit
> T9, 98, 87, 76, 65 suited (18% of all hands)

We've tightened a bit here by dropping five hands: A7 and A6 suited, A9 offsuit, and KT, suited or unsuited. The reasons are the same as before. We've retained the higher suited connectors and added some lower connectors because they add some deception that will be needed against the more perceptive opponents at these stakes.

Small stakes: Cutoff seat against passive button.

> Open raise with all pairs: AA-22
> AK to A2 suited
> KQ, KJ, KT, QJ, QT, JT suited
> AK to A6 offsuit
> KQ, KJ, QJ, KT, QT, JT offsuit
> T9 to 65 suited (25% of all hands)

How we handle the cutoff depends on what we know about the button. If he is somewhat tight or somewhat passive, the same range that we used at micro-stakes will work perfectly well. If he's aggressive, however, and likes to attack our cutoff range with loose calls or 3-bets, we're going to have to make a few changes.

Small Stakes: Cutoff seat against aggressive button.

> Open raise with all pairs: AA-22
> AK to A6 suited
> KQ, KJ, KT, QJ, QT, JT suited
> AK to A8 offsuit
> KQ, KJ, QJ, QT, JT offsuit
> T9 to 65 suited
> J9, T8 suited (22% of all hands)

Here's a slightly modified cutoff range in case we're dealing with an aggressive button. We've dropped the weakest aces which can be difficult to play out of position, but added a couple of suited one-gappers for deception. Overall, we've tighten our range from 25 to 22 percent, while creating a range that's a little harder to read.

Small stakes: Button against tight, passive blinds.

> Open raise with all pairs: AA-22
> All aces, suited or unsuited
> KQ, KJ, KT, QJ, QT, JT suited
> KQ, KJ, KT, QJ, QT, JT offsuit
> T9 to 54 suited
> J9 to 64 suited
> Q9 to 85 suited
> Q8 to 95 suited
> T9 to 54 offsuit (40% of all hands)

Our ideal opponents in the blinds are tight multi-tablers who will have checked the 'Fold' button long before the action gets to them. If you see a player like that in the big blind, raise your aggression level on the button. We're recommending 40 percent here, but you can get even more aggressive than that if they're not paying attention.

Notice that we're recommending an even wider range than at the micro-stakes. This might seem counter-intuitive, but it's not unusual to find small stakes players who actually *overvalue* position and are unwilling to play out of position, even against an obvious steal, without a solid hand. (You don't really want to be raising five-four offsuit if you can't take a player who called with jack-seven off his hand.)

Small stakes: Button against loose, aggressive blinds.

> Open raise with all pairs: AA-22
> All aces, suited or unsuited
> KQ, KJ, KT, QJ, QT, JT suited
> KQ, KJ, KT, QJ, QT, JT offsuit
> T9 to 54 suited
> J9 to 75 suited
> Q9 to 96 suited
> T9 to 87 offsuit (35% of all hands)

Even against loose aggressive blinds we still have to try and milk our positional advantage, so we're adapting here by eliminating 5 percent of our weakest hands. This includes all the three-gappers and the worst of some of the other low suited cards. The result is a 35 percent range and we certainly don't want to be intimidated into raising much less than that.

Small stakes: Small blind. In the small blind, we should use the cutoff seat range against an aggressive big blind. This situation is similar to the cutoff seat in that the player right behind us is guaranteed absolute position throughout the hand if he plays. At small stakes, that ensures a lot of action from many players in the big blind and until we have some evidence that the big blind is passive, we should stick to the tighter range. We can also limp, just to see what happens, with a variety of mid-strength hands and some of our premium pairs. Blind versus blind play is extremely opponent-specific, so don't rely too much on rigid guidelines.

Blind Stealing
and Blind Defense

If you read our opening hand section carefully, you noticed that our recommended range for open-raising on the button was actually a little wider for small stakes than for micro-stakes. At first glance that might seem strange since the players at small stakes are presumably better than at micro-stakes. While that's true, one of the ideas they're more knowledgeable about is the sheer value of position. As a result, they're more reluctant to call with worthless hands, which favors a wider range on the button.

For instance, suppose it's folded to you on the button and you raise. (We don't care about your cards right now.) The small blind folds and the big blind looks down at the

A micro-stakes player might go through the following thought process: *"Raise from the button. Obviously trying a steal. Hah! He can't pwn me. My queen's probably good. I call. EZ game."*

A small stakes player looking at the Q♣4♥ thinks more like this: *"Raising from the button. Probably an average hand, maybe above-average, and my price is good. But I'll be out of position the whole way. This junk isn't worth it. I'll wait and nail him to the wall later."*

The fact that players respect position and are generally less willing to call with junk makes stealing from the button even more profitable at these stakes than at the lower stakes. So be prepared to get involved in a lot of button versus blind battles with position on your side. Let's look at a couple of examples.

Example No. 1: You're on the button in a $100 NL 6-max game and it's folded to you. Your hand is the K♣8♦ and your stack is $100.

Before acting, you check the relevant HUD statistics for the blinds. Here they are:

Small blind: VP$IP/PFR = 15/10,
FBS ('fold big blind to steal') = 70.

Big blind: VP$IP/PFR = 12/8, FBS = 80.

These blinds will fold to a steal attempt at such a high rate that raising any two cards on the button becomes a theoretically profitable strategy. As a practical matter, you shouldn't do that; at these levels your opponents will notice and compensate by playing better poker. However, you should widen your raising range from the button considerably. Our king-eight offsuit is well outside our normal 40 percent button raising range, but here it's good enough. You raise to $3 and the blinds both fold.

Example No. 2 You're on the button in a $50 NL 6-max game, it's folded to you, and your hand is the T♠9♠. Your stack is $50, while the big blind has $46 and the small blind has $58. The statistics for the blinds are as follows:

Small blind: VP$IP/PFR = 30/18, FBS = 60.

Big blind: VP$IP.PFR = 23/14, FBS = 65.

These players have more normal statistics for blind defense and are both willing to put up a defense when they have some sort of a hand. The small blind is the looser player which is good because players don't defend as often from the small blind. (Their pot odds aren't as good as the big blind's, and they have one additional player who can act with position.)

Your hand is in our recommended opening range and you have no reason to hold back here, so you open for $1.50. The small blind folds but the big blind calls. The pot is $3.25.

The flop comes the Q♣7♦3♠ and the big blind checks. You'll almost always want to make a continuation bet after raising on the button and this flop certainly missed most of his range, plus you have a slight bonus in the presence of both a backdoor flush draw and two backdoor straight draws.

How big should your bet be? On a dry board like this, a smaller bet, perhaps about one-half the pot, is normally a good idea. Our opponent either hit the flop or he didn't; if he didn't, a small bet should get rid of him, and if he did, no bet will get rid of him. But here he has a greater than usual incentive to see another card since he'll suspect we're stealing. So in this case, something between $2 and $2.50 looks about right.

You bet $2.40 and he calls. The pot is now $8.30.

The turn is the J♣ and you should fire another barrel. Not only have you picked up a straight draw, but a lot of his calling range consists of medium to low aces (often suited) and small pairs, none of which will like the jack. A few years ago, continuation bets were sufficient to win a lot of pots. Now most players understand the point of continuation betting, so the turn bet is often the bet that takes down the pot. You bet $6 and the big blind folds.

Example No. 3: You're on the button in a $100 NL 6-max game, it's folded to you, and your hand is the

Your stack is $100, the big blind has $104, and the small blind has only $18. The statistics for the blinds are as follows:

Small blind: VP$IP/PFR = 12/8,
FBS = 85. He's playing 12 tables.

Big blind: VP$IP/PFR = 24/12, FBS = 65.

Given the small blind's stack size and super-tight numbers, he's probably playing a short-stack strategy of raising aggressively only with premium hands. It's a relatively easy strategy when you're multi-tabling and if he plays the hand at all, he'll probably push all-in and you'll have to fold. However, mostly he's already checked the 'fold' button and the big blind has normal numbers.

You raise to $3. The small blind folds and the big blind calls. The pot is $6.50.

The flop is the

and the big blind bets $2.50. Betting into the preflop raiser with a small bet is popularly known as a 'donk bet.' It generally means that the bettor has either a draw or a small pair, and prefers to bet out hoping to preclude a larger bet from his opponent. The best response is exactly what the big blind is trying to prevent, namely a sizeable raise.

You raise to $14 and the big blind folds. Here the raise was pretty easy because you actually had a hand, but it would have been a good move even if you had missed the flop.[6]

Blind Defense

If players are aggressively stealing from the cutoff or the button, you need a good strategy for defending your blinds, particularly the big blind. You can't be successful if people know they can just pound on your big blind at will. Let's consider a few approaches.

When you get raised from the button, you should be in the habit of paying special attention to three numbers in their HUD: their PFR, their ATS ('attempt to steal,' meaning an open-raise from the cutoff or button when first in), and their continuation bet percentage. The connections between these three numbers should tell you a lot about their approach to stealing.

- The PFR will converge more quickly than the ATS number, so use it as a guide to their level of aggressiveness when you only have a small amount of data. A PFR above 20 probably means a player whose real ATS is at least 30.

- A high ATS and a high continuation bet percentage usually indicates a player who is attacking your blinds with a lot of

---

[6] Be aware that as more people read this book, skilled players may begin to make this donk bet in the hopes that you will play the hand as given here. Therefore, against someone whose HUD statistics indicate a better player, this raise may not be as automatic as this example indicates.

weak hands. You're going to need to fight back and your main weapons will be 3-betting preflop, check-raising the flop, and floating the flop followed by leading on the turn. You'll be doing these moves with good hands and an appropriate number of bluffs.

If your opponent has a stealing percentage of 40, he's got a range that's similar to what we outlined in our previous section for the button. Against this range you can 3-bet for value more liberally than most people think. For instance, all the hands in the following range are a 55 percent favorite against a 40 percent range:

> Pairs: 77 and higher
> AK through A8 suited
> AK through AT offsuit
> KQ suited

That's 9.4 percent of your hands which is a pretty large number. Note that's it's about one-quarter of his range which is a typical relationship for making value 3-bets.

You then want to add a few more hands so that your opponent will not always be playing correctly by folding all but his premium hands to your 3-bet. So here's some additional hands to 3-bet with:

> Suited aces: A4 through A2
> Suited connectors: T9 through 65
> Suited one-gappers: T8 through 75

Those hands add about one semi-bluff for every two value hands and bring your 3-bet percentage from the big blind against a steal position raise to about 13 percent. Also, we've chosen these additional holdings for 3-betting because they have the potential of flopping a big draw, but they leave you plenty of high card combinations and pairs for calling.

The second line of defense is the check-raise bluff on the flop. This has the advantage of being less common than a 3-bet, and hence more threatening. It has the disadvantage of being about twice as expensive as a 3-bet.[7] The additional expense is partly balanced by the extra chance that it will actually work, and the somewhat bigger profit it makes when he folds. (Your profit at that point will be his preflop raise plus his continuation bet.) This bluff should definitely be part of your repertoire, but certainly less common than a straight 3-bet.

The final line of defense is to call preflop, check-call the flop, and bet the turn. That's exactly as expensive as the flop bluff-raise, but less risky since you acquire one more piece of information (the turn card) before making your last bet.

In short, you have several possible lines for defending your blind with a marginal hand or a straight bluff against an aggressive button. So when in the blind, the 3-bet should be your most common weapon. It's the cheapest possible move and has the merit of often ending the hand quickly negating your positional disadvantage.

---

[7] To see this, imagine that you're playing in a $0.50/$1 game and the button raises to $3. If you 3-bet to $10, you're putting an additional $9 in the pot. Now suppose you decide to check-raise the flop instead. You need to put in $2 to call his preflop raise which creates a pot of $6.50. Next, suppose you check the flop and he bets $4. A reasonable check-raise requires you to put about $15 more in the pot, for a total of $17, compared to the $9 you needed for a straight 3-bet.

3- and 4-Betting

One of the biggest differences between small stakes games and micro-stakes games lies in the handling of preflop reraising and re-reraising, better known as 3- and 4-betting. At the micro-stakes, 3- and 4-bets almost never happen; at small stakes they're a crucial part of the game, one you must understand well to be successful.

Why isn't 3-betting part of the micro-stakes world? Actually, it's not because the players are too scared to stick in a reraise. Instead, it's because the initial raising ranges are mostly so tight that only the most solid 3-bets can be profitable. Take a player whose VP$IP and PFR statistics are 30/3. That's a very tight raising range, but not that unusual in the micro-stakes world. He'll limp into lots and lots of pots, but only raise with the top 3 percent of his hands. Here's what that 3 percent raising range looks like:

Pairs: AA through JJ
AK, suited or offsuit

If you're sitting behind this fellow and he raises, what hands will make you a favorite against his range? Not many. Here's a look at how your top hands are faring against his range:

Hand	Result
AA	83.4%
KK	62.2%
QQ	47.3%
JJ	36.5%
AKs	42.8%
AKo	39.8%

If you want to 3-bet for value, only a pair of aces or kings are an actual favorite against his range. And if you intend to bluff him with a 3-bet, which hands in his range do you think he'll lay down? Probably only a pair of jacks. That's because players who only raise with premium hands won't be raising with hands they will be eager to laydown.

But by the time players graduate to small stakes, their raising ranges have become much wider which in turn makes possible a wider range of 3-bets, both value bets and semi-bluffs. Let's now take a closer look at the strategy for this important and fascinating phase of the game.

Responding to an Opening Raise

An opponent raises, and the action comes to us. We can 3-bet, call, or fold. If we 3-bet, we can 3-bet for value or as a semi-bluff. Before we get into the specifics of what ranges we need for what actions, let's make a few general comments about 3-betting.

1. Check the initial raiser's 'fold to 3-bet' number in your HUD. If it's high (75 to 80 percent) and based on enough data, then you could theoretically make money 3-betting him with any two cards. You'll need to be careful, however, because other players at the table will see this number as well and be suspicious of what you're doing. Your brilliant 3-bet with the

might be followed by a crunching 4-bet right behind you! Use this number instead as a guide to 3-betting, but don't get too far out of line.

2.   3-betting in position is always stronger than 3-betting out of position. Add more light 3-betting hands to your range when you're in position.

3.   The more players there are that called the initial raiser, the stronger your 3-bet. We call a 3-bet after at least one caller a 'squeeze play.' They are stronger than heads-up 3-bets simply because there's more dead money in the pot. Remember, if the caller had a hand good enough to call a 3-bet, he could have 3-bet himself with a better chance of winning the pot.

Now let's take a look at the central problem: constructing a range of responses to an opening raise.

A Sample Situation

We'll start with a very basic situation. In a $100 NL 6-max game, Player B open-raises from middle position after the under the gun player folds. The cutoff folds and it's your turn to act on the button. Player B is loose-aggressive. His overall VP$IP/PFR numbers are 30/26 and his 'fold to 3-bet' is 60 percent. You believe that from middle position, his raising range is about 20 percent. So how should you respond?

We outlined a 20 percent range back in "Part Three: Ranges and Distributions," but let's review it here. A 20 percent range looks about like this:

All pairs
Suited aces: AKs through A7s
Offsuit aces: AKo through A9o
All suited Broadways: KQs, KJs, KTs, QJs, QTs, JTs
Offsuit Broadways: KQo, KJo, QJo
Suited connectors: T9s through 65s
Offsuit connectors: JTo and T9o

Precision isn't essential here. Players will have slightly different 20 percent ranges, but typical hands will behave about the same against any range as wide as this.

So against this range, we're going to take one of four actions:

1. 3-bet for value
2. Call
3. 3-bet semi-bluff
4. Fold

We'll build our ranges in a straightforward way. We'll 3-bet for value with our best hands. We'll call with our next strongest hands. We'll 3-bet semi-bluff with the next group, the best hands which aren't good enough for either value raising or calling. Finally, we'll fold the remaining hands. In a really tough game, we'd move a few of our 3-bet value hands down into our calling range so that our opponents couldn't exclude a premium hand just because we called. However, that's a refinement which is not strictly necessary at the small stakes level.

Next, let's answer this key question: With what possible hands should we take each action? Let's start with 3-betting for value and work our way down.

To 3-bet for value, we need to have a hand that's an actual favorite against this range. But simply being a 51 percent favorite isn't enough; there are two players to act behind us, and either one could cause a problem. On the other hand, demanding to be a 60 percent favorite is too much and if we insist on hands that good, we'll end up mostly 3-betting with only aces and kings.

My standard for 3-betting for value is about 55 percent. Hands that are around that big a favorite are the ones I feel comfortable making this play; weaker hands seem dicey to me. Other players might be comfortable with a different figure, but that's mine, and I recommend it as a good starting point. Remember, we'll have plenty of weaker hands that we'll be using for bluffing.

Against that 20 percent range of our opponent, what hands cross the 55 percent threshold? Let's take a look.

Hand	Result	Hand	Result
AA	83.6%	AKs	61.2%
KK	76.6%	AKo	59.2%
QQ	72.2%	AQs	58.3%
JJ	67.5%	AQo	56.0%
TT	62.1%	AJs	55.5%
99	57.2%	AJo	53.2%
88	54.2%	KQs	50.5%

That table gives us our range for being a 55 percent favorite against his range. It looks like this:

> Pairs: AA through 99
> Suited aces: AKs, AQs, and AJs
> Offsuit aces: AKo and AQo

That range amounts to 5.4 percent of all possible hands. Since his range is 20 percent, we're 3-betting a range that's about one-quarter of his range. That's a typical relationship as long as the initial raiser has a reasonably wide range. 3-betting a range that's about the top one-quarter of his range will yield a set of hands that are about 55 percent to win. This relationship allows you to pick your set of value betting hands pretty quickly. Since there are 1,326 possible different hold 'em hands, with each pair having six combinations, and each non-pair having 16 (four of which are suited), all you need to know is that 5 percent of all possible hands is 66 hand combinations, and you can quickly put together a list of candidate hands that won't be off by more than a combination or two.

Once we have our set of value 3-betting hands, our next step is to select our range of calling hands which will be our next strongest group of hands. For calling, I like to pick hands that are better than 45 percent to win against his range if I'm in position, and better than 48 percent to win if I'm out of position.

Again, these ranges are based on my experience and I'll pick a group of hands that are a comfortable calling range given that I'm getting some good pot odds to play. For instance, if the opener raises to three big blinds, the pot at that point will be 4.5 big blinds, and it will cost me three to call, so I'll be getting 1.5-to-1 on my call. Those are comfortable odds, even allowing for the possibility of a raise behind me.

In our example, we're in position on the original raiser. So what set of hands are 45 percent or better against his range? (Excluding, of course, the hands we're already using for 3-betting.) Let's take a look.

Hand	Result	Hand	Result
88	54.2%	A7s	45.2%
77	51.7%	AJo	53.2%
66	49.3%	ATo	49.7%
55	47.3%	KQs	50.5%
44	45.3%	KJs	47.8%
ATs	52.2%	KTs	45.8%
A9s	48.0%	QJs	45.5%
A8s	46.1%	KQo	47.8%

That set includes about 7 percent of our hands which seems about right given that we're in position. Out of position, we're looking for 48 percent, which would restrict us to a small range of calling hands: 88, 77, 66, ATs, A9s, AJo, ATo, and KQs, only about 4 percent of all hands. Again, this seems about right since we should be relatively reluctant to be calling out of position.

One very important point needs to be mentioned about calling, whether in or out of position. You can't call simply with the idea of continuing with the hand only if you hit the flop in some way. Whether you call with two high cards or a medium/low pair, you won't hit the flop often enough and you won't win enough money when you do hit to make the play profitable. You need to be prepared to bluff at least sometimes on the flop in order for your call to be better than just folding. The prime targets for your bluffs, of course, will be players with a high continuation-bet percentage, but recognize that some post-flop bluffs with a calling hand need to be part of your bag of tricks. Note that bluffing after a call is another big difference between micro-stakes and small stakes play. In micro-stakes, you could make money on your calling hands when your passive opponents shut down on the flop, indicating that they had no hand. Then you could often just pick up the pot with a bet on the turn. At small stakes the overall level of aggression is higher, and you need to counter that by introducing a little more bluffing into your game.

So far we've selected our value 3-betting hands and our calling hands. What about our 3-bet semi-bluffing hands? How many should there be and what kinds of hands should they be?

Let's start with the question of how often we should 3-bet bluff. There isn't a trivially simple answer to this question because it's going to vary with some other factors. We'll lay out the factors we want to consider, and then give some concrete examples of how often to 3-bet light. Here they are:

1.   His PFR and our 3-bet for value range.

2.   His 'fold to 3-bet' number.

3.   Whether we are in or out of position.

4.   The number of players yet to act.

5.   The number of callers in the pot.

That's a lot of factors, but the process really isn't as difficult as it might appear. First, let's see how each factor affects our decision.

1.   The tighter his PFR and the smaller our 3-bet for value range, the less we want to 3-bet light. Against a really tight opening range, like 3 to 4 percent, we're not going to 3-bet light at all. We'll just 3-bet for value, call, or fold.

2.   The bigger his 'fold to 3-bet number,' the more we want to 3-bet light.

3.   In position, we'll 3-bet light less and call more. Out of position, we'll call less and 3-bet light more.

4.   The more players left to act, the less we will 3-bet light.

5.   The more callers of the initial raiser in the pot, the more we will 3-bet light.

With these ideas in mind, let's return to our original problem and see what we would do.

In our original problem, Player B raised from middle position and we were on the button trying to map out our responses. Player B, we estimated, had a PFR of 20 percent in middle position. His 'fold to 3-bet' was 60 percent, an average number. So far we've decided that we're going to raise for value with a range equal to about 5.4 percent of our possible hands, and call with a range of about 7 percent.

Against a generically aggressive opponent with a PFR between 10 and 20 percent (adjusted for his position) I like to 3-bet light about half as many hands as I will 3-bet for value. That's not particularly loose or tight, and it would be hard to exploit even if an opponent knew exactly my strategy. Since I'm 3-betting 5.4 percent for value here, my starting point will be 2.7 percent light 3-bets.

Once you have your starting number, adjust it up or down depending on the factors listed above. Here there's not much adjustment to be made. His PFR is in our generically aggressive range. His 'fold to 3-bet' is pretty average. There are no callers so far. There are two players left to act, but they're the blinds and you'll have position on them. Let's stick with our 2.7 percent number, and try to figure out what hands we'll put in that range.

With a little mental arithmetic, we can calculate the number of hand combination needed pretty quickly. There are 1,326 possible two-card combinations. Ten percent of that number is 133. Notice that 2.7 percent is just a little more than one-quarter of 10 percent. Dividing 133 in half, and then in half again, yields 33 combinations. To move from 2.5 percent to 2.7 percent, add a few more hands, and we end up with about 36 combinations, which is pretty close to 2.7 percent of 1,326.

The next point to notice is that our light 3-betting hands will only consist of pairs or suited cards. Remember, we're looking for hands which are both:

1. The best of the hands still available.

2. Semi-bluffs which can improve to monsters with a little luck.

And three categories stand out as obvious candidates:

1. Pairs, which can improve to sets.

2. Suited aces, which can improve to the nut flush or the nut flush draw.

3. Suited connectors, which can improve to straights, flushes, or draws.

And since we have plenty of hands to choose from, there's no need to be semi-bluffing with unsuited cards or high card/low card type hands.

Here's a hand range which will give us our needed 36 combinations and meet our other criteria at the same time:

Pairs: 33 and 22 (12 combinations)
Suited aces: A5s and A4s (8 combinations)
Suited connectors: JTs, T9s, 98s, 87s (16 combinations)

These are the best hands available and give some representation in each category. (Note that we've left out A6s but included A5s. Since A5s has some straight possibilities, it's a better hand for our purpose.) The rest of our hands, of course, we'll be folding.

That finishes our little exercise. We've picked out a set of value 3-betting hands equal to about one-quarter of our opponent's raising range, a set of light 3-betting hands equal to about one-half of our value bets, and a set of calling hands that have between 45 and 54 percent winning chances against our opponent's range.

In a high-stakes game, we'd have one more modification to make. We would for balance move a few of our strongest hands from the value reraising range into the calling range. We wouldn't need to move a lot of these to accomplish the purpose. We might, for instance, move the pairs of red aces and red kings, the pairs of black aces and black kings, and any ace-king with the ace of spades. That's a total of eight hands. But it's an overly sophisticated move for small stakes play, so we won't bother with it.

So how big should our 3-bets be? If the initial raiser raised to three big blinds, a pot-sized 3-bet would be 10.5 big blinds. But a full pot-sized bet isn't really necessary. Therefore, a simple rule is to just triple his initial raise. That will get you closed to a pot-sized bet with a minimum of effort. If there has been a caller after the initial raise, then increase the amount of your raise to about four times the initial raise.

A Second Example

Now let's look at a second example. We'll leave out a lot of the intermediate calculations here and just show what our ranges look like and why we made some adjustments to our original example.

Example: In a $100 NL 6-max game, Player D open-raises from the button after three folds. The small blind folds and we act from the big blind. Player D is loose-aggressive, his overall VP$IP and PFR numbers are 32/25, and his 'fold to 3-bet' number is 70 percent. We believe that from the button his raising range is about 35 percent. How should we respond?

We first note that 35 percent is a wide range, roughly consisting of all pairs, all aces, all Broadways, and most suited connectors, suited one-gappers, and offsuit connectors. Our 3-betting for value range looks like this:

Pairs: AA through 77
Suited aces: AKs through A9s
Offsuit aces: AKo through ATo (116 combinations)

These are the hands that are 55 percent to win against his range. It's a modest set, but it still amounts to an 8.7 percent range, almost exactly one-quarter of his 35 percent raising range, so our relationship holds.

We're going to be out of position on the flop, so our calling range tightens to include only hands that are between 48 and 55 percent to win. That range looks like this:

> Pairs: 66 through 44
> Suited aces: A8s through A4s
> Offsuit aces: A9o, A8o
> Suited Broadways: KQs, KJs, KTs, QJs, QTs
> Offsuit Broadways: KQo (88 combinations)

This is a slightly smaller calling range than our first example, comprising 6.6 percent of all hands. His range got wider, but being out of position tightened our requirements.

What about our range for 3-betting light? Our generic rule of thumb is to 3-bet light with about half the number of hands that we would value 3-bet. In here, we are going to make some adjustments.

1. His 'fold to 3-bet number' is 70 percent, which is on the high side. This means we want to increase our light 3-bets.

2. We're out of position in this hand, so we want to reduce our calls (which we've already done), and increase our light 3-bets.

3. No one can act behind us, so we want to increase our light 3-bets.

That's a lot of reasons for increasing the number of light 3-bets. And of course, the sheer size of his raising range (35 percent) indicates that he will fold a lot of his hands. At a minimum, our number of light 3-bets should equal our number of value 3-bets. Even light 3-betting a little more than that wouldn't be unreasonable.

Since our value 3-betting range included 112 hands, let's aim for 116 hands or about a 9 percent light 3-betting range. And here's what that range looks like:

Pairs: 33 and 22
Suited aces: A3s and A2s
Suited connectors: JTs through 76s
Suited one-gappers: J9s through 75s
Suited two-gappers: Q9s through 85s
Offsuit Broadways: QJo, QTo, and JTo (116 combinations)

Notice that we were running out of reasonable suited cards, so we included the best of the offsuited combinations that hadn't been chosen yet.

Attacking Weak Raisers

Occasionally you'll meet some players who just don't understand the 3-betting idea and have grossly distorted 'fold to 3-bet' numbers, sometimes 80 percent or more. Theoretically, you could 3-bet these folks 100 percent of the time and show an immediate profit. In practice, you can't. The problem is not that the initial raiser will figure out what you're doing; after all, if he's folding 85 percent of the time, he hasn't done well so far in the 'figuring out' department. The problem is the other players at the table who have his 'fold to 3-bet' number on their HUD screens as well, and can see what you're doing.

The best approach is to increase the number of your light 3-bets but without going completely crazy. Try 3-betting light with a range twice the size of your value 3-betting range; that should make a nice profit without raising too many red flags around the table.

Responding to a 3-bet

Sometimes, of course, you'll be the one who opens the pot with a raise and then gets 3-bet. Responding here can be a little tricky, so let's go through the main issues involved.

Roughly speaking, your opponents at small stakes will fall into two main groups:

1. Group A consists of players who, like most micro-stakes opponents, will 3-bet only with a tight range, about 3 percent or less. A 3 percent range consists of pairs, jacks or better, and ace-king, suited or unsuited. They may fold some of this range to a 4-bet, but more likely they're prepared to get all-in once they've 3-bet. As you move up the scale from $25 NL to $50 NL to $100 NL, you'll encounter fewer players in this group. But you'll still find some, even at $200 NL.

2. Group B consists of players who play more or less as we described earlier in this chapter. They'll raise for value, call some hands, and semi-bluff with a few more. Their exact approach will vary from player to player, but they'll be 3-betting with something like 6 to 10 percent of their hands.

The most important skill in responding to a 3-bet is to place your opponent in either Group A or Group B. Once you know where an opponent belongs, your strategy is pretty straightforward.

Against Group A, you fold everything but your premium hands. This can be difficult because it will feel like you're being exploited. But in fact, you're the one doing the exploiting. They've told you what they have, and you're sidestepping the trap of losing your whole stack with jacks or ace-queen.

Against Group B, you treat your 4-bet decision exactly as you treated your 3-bet decision in the previous section. You're going to 4-bet for value with your best hands, call with some others, and 4-bet semi-bluff with the best hands that are left.

Example: In a $100 NL 6-max game, you open from middle position for $3. Your opening range from this position at these stakes is 18 percent, consisting of these hands:

> All pairs
> Suited aces: AKs through A8s
> Offsuit aces: AKo through ATo
> Suited Broadways: KQs, KJs, KTs, QJs, QTs, JTs
> Offsuit Broadways: KQo, QJo, JTo
> Suited connectors: T9s through 65s
> Suited one-gappers: J9s and T8s (238 combinations)

Your 'fold to 3-bet' number for this session so far is 60 percent. Everyone folds around to the small blind who reraises to $10. You have a couple of hundred hands of data in his HUD, and his 3-betting percentage is 8 percent. So far, he appears to be a very competent player who has always shown down reasonable value. The big blind folds. So what should your ranges look like for 4-betting for value, calling, light 4-betting, and folding?

We'll proceed here exactly as we did in our 3-betting discussion. The first step is to assign him a 3-betting range, given what we know.

His overall 3-betting range is about 8 percent. Since we think he's a competent player, we expect him to adjust his range up or down a bit just as we would.

- Since we raised from middle position, our raising range will be a little tighter than our overall PFR. He will tighten his 3-betting range accordingly.

- Since he'll be out of position after the flop, he wants to 3-bet light a little more, and call a little less.

- There are no callers in the pot, and only one player to act behind him. These two effects should cancel out.

- He's seeing a 'fold to 3-bet' for us of 60 percent, about an average number.

The net result of all these factors looks like a wash, so we'll assume his 3-betting number in this situation is no different from his average, about 8 percent. If he uses the same criteria we would (a loose assumption, but we don't have any information that would let us make a different assumption), his 3-betting range would look like something like this:

3-betting for value:

> Pairs: AA through 99
> Suited aces: AKs and AQs
> Offsuit aces: AKo and AQo (68 combinations)

3-betting light:

> Pairs: 55 through 22
> Suited aces: A9s and A8s
> Suited connectors: QJs and JTs (40 combinations)

Hands in between the value bets and the light bets are, of course, his calling hands.

Against that 3-betting range, what would the ranges for our various responses look like? First, let's note that when we 4-bet, we'll fold out the light 3-bets in his range, so we just need to look at how our prospective hands fare against his value range. Here are the hands we can 4-bet for value, which are 55 percent against his value 3-betting range.

4-bet for value:

Pairs: AA through QQ (18 combinations, 1.4%)

Calling becomes a little different. We're still trying to call with hands that are 45 to 55 percent against his range. However, when we call, we keep his whole range in the hand rather than folding out his weakest cards. As a result, it's easier for hands to pass our calling criteria than our raising criteria, so we have relatively more hands in this group than previously. And as before, we are going to have to bluff with some of these hands post-flop to avoid being exploited.

Call his 3-bet:

Pairs: JJ through 55
Suited aces: AKs and AQs
Offsuit aces: AKo (62 combinations, 4.8%)

Finally, we still need some light 4-bets which are the best hands below our calling hands.

4-bet bluff:

Suited aces: AJs and ATs (8 combinations, 0.7%)

Somewhat surprisingly, our range of playable hands after his 3-bet is almost as large as his 3-betting range! This seems surprising at first but makes complete sense. Imagine a pot-limit game with stack sizes that are enormous compared to the initial bets, and two players who keep raising each other. At first, each raise reduces the hand range enormously as all the junk hands are filtered out. With subsequent raises, however, the number of dropped hands falls off as the curve flattens. Eventually the players are reraising with the identical range of hands: aces and kings at first, and then only aces.

One last point about 4-betting: The size of a 4-bet can be constrained by the stack sizes that remain. Imagine a game where both players in the hand have stacks of 100 big blinds. Let's say one player raises to 3.5 big blinds and his opponent 3-bets to 12 big blinds. If the first player now 4-bets to 40 big blinds and his opponent 5-bets all-in, the pot becomes 140 big blinds (ignoring the initial blinds) and the first player has only 60 big blinds left. The pot is offering him 2.3-to-1 odds to call. Given the hands in his 4-betting range, he's essentially made himself pot-committed with most of his range. A better course would be to make a smaller 4-bet to something like 30 or 32 big blinds which would still chase away a lot of bluffs, but would leave some room to get out of the hand if your opponent decided to push all-in. The smaller the initial stacks, the more important this issue becomes.

Flop Tactics
at Small Stakes

Your strategy in a heads-up flop depends not only on the exact hand you flopped but also on what happened during the preflop betting. If you were the aggressor preflop (you bet and your opponent called) then you will most likely take the lead, whether or not you improved your hand, with a continuation bet. If you were the defender preflop (your opponent bet and you called) then you will usually face a continuation bet and need to decide how to respond.

You Were
the Aggressor Preflop

At small stakes you have to be a little more circumspect than at micro-stakes. In the smaller games, the players are usually playing their own hands and not paying too much attention to what you've been doing. But in small stakes games, you can expect a lot of your opponents to be using HUDs. Consequently, if you overdo your continuation betting, your opponents will notice and start to target you for bluffs or other plays. Therefore, you need to bet most, but not all, of your good hands. This way, your checks don't guarantee weakness. You'll also need to check some of the hands where you miss the flop completely. In general, if your continuation betting exceeds 80 percent, you're setting yourself up for some difficulties. So with these general ideas in mind, let's look at how to play some specific categories of hands.

Playing Big Hands

For our purposes, a 'big hand' is anything larger than an overpair. Full houses, flushes, straights, sets, and two pair without a pair on board all qualify. When you flop a big hand, you're in a pleasant situation. You almost certainly have the best hand at the table, and your main goal is building a pot.

Mostly, you want to bet your big hands. One of your goals in no-limit hold 'em is to create situations where you can win your opponent's whole stack, and these hands give you a chance at doing that without too much risk.

This means that slowplaying should be an occasional variation, rather than your main strategy. Consider the following situation: After the flop you have a monster holding, but your opponent has a hand which is good enough to allow him to call a three-quarter-pot sized bet, but which he will check behind if you fail to bet. Let's say that on the flop, the pot is 8 big blinds and there is no bet. On the turn you try to make some money, so you bet 6 big blinds and he calls. On the river the pot is 20 big blinds, so you bet 15 big blinds and he calls again. You win and your profit is 21 big blinds.

Now suppose you don't slowplay the flop but bet instead and get called down. This time you make 6 big blinds on the flop and 15 on the turn and by the river, the pot is 50 big blinds and your three-quarter pot bet is now 37 big blinds. If called, you have just won an additional 37 big blinds compared to the slowplaying strategy. This is an increase of 176 percent!

But slowplaying becomes preferable when your hand is so strong and the board so dry that it's likely no one can stand up to you. In that case, checking may allow your opponent to make some sort of hand which might enable him to call a bet somewhere down the road.

So when you bet, how big should your bet be? This depends entirely on the chance that someone has a hand that can play with you. The larger that chance, the more you should bet. The smaller the chance, the less you should bet. Let's look at a few examples and in all of these examples, we'll assume that you raised preflop and got called, the pot is about 8 big blinds, and the effective stack is about 100 big blinds.

Example No. 1: Your hand is the

and the flop is the

(three suits). While you've basically won the hand, the chance that your opponent has a holding of value is tiny since only one ace and two tens remain, and the only possible draw is a gutshot. You should check the flop. If the turn comes with a king, queen, or jack, you can bet half the pot in the hope that card hit your opponent and he'll give you credit for a possible steal attempt. If the turn is a blank, check again and try to make some money on the river.

Example No. 2: You have the J♥J♦ and the flop is the J♣T♥T♣ (two suits). This is completely different from the previous example. While you again have a full house, many draws are possible. So it's best to lead out for about a half-pot bet and hope your opponent has a draw and will come along for the decent odds that you're offering. If a card then hits on the turn or river which seems to complete a draw, bet strongly. You now have a chance to win his entire stack, and that possibility will outweigh other considerations.

Example No. 3. You have the A♠T♠ and the flop is 9♠8♠4♠. Although many players are tempted to check, this is a good spot to bet. Your opponent's hands fall into one of five categories:

1. He has a worse flush.

2. He has a flush draw with a high card, like the K♠ or Q♠.

3. He has a flush draw with a low flush card.

4. He has a made hand or a straight draw with no spade.

5. He has nothing.

Most players will interpret your flop bet as either a flush draw or a bluff. You'll frequently get a call from hands in the first four categories, and you'll only fold out the last category where you're unlikely to ever make any money anyway.

If a fourth suited card comes on the turn, you'll make another bet from categories Nos. 1 through 3, and probably fold out category No. 4. And regardless of what happens on the river, it's easy to see that betting the flop is going to dominate not betting the flop.

Playing Top Pair, Top Kicker/Overpair Hands

At micro-stakes these hands are your bread-and-butter profit centers. You'll often get three streets of value as your bets get called by second pairs, third pairs, underpairs, or all sorts of draws including gutshots. At micro-stakes, you need a compelling reason to stop betting your top pair or overpair hands and frequently, your opponents in these games will give you such a reason by raising on the turn or betting big on the river, signaling a big hand.

At small stakes, your opponents in general are better and they'll start to take into account what your bets are saying. Better players will not call three streets if they can't beat the top pair sort of hand that you're representing unless they have reason to think you are semi-bluffing. So you're going to need to mix up your play more, and you're going to need to identify the good players from the weak players so you can still extract value from the weak ones, while not walking into traps from the good ones.

In general, top pair, top kicker is a good hand and you'll want to bet it on the flop. However, there are reasons why not betting it can be a good play as well. Let's look at some of these pros and cons.

Advantages to betting top pair:

1. **Weaker hands will put money in the pot.** Most players won't lay down a pair on the flop to a continuation bet. In general, you'll have to bet again on the turn to make them fold.

2. **Drawing hands need to pay to play.** By betting, you force most draws to put money in the pot to see if their draw hits. If you make a normal-sized bet (say two-thirds of the pot), they won't be getting the right expressed odds to call. For instance, if the pot is $9 and you bet $6, they'll be getting 15-to-6 or 2.5-to-1 odds to call. Those aren't enough to justify calling with a straight draw or a flush draw unless they can count on winning more money when they hit their draw, and if their draw is obvious, you may not pay them off.

Advantages to not betting top pair:

1. **Balance:** Against more perceptive players, playing straightforward poker makes you a juicy target. By checking, you ensure that your range of checked hands includes some strong ones, so your opponents can't attack you with impunity.

2. **Pot control:** In games with good players, top pair, top kicker isn't a hand you want to play for your entire stack. If you get to the river with nothing but top pair and all the money goes in, your hand isn't likely to be best. Checking the flop is a good way to control the final pot size by removing one round of betting.

3. **Hand stability:** If the board doesn't have any draws, and you're currently the favorite, your lead is pretty safe. Imagine that you have the

and the flop was the

If your opponent now has the

he only has two outs on the turn, just over a 4 percent chance of outdrawing you (on that round). If he has the 7♠6♠, he has an 11 percent chance, and if his hand is the K♠Q♠, he's got less than a 7 percent chance. In short, if you're ahead and there aren't any draws, it's likely to stay that way on the turn and the river.

4. **Allowing improvement:** Your opponent might have nothing but catch something on the turn, in which case you may win a bet you wouldn't have gotten had you bet the flop.

The advantages to betting are straightforward and perfectly valid. Most of the time, you'd rather bet top pair than not. However, not betting has some positive aspects as well.

So given that you mostly want to bet but sometimes it's best to check, how should you choose? Once again, it's a combination of assessing the flop and your opponent.

Good checking flops, like K♠8♣3♦ or 8♣8♦4♠, are flops lacking any draws. If you have top pair or an overpair on these boards, and your opponent has some lower pair, it's unlikely they can draw out on you.

On the other hand, you want to bet flops, like J♠T♥3♠ or 9♥7♥6♣, that have draws. Top pair or an overpair on these flops are vulnerable to draws, so go ahead and bet.

Another key idea is exactly how strong your top pair is. Suppose you have the

and the flop is the

You have top pair, top kicker and only one overcard to your queens can arrive to bother you, namely a king. In that case, checking presents little risk. On the other hand, if you have the T♥9♥ and the flop is the T♣3♠2♠, you have top pair but won't be happy if an ace, king, queen, or jack arrives on the turn. Therefore, betting here is very important.

In terms of your opponent, the best ones to check against when you are out of position are those with high flop and turn aggression factors. They're most likely to interpret your check as weakness and take the lead themselves. However, against passive players you want to bet since they're unlikely to bet anything but strong hands, yet they'll frequently call your bet with hands you can beat.

Playing Draws

At micro-stakes, you tended to play draws conservatively because the folding equity was low. Checking and calling were generally preferable to actively semi-bluffing.

At small stakes, drawing hands offer a lot of flexibility in how to continue on the flop. If you have a simple flush or straight draw with no other ways to win, against a player with a strong pair, you're typically between 35 and 40 percent to win the hand, while a flush draw plus two overcards against a top pair hand is a slight favorite. So depending on your position, you can do any of the following:

If you are out of position:

1. **Bet:** This operates as a straight semi-bluff. With a weak draw (eight to nine outs) you're happy to take the pot down right now. If your opponent calls and you miss the turn, you'll often have a bit of a problem. Your chances of hitting a weak draw now drop to the 20 percent range, but your chance of taking the pot by firing a second barrel will be higher against most opponents. If your opponent raises your flop bet, reraising all-in is a strong option.

2. **Check-raising:** Check-raising is a strong alternative to betting. The probability of taking down the pot goes up while the probability of hitting your hand remains constant. If your check is met by a check, you get to draw for free.

If in position:

1. **Bet after a check:** This is the standard line. If your opponent was the preflop aggressor, his check shows weakness and your chance of taking down the pot are usually high. If he has an aggressive profile and check-raises, pushing all-in becomes a strong option in reserve as long as you have reason to believe he will frequently make these check-raises with semi-bluff type hands. If you were the preflop aggressor, this is just a standard continuation bet.

2. **Check after a check:** This line conceals your hand well and lets you draw for free, never a bad deal. It's especially

effective against an aggressive opponent who is more likely to be going for a check-raise with little probability of semi-bluffing.

3. **Call after a bet:** While this is a cheap way of seeing another card, small stakes players are more likely to interpret calls as possible draws, so your implied odds may be smaller than you think when your card comes in. But this is a good play against an opponent whose aggression factor is much higher on the flop than the turn because you retain a better chance of stealing the pot on a later street.

4. **Raise after a bet:** This is a good play with either a strong or weak draw. Your fold equity is higher since you'll be playing your sets and two pairs this way. In addition, your chance of seeing both the turn and the river cards is higher because if your opponent calls your raise he'll likely check the turn and you'll have the option of seeing the river for free or betting again.

Example: In a $100 NL game, your opponent open-raised to $3 preflop from the cutoff seat. You called from the big blind with the

The effective stack is now $80, the pot is $6.50, and the flop is the

You have a strong hand with a pair plus a flush draw and a runner-runner straight draw. Against a hand like A♠K♠, you're a 51-to-49 favorite, and even in the unlikely case he holds top set, you still have a 30 percent chance to win.

Your choices are betting out or checking with the idea of check-raising, and it's my opinion that check-raising is a stronger overall line, so make that play the majority of the time. You should base your decision, however, on his 'continuation bet' and 'flop aggression' numbers. If his continuation bet percentage is unusually low (less than 50 percent), just bet out because he may not bet if you check. But if both his continuation bet and flop aggression numbers are high, you can also bet and make it something like a half-pot bet or even a little less. Now there's a good chance he will assume you're bluffing or holding some weak low pair-type hand and raise, after which you can reraise.

If his continuation bet and flop aggression numbers are more normal, just check and be prepared to check-raise. Remember, a pair and a flush draw is a strong hand and thus warrants this type of aggressive action on your part.

Playing Weak
Hands or Nothing Hands

When you either miss your hand completely or flop something like bottom pair or an underpair, you're going to have to bluff sometimes and check sometimes. In general, you want to bluff favorable flops and/or favorable opponents.

A favorable flop is one that's either likely to hit you, given that you took the lead preflop, or likely to have missed your opponent. Let's take a look at some favorable and unfavorable bluffing flops.

1. **Q♣7♦2♥ — favorable:** A dry flop with a single high card is one of the best bluffing flops. No draws are possible and most of your opponent's range will just miss. Unless he originally called with a pair, he'll probably fold.

2. **9♦9♥3♠ — favorable:** A dry paired flop is also an excellent bluffing flop. Again, unless he has a pair, he'll probably fold.

3. **A♠9♥2♦ — favorable:** This is an excellent bluffing flop at lower stakes where players will call with a wide range that doesn't include a lot of aces. They'll assume that if you bet this flop, you probably raised preflop with an ace. But bluffing here becomes less and less effective as you move to higher stakes where players understand its bluffing potential and may elect to play back at you.

4. **T♠9♠3♦ — somewhat unfavorable:** This flop offers a lot of draws and hits a lot of calling ranges. At the same time, it doesn't hit a lot of preflop raising ranges.

5. **J♥T♣9♥ — unfavorable:** If this very wet flop didn't connect with your hand, it's best to let it go.

A favorable opponent for continuation bet bluffing is a player with either a high 'fold to c-bet' percentage (over 70 percent is good) or a player who's generally passive (with low aggression factors). A high fold percentage is obviously good, while low aggression factors help because you can be reasonably confident that a raise from him actually represents a big hand and lets you fold with certainty.

Defending Against a Continuation Bet

As we've mentioned before, you can't call a raise preflop with the simple hope of hitting the flop and then taking down the pot. Since you'll miss the flop about 70 percent of the time, this fit-or-fold approach lets too many pots slip through your fingers. You can play that way at micro-stakes, not because it's profitable in itself, but because you're collecting so much money on your value bets that you won't notice these small losses. But at small stakes, your value bets won't be as profitable, so you'll need to pay attention to fighting for pots where you miss the flop.

Suppose you called a raise preflop and now you're in position in a heads-up pot, and flop nothing. Your opponent leads with a continuation bet. Do you want to defend now or let this situation go? How do we decide?

First, we want to look at the flop. Some flops are good to bluff at while others aren't. Here's a bad flop:

Our opponent led preflop, so he's supposed to have high cards and aces in his range. Hence bluffing at this flop is probably going to be a disaster.

Here's another flop we don't want to bluff:

True, it doesn't have an ace or a king, and you can image an opponent who raised preflop with ace-king not liking it. But pretty much every other high card hand hit this flop in some way, and if your opponent has the A♠ or K♠, he's drawing to either the nut flush or the second-nut flush. In addition, most of the pairs in his range now have either an overpair, a set, a straight draw, a flush draw, or some combination of these. If you missed this flop with your small or medium pair, just let it go.

But this flop presents a different problem:

While it will miss most of an aggressor's range, it's also telling a story that you don't need told. Your opponent can look at this and say "Well, I missed this but so did he. His bet probably represents a flush draw, or maybe he has a straight draw with something like a seven-six. I can push him off these hands."

On the other hand, here are two good bluffing flops:

and the

Neither of these permit any draws, and eliminating draws from your bluffing narrative is good for you. Either you have a pair, a set, or you don't. If he has nothing, it's a lot easier to just let his continuation bet go than chase you down and perhaps lose his whole stack in the process.

(A word of caution about this advice. It's good advice for small stakes games, *but it's only good for small stakes games.* It's bad advice for micro-stakes because it's a hard way to make money, and you'll find many easier ways later in the session. Why sweat to make a buck when money grows on trees? In high stakes games, it's not terrible advice, but it's only a starting point. High stakes players know these are good bluffing flops, and they're perfectly capable of reraising your bluff-raise.)

Besides the flop, you also want to consider your opponent. Is he generally tight with a narrow range, or generally loose with a wide range? Narrow ranges will hit some flops hard, but many others not at all. Wide ranges contain many hands that will hit many flops to some extent, but weakly. Loose aggressive players are good targets because they'll often show up with nothing, and at these stakes they're more capable of letting the hand go than their micro-stakes brethren.

Lastly, consider the stack sizes. Deep stacks are better for bluffing because your opponent has a lot more to lose if he guesses wrong. Shallow stacks encourage a "what-the-hell" attitude that's a problem if you're trying to run a bluff.

Example No. 1: You're in the big blind holding the K♠J♥ in a $100 NL 6-max game. The first three players fold and Player D, on the button, raises to $4. He's loose and aggressive with VP$IP/PFR numbers of 31/31 after 52 hands. His 'attempt to steal' number is 39 and his continuation bet percentage is 80. Your own VP$IP/PFR numbers for this session are 22/18 and the two of you have yet to tangle in any significant pots. The small blinds folds and the action is on you.

It's reasonable to think that his opening range on the button is about 40 percent of his hands. Here's how a typical 40 percent range breaks down into hand types:

Hand	Frequency
Pairs	15%
Aces	35%
Other Hands	50%

Your king-jack offsuit is almost exactly even money against that range right now and you have the choice of 3-betting immediately or just calling and seeing the flop. Either is reasonable. But since you've already tossed in a few 3-bets this session, you elect to call knowing that in order to call, you will sometimes have to bluff post-flop on good bluffing flops.

You call. The pot is $8.50 and the flop is the 5♥4♠4♦.

Here's an interesting fact. With his hand range, you're now actually about a 3-to-2 underdog post flop! All of his pairs are beating you, and his aces are still ahead. In addition, some of the low parts of his range actually hit that flop. However, you're not going to simply give up. Only about one-seventh of his starting hands were actually pairs, so most of his range doesn't know it's ahead. Therefore, it's a reasonably good spot for bluffing, and if you want to play on, you have three lines to consider:

1. Leading out (donk betting).

2. Check-raise his inevitable continuation bet.

3. Check-call, and then lead on the turn.

Let's assume that we're willing to make one stab at this pot, and we'll evaluate these three lines in terms of cost and effectiveness.

1. Donk betting is the cheapest. With an $8.50 pot, a good bet size would be about $6. It's also the least effective. It's hard to convince an opponent that a donk bet really represents a strong hand since if you had a strong hand, why wouldn't you attempt to check-raise him? So this would be my least favorite choice.

2. Check-raising is more expensive than donk betting, but also conveys more strength. If your opponent bets $6, your check-raise will be to about $21.

3. Checking and calling the flop and leading out on the turn is about as expensive as check-raising. You'll need $6 to call his flop bet, creating a $20.50 pot. Then $15 will be a good bet on the turn, making your total investment again $21.

Both check-raising and check-calling-betting cost about the same and indicate real strength. (In my experience, check-calling and betting the turn actually conveys a little more strength, but that's a subtle point.) Betting the turn, however, does offer one strong benefit. You get to see the turn card, and if it's an ace, you might elect to back off since a big chunk of his range will contain an ace. Alternatively, the turn might let you bet for value or it might actually hit his hand.

All other things being equal, betting the turn is a slightly better line than check-raising the flop, but in a tough game you need to do both to balance your attack. Having bet the turn in an earlier hand (although not against this player), you elect to go for the check-raise.

You check and your opponent bets $6. You check-raise to $20 and he pushes all-in with his last $90.

Oops. Not this time. Even a loose player can hit a hand. You're not sure what he has, but you said you had a strong hand and your opponent was willing to push, so you're pretty sure your king-high isn't good.

Example No. 2: You're on the button holding the 6♠6♦ in a $50 NL 6-max game. The first player folds and Player B, in middle position, raises to $1.50. He's active, but not so much to qualify as 'loose,' and fairly aggressive with VP$IP/PFR numbers of 23/23 after 75 hands. His 'attempt to steal' number is 35 and his continuation bet percentage is 75. Your own VP$IP/PFR numbers for this session are 24/21 and you don't have any particular history with this player. The next three players fold, the action is on you, and you both have stacks of about $50.

His PFR numbers are probably skewed a bit by his aggressiveness in late position. A reasonable guess for his middle position range is something like 15 to 18 percent, so let's take 16 percent as a good estimate. That range looks something like this:

> All pairs
> Suited aces: AKs through A8s
> Offsuit aces: AKo through ATo
> All suited Broadways
> Offsuit Broadways: KQo and KJo
> Suited connectors: T9s through 76s

Your pair of sixes is 48 percent against this range, good enough to call. But as before, you can't call with just a plan of hitting your set, so you're going to need to attack on a suitable flop. His continuation bet percentage is 75, not absurdly high, but high enough to indicate that a lot of his bets will be bluffs.

You call $1.50 and the pot is $3.25. The flop is the K♣7♠3♦.

That's a good flop for your hand given that you didn't hit a set. There are three widely separated cards and no draws. On this board, your low pair is just a slight (53-to-47) underdog against his range. Therefore, it's a good flop for making a move.

So what's the best line to choose? Unlike the previous example, an immediate raise is the best play. The reason is that our hand has fewer outs: only two cards can improve it to a set, whereas in the previous hand we had six cards that could improve us to top pair. So seeing a turn card has less to offer, and the fast track looks more appealing.

Your opponent bets $2.25. You raise to $6.50 and he folds.

Value Betting
in Small Stakes Games

As we described in "Part Four: Beating Micro-Stakes Games," value betting is the art of making bets that will get called when you probably have the best hand. At micro-stakes, good value bets were the source of most of your profits. This will be true at small stakes as well, but the nature of value betting undergoes a subtle shift in transitioning from micro-stakes to small stakes, so we need to reexamine the topic a bit.

Value betting is fairly simple at micro-stakes because those games offer you so many profitable opportunities to bet. You flop top pair plus a flush draw and bet; your opponent calls. You hit your flush on the turn and bet; your opponent calls again. You bet the river and get called a third time; your opponent shows second pair and you win. Why did he call three bets with second pair? Because his hand might have been good if you were bluffing.

We call this kind of value *fat value*, and it's prevalent at the micro-stakes. But at small stakes your opponents are going to put up more of a fight, and often you'll get to the river thinking that you might be good, you're probably good, but you can't be really sure. Making river bets under these circumstances is what's called *extracting thin value*, and you'll need to become good at recognizing thin value and extracting it to succeed at small stakes games.

Trouble
on the River

Problems with betting the river occur because three reliable no-limit hold 'em principles come into apparent conflict. Here's the first principle, which we called "The Strength Principle" in "Part One: Basic No-Limit Hold 'em Concepts."

> In general, you want to bet your strong hands, check or call with your hands of middling strength, and fold or bluff with your weak hands.

The second principle is even more succinct:

> Big hand, big pot; small hand, small pot.

And finally, here's the third principle:

> When you think you have the best hand, you want to get more money in the pot.

Individually, all these principles make sense. But what happens when you get to the river with a hand like top pair, top kicker and your opponent has called your bets to this point? Your hand may still be best since your opponent hasn't given any sign that his is better, so the third principle argues for a bet. But if you bet, the pot will have gotten large, and the second principle says that a one pair hand on the river is pretty modest, and deserves only a small pot. Furthermore, the first principle supports the second principle: if you check you can at least try to capture the value represented by your pair, while if you bet you might get raised off the hand with a bluff.

The situation is a real conundrum, one that leads many players to forgo river bets with modest but probably good hands. It's an easy decision to rationalize while playing since almost any board can look threatening by the river. *"What if that deuce just*

gave my opponent a set? Or two pair? If he started with five-trey,
he just made a straight! Lots of things can beat me. I check."

So what's the solution to this problem? First, let's note that
learning how to extract value on the river is a key skill whether
you have a monster hand or a modest one. So if you're going to be
successful at small stakes hold 'em, you're going to have to be
efficient at harvesting the value that's available when all the cards
are out, where the bets are larger, and where your opponent has no
chance of drawing out if he's behind. Here are some guidelines to
help capture river equity:

1. **Plan your hands.** Top pair is a nice hand on the flop but a
    modest one by the river. Don't feel you have to build a big
    pot by betting all three streets with top pair. It worked at the
    micro-stakes when you could get called all the way by
    bottom pair; it won't work so well against better opponents.
    Instead, vary your betting by sometimes checking the flop
    and betting the turn, or betting the flop and checking the turn.
    Either line will bring you to the river with a pot that's much
    smaller than your stack, which in turn gives you plenty of
    flexibility to bet the river without committing your whole
    stack. In addition, these different lines will diversify your
    play and make you difficult to read.

2. **Analyze the hand.** Hand-reading is not only an art, but it's
    crucial for small stakes play. Start with your opponent's
    preflop range and try to narrow it after the flop by eliminating
    hands as you see actions from your opponent. Would he
    really bet the turn with a draw? Could he check a set in that
    spot? By the time you reach the river, you should have
    narrowed your opponent's range to a manageable number.

3. **Make sure he can call with hands you beat.** There's no
    point to betting the river if he can't call with a worse hand.
    For example, if an ace, king, and jack have hit the board by

the river, there aren't going to be any low pairs in his calling range. If you can't find any such hands, check and see what happens.

4. **Bluff raises on the river aren't common at these stakes.** Players often refuse to bet a modest hand on the river for fear of running into a check-raise bluff, and having to fold a hand with some value. Resist this fear! Your opponents aren't supermen. Small stakes players are much better than micro-stakes players, and they do many things well, but bluff-raising the river isn't one of them. That's a ploy you'll find in higher-stakes games. Of course, there can always be an exception. But players like these are normally playing in larger games.

Being able to bet the river with hands of modest value has another benefit as well. By betting these hands, you avoid the problem of creating an excessively *polarized range*. That is a range of betting hands that includes strong hands and bluffs, but no medium strength hands. When you have a polarized betting range on the river, your opponent knows that your checking range consists of a combination of medium-strength hands and hands that were a little too strong to bluff. This knowledge lets him value bet more effectively, eliminating a lot of the value of your modest hands.

Example No. 1: You're under the gun with a $320 stack in a $200 NL 6-max game holding the

It's a bit outside your normal raising range for under the gun, but you've shown down several big hands in the last hour and think the table is giving you a lot of respect, so you raise to $6. The small blind, with a $170 stack, calls $5, and his VP$IP/PFR numbers after 28 hands are 50/22. The big blind folds and the pot is $14.

The flop is the

The small blind checks and since the board is pretty dry, you make a small continuation bet of $6. The small blind calls and the pot is $26.

The turn is the 7♠ and the small blind checks. Since you don't have anything and aren't sure you can bet this player off a low pair, you check as well. The pot stays at $26.

The river is the J♠ giving you second pair and the small blind bets $10. Right now, you think it's likely your hand is best. It's hard to put the small blind on a queen since he just called preflop and checked both the flop and the turn. It's not impossible that he hit a backdoor spade draw, but it's unlikely. And two pair hands are unlikely on this board as well.

At micro-stakes, a raise would be a reasonable play since a loose player could call with a lot of medium or small pairs despite the queen and jack on board. However, at small stakes a raise doesn't really make sense since the only hands that can call are those that are beating you. That's because loose players, in this type of situation at the small stakes are capable of throwing away something like a pair of eights if you raise them on the river. Therefore, calling is the best play even though your hand is probably good. You call and your opponent shows the 9♥9♠ and you take the pot.

Just because you've read the hand and decided you're probably best doesn't guarantee a good "thin value" bet or raise. Your opponent also has to be able to pay off.

Example No. 2: You're in the big blind with a $260 stack in a $200 NL 6-max game holding the Q♣7♥. The first three players fold and the button makes a min-raise to $4. He's the same 52/20 player you faced in Example No. 1, but his stack is now $150. The small blind folds and getting 3.5-to-1 pot odds against a loose player, you elect to call. The flop is the Q♠6♣5♦.

Your hand is certainly ahead of most of his range, but leading out on this dry flop with a single high card telegraphs the kind of hand you actually have. Checking and calling his continuation bet tells him little about what you're doing, and that's a better choice.

You check. Your opponent bets $6 and you call. The pot is now $21 and the turn is the 9♥.

While your hand isn't a powerhouse, you have no reason to think you're behind, and your call on the flop may slow him down if he has something like ace-six or five-four, so you need to take the lead now. Since a draw is unlikely, you don't need to make a big bet; you just need to keep building the pot, but in a way that a medium pair feels justified in hanging around.

You bet $8 and he calls. The pot is now $37 and the river card is the 2♦.

That's a good card because it's hard to assign your opponent a hand that the deuce can help. So betting is still good even though your hand is modest. That's because your opponent's hand is probably worse. Your flop check has, to some extent, disguised your actual hand. Hence you should bet on the end, but you need to make a small enough bet, like one-third the pot, so a hand like a pair of sixes can call.

You bet $12. Your opponent calls and shows the A♠6♠, and you take the pot.

Don't confuse this situation with some of the "small hand, small pot" advice we gave earlier. It's true that we have a small hand here, and yet we're betting the river. That's simply because, as best we can determine, our opponent has even less. In addition, we did keep the pot small by making small bets throughout. If your hand reading skills are good, you'll encounter many situations where your modest hand on the river still rates to be best, and can still be called by hands that your opponent could plausibly hold. Developing those skills is the essence of "thin value" betting.

Example No. 3: You're in the big blind with a $120 stack holding the J♥T♥ in a $100 NL 6-max game. The first four players fold and the small blind just calls for another $0.50, and his VP$IP/PFR numbers after 22 hands are 42/20.

You elect to raise to $3. You have a decent hand, are in position, and your opponent looks like he limps with a lot of mediocre hands. He calls another $2 and the pot is $6.

The flop is the J♠7♦6♠ giving you top pair, weak kicker. Somewhat unexpectedly, your opponent bets $3. A raise on your part would be an aggressive play given your hand strength, and any ace, king, or queen on the turn could be troublesome. So you call $3 making the pot $12.

The turn, the 4♠, is a bad card for you. It completes a flush and might give him a straight draw. This time your opponent again bets $3, just one-fourth of the pot.

Odd bets like this could represent weakness, or they could be attempts to lure you into a bigger pot, but you can't fold top pair getting 5-to-1 odds, so you call. The pot is now $18.

The river is the 4♦ which only hurts you if your opponent had a hand like five-four. This time he checks.

Despite your modest hand of top pair, weak kicker, it's time to make a bet. Lots of hands beat you, but the evidence of the betting is that your opponent doesn't have one of those hands. He could be trapping with something big, but that's what "thin value" betting is all about: reading the hand assuming that his actions mean something. In this case, what they mean is that you're ahead. You bet $10 and your opponent folds.

Unlike some of our other hands, this one played out much the same way as it would have at the micro-stakes since your play was pretty much predicated on your opponent's loose statistics. Players with similar statistics are common at micro-stakes but less common at small stakes. The ones you find, however, will tend to play the same way and make similar mistakes.

Extracting Value with Bigger Hands

When you have a strong hand, you want to manage the action so as to extract as much value as possible. The key questions are whether to bet or check, how much to bet, and how to handle the river. Unlike micro-stakes games, where your opponents were primarily focused on their own hands, now your opponents will be giving some thought to just what your bets represent. You want to keep their range in mind, and your bets should try to tell a story that some parts of their range can beat.

Example No. 1: You're on the button with a stack of $220 holding the in a $200 NL 6-max game. The first three players fold and you raise to $6. The small blind calls $5 and the big blind folds. The small blind has an odd set of statistics: VP$IP/PFR of 36/5, ATS of only 9, overall aggression of just 0.8, but a 3-bet of 10, all based on 55 hands. The pot is now $14.

The flop is the

and the small blind just checks. Your top set is obviously a monster hand. The real question becomes "How do we extract the most value against this opponent?" Looking at his statistics, it's apparent that the numbers are consistent except for the 3-betting number of 10 percent, which stands out as an anomaly. Since the numbers are based on only 55 hands, we'll just disregard the 3-bet number as representing a couple of fluke big hands, and base our strategy on the others. We think our opponent is passive overall and not positionally aware because of the low 'attempt to steal' number.

Since he's passive, we can't really expect him to take the lead or semi-bluff in any way. Therefore, the best idea is to make small bets in the hope that he has just enough of a hand to hang around. From his 36 percent VP$IP number, we know he likes to be involved in hands, so let's offer him a cheap price to stick around. But that strategy comes with a risk: If he's actually on a flush draw, we'll be offering him a good price (probably a correct price) to stay. But if he's on any other hand, he's getting the wrong price, and since that's the most likely situation, that's what we'll assume.

We bet $4 and the small blind calls. The pot is $22.

We got a nibble on the line, so he probably has something: maybe a small pair, a draw, two overcards, or even just one overcard! By betting small, we lose our ability to narrow his range, but since our hand is strong we don't care. The turn is the T♥ and this player checks again.

The flush didn't hit, and if he has a low pair, he may be afraid of two overcards on board. On the other hand, if he had exactly jack-ten, we'll get his whole stack. Let's make another small bet and see what happens.

We bet $8 and he calls. The pot is $38 and the effective stack is $37. Also notice that we bet just enough so that we can put him all-in on the river with a pot-sized bet.

The river is the K♣ and the small blind checks again. Notice that we have two ways to go here. We could make another small bet in the hope that a weak pair might look us up because of the big odds, or in the hope that a busted flush might try to bluff us. Or we could put him all-in with the hope that our play looks like a bluff, that he just hit a king, or that he collected two pair along the way and can now call.

Of the two approaches, putting him all-in is clearly better. Given his passive statistics, we can't count on him ever bluffing us, and if he has nothing or a low pair, even a small bet may not get called. Let's hope he has something like the K♦x♦, or maybe king-ten or king-jack, in which case we want him to call as big a bet as possible.

We bet $50 and our opponent folds. Dry hole, but we did the best we could.

Example No. 2. You're in the cutoff with a $240 stack in a $200 NL 6-max game holding the 7♣7♥. The under the gun player folds and Player B in middle position, with a stack of $112, calls $2. Player B who just joined the table has VP$IP/PFR numbers of 40/0 after only five hands, and he's just lost two big pots and may be on tilt. So you attack Player B and raise to $8. The button and small blind fold and the big blind, with a stack of $192 and who after 15 hands has VP$IP/PFR statistics of 20/0, calls. Player B also calls and the pot is now $25.

The flop is the Q♠Q♥7♠ and you've hit a full house. The big blind checks and Player B bets $14.

You're going to call. Raising would only make sense if you could reliably put him on a big pair or a queen, which at this stage of the hand would be almost impossible Calling also gives the big blind a chance to make a squeeze play, which is unlikely but not impossible since either player could have a flush draw at this point. If Player B is really on tilt and has something like a medium pair, calling gives him a green light to continue betting. You call $14, the big blind folds, and the pot is $53.

The turn is the T♥. Player B now bets $32 and the effective stack is now $58.

At this point, the right play is to push all-in. This may be surprising to many players who might think that continuing to show weakness by calling must be the right idea. However, let's look at the real hands he might have and see how they would react to a turn push or a turn call followed by a river bet.

1. **He has a flush draw.** If we push, the pot will be $175 and he'll need $58 to call. Those are about 3-to-1 odds. It's not enough, but if he has a draw with an ace or a king, he may rationalize that the high card gives him extra outs. If we wait, we'll only get his money if he hits the flush, or if he misses and decides to bluff. He might realize, however, that his stack is so small that the bluff won't be effective, and just save his money. Also note that he could have a flush draw in either hearts or spades, so this variation is more likely than usual. Big edge to pushing.

2.   **He has a queen.** Either play will get his money, or cost us our whole stack if he pairs his kicker or the ten pairs. No difference.

3.   **He has a pair below queens.** Waiting could be costly. Unless he has a pair of jacks or a ten in his hand, he'll probably fold to a push. He'll also fold those same hands to a river push unless he has nines or eights and hits a queen or his card on the river, in which case he beats us. Edge to pushing.

4.   **He has nothing.** If we wait it's possible he'll bluff off the rest of his stack on the river, but if we push now he'll go away. Edge to waiting.

In short, waiting only gains if he has nothing and is inclined to bluff the rest of his stack; pushing now is a better play.

We push, and he calls and shows the A♥6♥. The river is the 8♠ and we take the pot.

The Problems

Problem 5-1

Table layout:

UTG	Player A $106	
MP	You $184	Your HUD (This session) You / (28) / +42 VP 32 / PF 26 Your HUD (Overall) You / (many) / +6 VP 16 / PF 12
CO	Player B $82	B's HUD Player B / (252) / +6 VP 20 / PF 15
BTN	Player C $102	C's HUD Player C / (512) / -2 VP 28 / PF 14
SB	Player D $112	D's HUD Player D / (28) / -12 VP 22 / PF 18 / AS 10 / FB 100 3B 0 / F3 -- / AF 2 / 3 / 0 / 0
BB	Player E $66	E's HUD Player E / (356) / +3 VP 16 / PF 12

Situation: Online $100 NL 6-max table. Blinds are $0.50 and $1.00.

Your hand: J♠J♥

Action to you: Player A folds.

Question: *What do you do?*

    Answer: Of course you'll raise. We've included two HUDs for you because the action at the table so far has been unusual. Your first HUD, labeled 'This session,' shows what's happened so far: you've had a good run of cards, played a lot of hands, and almost doubled your money. The second HUD, labeled 'overall,' shows what an opponent would see if he had played many sessions with you: in fact, you're a pretty tight, conservative player, with VP$IP/PFR numbers of only 16/12.

    These two HUDs are important because as we look at the rest of the players to act, we notice that their HUDs for us will be showing very different numbers. Player D in the small blind has only played with us at this table. He sees our HUD based on just 28 hands and probably thinks we're a very aggressive player who's been pushing the table around. Players B, C, and E have played against us many times; they see our style for what it is: tight and conservative, and they're unlikely to believe that we have suddenly changed our stripes.

Action: You raise to $3 and the next two players fold. Player D in the small blind reraises to $8.50 and the big blind folds. The pot is now $12.50.

Question: *What do you do?*

    Answer: Player D's HUD doesn't help much because based on the 28 hands we've played so far, there isn't much information. His PFR number of 18 pegs him as somewhat aggressive, but his 3-bet percentage of 0 isn't meaningful.

Most likely he's had three or four opportunities to 3-bet and hasn't done anything yet.

What is helpful is his impression of our statistics. To Player D, we must look like a wild man with our VP$IP/PFR numbers of 32/26, and he must believe we'll be stealing pots with a lot of marginal hands. As a result, we can credit him with a wide 3-betting range and here's how our jacks are doing against three possible ranges:

1. Against a 4 percent range of AA through TT, AKs, AKo, and AQs, we're 44 percent.

2. Against a 7 percent range including all those hands plus 99, 88, AJs, KQs, AQo, and AJo, we're 55 percent.

3. Against a 10 percent range including all those hands plus 77, 66, ATs, KJs, QJs, and KQo, we're 58 percent.

The last range, given what we know, is probably a better guess of his true range than any other. And since we're favored against his range and there are a lot of cards we don't want to see on the flop, we should 4-bet. So given his stack size, I would 4-bet to $30, and if he decides to 5-bet by pushing all-in, which in turns lets us narrow his range substantially, we can get away from the hand.

Action: We 4-bet to $30 and Player B, after thinking for awhile, folds.

Problem 5-2

Table layout:

UTG	Player A $218	
MP	Player B $217	
CO	Player C $103	C's HUD Player C / (3) / -150 VP 33 / PF 33 / AS na / FB na 3B 0 / F3 100 / AF inf / inf / na / na CB 100 / FC na / FT na W$F 0 / WtS 100 / W$S 0
BTN	Player D $200	
SB	Player E $35	
BB	You $200	

Situation: You have just sat down at an online $200 NL 6-max table. Blinds are $1.00 and $2.00.

Your hand: 5♣4♣

Action to you: The first two players fold. Player C opens for $6 and Player D and the small blind fold. The pot is $9.

Question: *What do you do?*

    Answer: We're playing our first hand at this table and know essentially nothing about our opponent who raised from the cutoff seat. With so little data, we can't narrow his range much except to say that his hand is probably better than average.

    With no hard information, we need to fall back on first principles, so let's list what we know:

1.   We have a hand with some promise (low suited connectors).

2.   We need to put in $4 to call, so we're getting 9-to-4 odds, or 2.25-to-1.

3.   We'll be out of position after the flop.

4.   Our opponent's stack is just over 50 big blinds, about 13 times the size of our call.

    In general, we want to defend our blinds. If you're a typical player, you'll discover over time that at a 6-max table you tend to win money in the four non-blind seats (with the most money being won on the button) while losing money in the blinds. Since you're required to post a blind no matter how bad your hand may be, and since you're out of position in the subsequent play, you can't expect to show a profit in the blinds.[8] You can, however, work to reduce your losses, and the best way to reduce your losses is to take advantage of

---

[8] If you don't include the blind money already in the pot, you should also be winning money from the blinds. That's because the alternative of folding produces an expectation from that point on of $0.00, and you should only play hands that do better than this. But your overall expectation will still be negative due to the required blind bet.

generous pot odds when offered and call with playable hands. With odds of 2.25-to-1, suited connectors are an easy call here.

When you call in the blinds with suited connectors and other playable cards, don't be discouraged if the flop comes with three high cards and you have to fold. Your compensation for calling won't necessarily come immediately. It can come further down the road when you hit disguised monsters on the flop, or when your image as a player with a wide calling range lets you pull off some unlikely bluffs. All good players actively defend their big blinds; you should too.

Now let's note a couple of caveats. If the initial raiser had a short stack, say 20 big blinds or so, you can fold this hand since the implied odds you need to make the call worthwhile won't be there. If the initial raiser had made a bigger raise, say to four big blinds instead of three, then you're only being offered 11-to-6 odds, or less than 2-to-1, to call. In that case, you need to tighten your calling requirements somewhat and it might be best to let the five-four suited go, but I would still be happy to call with a seven-six suited.

Action: You call another $4 and the pot is now $13.

Flop: Q♦T♥8♣

Question: *What do you do?*

    Answer: We can't put Player C on much of a range yet, but this flop has enough high cards to have hit a lot of ranges pretty well. We, on the other hand, have whiffed completely. Betting here is a little silly, so let's check and see what happens.

Action: You check and Player C checks as well.

Turn: T♦

Question: *What do you do?*

Answer: How you play now depends mostly on what level of game you're playing. At micro-stakes, a bet here would take down the pot a good percentage of the time. That bet would say "I have a ten and I didn't bet the flop because of the overcard, but now I have trips, so you're toast." A lot of micro-stakes players would believe you and go away.

But more sophisticated players are suspicious of a betting line that goes "check - check - board pairs - I bet." You're unlikely to actually have a ten, but much more likely to see the chance for a move. A good player will often play back at you in this case or call down with just an ace.

Here we're in a $1/$2 game against an unknown opponent. We don't know his level — either his level of thinking or his level of skill. A bet certainly has some value, but that board is supposed to have come somewhere near his hand and a lot of his range should have connected in some way. So considering we're out of position, know nothing about Player C, and it's still early in the session, there's no harm in conceding this hand. Yes, it's good to be aggressive. But it's better when I have some information to inform my decision and this isn't that place.

Action: You check and fold after Player C bets $8.

Problem 5-3

Table layout:

UTG	Player A $250	
MP	Player B $510	
CO	Player C $60	C's HUD Player C / (15) / +31 VP 33 / PF 33 / AS 100 / FB na 3B 33/ F3 100 / AF inf / inf / na / na CB 100 / FC na / FT na W$F 50 / WtS 0 / W$S na
BTN	Player D $240	
SB	You $220	
BB	Player E $140	E's HUD Player E / (55) / -70 VP 36 / PF 5 / AS 9 / FB 50 3B 5 / F3 100 / AF 0.8 / 2 / 0 / 0 CB 0 / FC 60 / FT 0 W$F 39 / WtS 28 / W$S 40

Situation: Online $200 NL 6-max table. Blinds are $1.00 and $2.00.

Your hand: 9♦7♦

Action to you: The first two players fold. Player C min-raises to $4 and Player D folds.

Question: *What do you do?*

Answer: In the right circumstances, you certainly wouldn't mind calling with a hand like nine-seven suited. Ideally, you'd like to be in position against a loose-passive player with a big stack. The big stack would give you the implied odds needed with a suited one-gap hand, and a loose-passive style means that he'll likely call at least a bet or two when you hit your hand and give you the choice between semi-bluffing or just taking a free card when you need it. (Against most loose-passive players you'll be taking the free card since semi-bluffing won't work as often as you'd like.)

Here, however, you're against a loose but very aggressive player with a short stack. The loose part is nice because you're almost getting the pot odds you need to call right away. (Your hand is 38 percent against a 40 percent raising range which is probably about right for this player in the cutoff.) But his short stack and his 100 percent continuation betting frequency means that this hand will tend to be decided early, rather than late. When there's a good chance that the hand will be settled on the flop, you'd rather be playing a high-card hand which has a better chance of making top pair than a medium-card hand that tends to make second pair or a draw.

So calling here with nine-seven suited certainly wouldn't qualify as a blunder, but I'd wait for a better position against a bigger stack. If Player E, instead of Player D, was the one raising in the cutoff, you'd have an easy call.

Action: You fold.

Problem 5-4

Table layout:

UTG	Sitting Out	
MP	Player A $120	A's HUD Player A / (21) / +26 VP 14 / PF 5 / AS 0 / FB 50 3B 17 / F3 na / AF inf / inf / inf / na CB 100 / FC na / FT na W$F 75 / WtS 0 / W$S na
CO	You $210	Your HUD You / (37) / +4 VP 27 / PF 22 / AS 31 / FB 50
BTN	Player B $250	
SB	Player C $130	
BB	Player D $240	D's HUD Player D / (40) / +19 VP 28 / PF 25 / AS 33 / FB 100 3B 22 / F3 50 / AF 3 / inf / 1 / na CB 100 / FC 100 / FT na W$F 33 / WtS 17 / W$S 100

Situation: Online $200 NL 6-max table. Blinds are $1.00 and $2.00.

Your hand: A♣7♣

Action to you: Player A raises to $8 and the pot is $11.

Question: *What do you do?*
    Answer: Fold. You don't really have any good options here. Ace-seven suited isn't strong enough for calling a raiser with a narrow range since many of his hands will dominate you. So against a 5 percent raising range, for instance, your raw winning chances, assuming the players behind you all fold, are only about 30 percent preflop.
    Against wider opening ranges, ace-seven suited appears to offer reasonable chances. For instance, here's how you're doing against some wider ranges:

Opponents Range	Your chance
15%	43%
20%	46%
25%	48%

    But you're actually not doing as well as it appears. Since there are three players yet to act (including one aggressive player in the big blind), you will sometimes be squeezed off your hand. And since you're often dominated, you can hit your hand and still lose a reasonably big pot.
    However, when calling is a losing play, 3-betting can be attractive. Here, a 3-bet is essentially a bluff, but your hand works well. You would obviously fold to a 4-bet whose range includes many of the hands that crush you. But against a wide range, your 3-bet would induce many folds. Finally, most of the hands that call would be medium pairs, and against that range you will generally know where you stand after the flop.
    Unfortunately, 3-betting still doesn't work well here because your opponent's raising range (5 percent) is so tight that you can't make him fold enough hands for it to be profitable. If his PFR were 15 percent or higher, 3-betting would be your best option. Therefore, you should just fold.

Action: You fold.

Problem 5-5

Table layout:

UTG	Player A $462	
MP	Player B $333	
CO	Player C $156	C's HUD Player C / (58) / +14 VP 31 / PF 12 / AS 28 / FB 80 3B 5 / F3 25 / AF 1.7 / 1 / inf / inf CB 60 / FC 50 / FT 60 W$F 43 / WtS 14 / W$S 100
BTN	Player D $109	
SB	You $198	Your HUD You / (58) / -1 VP 24 / PF 18
BB	Player E $43	E's HUD Player E / (22) / +1 VP 10 / PF 8

Situation: Online $200 NL 6-max table. Blinds are $1.00 and $2.00.

Your hand: K♣K♥

Action to you: The first two players fold. Player C in the cutoff min-raises to $4 and Player D folds.

Question: *What do you do?*

   Answer: We'll certainly 3-bet our kings, but first it's a good habit to look and see what our opponent might have. His PFR of only 12 indicates he likes to have a pretty good hand when he raises. His ATS of 28 shows that he's positionally aware and doesn't need a great hand to raise in a stealing position, but he won't just be raising with any two cards. His 'fold-to-3-bet' number is also a low 25 which may just reflect a small sample, but certainly hints that he won't necessarily go away when we reraise him. So even from the cutoff, we can probably put him on a raising range of something like 15 to 17 percent of his hands, a range which looks roughly like this:

> All pairs
> Suited aces: AKs through A8s
> All suited Broadway cards
> Offsuit aces: AKo through ATo
> Suited connectors: T9s and 98s
> Offsuit Broadways: KQo, KJo, QJo

   As an aside, against this range our kings are currently a little more than a 3-to-1 favorite. We've been playing about an hour and haven't yet tangled with this player in a big pot, so history isn't really an issue. He has, however, been a solid winner at the table although he's shown down very few hands.

Action: We raise to $14 and the big blind folds. Player C calls another $10 and the pot is $30.

Flop: J♠J♣4♥

Action to you: We act first.

Question: *What should we do?*

    Answer: Let's start by adjusting his range given that he called our 3-bet. Normally, this would reduce a player's range quite a bit. Here, we can't be so sure because he seems to like to call 3-bets once he puts some money in the pot. So let's keep all medium to high pairs, the high suited aces, and the high offsuit aces. We'll also keep aces and queens (and the lone remaining pair of kings) on the theory that a player who calls a high percentage of 3-bets may be calling rather than 4-betting with some very good hands. And his new range looks like this:

> Pairs from AA to 77
> Suited aces: AKs through ATs
> Offsuit aces: AKo through AJo

That's about 7.5 percent of his total hands.

    We're obviously doing well against that range. We're ahead of all his hands except aces (which might not be in the range at all), as well as ace-jack, suited or not. Interestingly, our 3-bet preflop actually should have chased away most of the hands which would now be beating us.

    So far, we've been continuation betting about 70 percent of the time with our bets varying between 50 and 75 percent of the pot. Since we've been continuation betting on flops we missed, we also need to make sure we bet on flops that helped us, or at least didn't hurt us.

    In addition, our continuation bet here is a straight value bet, charging the aces and lower pairs that make up most of his range. Since this flop must appear (to him) to have missed much of our range as well, our bet is likely to get a call.

Action: We bet $18 and our opponent calls. The pot is now $66 and the effective stack is $124.

Note that his flop call doesn't narrow his range. Virtually all hands left in his range would call given the forced nature of our bet and his positional advantage. Thus another reason to bet a pair of kings.

Turn: 2♣

Question: *Now what?*

Answer: That deuce didn't help any part of his range, so our relative situation remains unchanged and we need to think about how to extract additional value from the majority of his range that we're beating. But a bet probably isn't the right way to do that. All it will do is fold out a lot of his hands, while a check will allow him to bluff.

Notice that his turn and river aggression factor numbers are infinite, meaning that we haven't seen him call on the later streets, but we have seen at least some bets or raises. His 'went to showdown' number, which is probably based on very little data, is only 14, but like the aggression factor number it gives us a hint that he might be willing to stick in a bet. None of this evidence is conclusive, but checking to try and induce a bluff looks like the right way to go.

Action: We bet $26 and he folds.

Even a small bet, offering good odds, was more than his hand could take. Most likely he floated the flop with a small pair or an ace-x type hand with the idea of taking the pot away if we couldn't fire a second barrel.

Problem 5-6

Table layout:

UTG	Player A $210	
MP	You $350	Your HUD You / (55) / 68 VP 36 / PF 29 / AS 30 / FB 66
CO	Player B $180	
BTN	Player C $170	
SB	Player D $250	D's HUD Player D / (44) / +38 VP 29 / PF 24 / AS 67 / FB 100 3B 10 / F3 50 / AF 3 / 4.5 / 1 / 2 CB 66 / FC 40 / FT 60 W$F 50 / WtS 22 / W$S 75
BB	Player E $200	

Situation: Online $200 NL 6-max table. Blinds are $1.00 and $2.00. You've had a great run of cards to start the first hour of this session, played a lot of hands, and won a lot of pots. So far you're up $150.

Your hand: K♣T♠

Action to you: The first player folds.

Question: *What do you do?*

    Answer: Raise unless you're a tight player. King-ten offsuit will show up in your range at about the 17 to 19 percent level. In middle position, you'll be raising a hand like this if your overall PFR number is in the mid-twenties. That's an aggressive PFR, but not an absurdly aggressive one, and you'll face some difficult post-flop decisions with this hand, but that's what aggressive players learn to do.

Action: You raise to $6 and Players B and C fold. Player D in the small blind reraises to $22 and the big blind folds. The pot is now $31.

Question: *What do you do?*

    Answer: When confronted with a 3-bet, we need to ask ourselves a few questions. Here are the most important:

1.   What's our estimate of him and his 3-betting range?

2.   What's his impression of us and our raising range?

3.   How good is our hand in relation to our whole range?

4.   How do position and stack sizes factor into our decision?

    Let's look at these questions one at a time.

1.   **Our estimate of him.** We have just enough data on Player D to start putting together a preliminary picture. He's loose and aggressive; his VP$IP and PFR numbers are 29/24, definitely on the high side. His 'attempt to steal' number of 67 and his aggression factor of 3 are just more confirming information, as is his 3-bet

percentage of 10. He definitely likes to put pressure on the other players.

If 10 percent is his real 3-betting percentage, then his range looks something like this:

> Pairs from AA to 55
> Suited aces: AKs to ATs
> Offsuit aces: AKo to AJo
> Other Broadways: KQs, KJs, KQo

Against that range, our king-ten offsuit is about 33 percent to win.

2. **His impression of us.** If he's been tracking us this session our VP$IP/PFR stats of 36/29 probably makes him think we're even looser and more aggressive than he is. So if he puts us on a 25 percent raising range (from middle position), it would look like this:

> All pairs
> All suited aces
> Offsuit aces down to A5o
> All suited and offsuit Broadways

That's a pretty big range and he can reasonably expect us to fold most of it.

3. **How good is our hand in relation to our whole range?** Our king-ten offsuit is near the bottom of our actual range for this position. Even given our opponent's probable assessment of our range, which should be looser than our real range, this hand still ranks near the bottom.

4. **How do position and stack sizes factor into our decision?** We have position on him which is an advantage if we decide to play. His stack was 125 big blinds to start the hand, and we had him easily covered. That's moderately deep. However, we don't really have the sort of hand that benefits from big implied odds, in contrast to, say, a low suited connector. Stack sizes are therefore neutral to unfavorable for our hand.

So what do we do? Clearly we can't 4-bet for value; our hand is too weak for that. Calling isn't an appealing option either. Although we have position, our hand is weak, and if we hit it we won't be sure if our hand is good or dominated and walking into a trap.

If we eliminate 4-betting for value and calling, we're down to just two possibilities: folding and 4-bet bluffing. Folding is fine and no one could criticize you for tossing this hand in the muck. However, notice that this is an excellent spot for 4-bet bluffing! A number of factors make the bluff reraise especially strong here:

1. Your opponent is aggressive and has a wide range.

2. You've appeared more aggressive than you are, and his action may be based on that perception.

3. You have position which may make him more reluctant to call.

4. A 5-bet on his part essentially commits him to the pot.

After a bluff 4-bet on your part, your opponent may conclude that his choices have been reduced to pushing or folding, in which case he may choose to fold a big chunk of his range. Also, you need to 4-bet bluff some of the time against regular opponents, and even though he isn't a regular (yet), it's still a good spot. Raise to $60 or $65 and see what happens.

Action: You 4-bet to $60 and after a long pause, Player D folds.

You may well have folded out a better hand, something like AQ, AJ, AT, KQ, or the medium or small pairs. Whatever he had, it wasn't a hand that he wanted to play for his whole stack.

Problem 5-7

Table layout:

UTG	Player A $217	
MP	Player B $109	
CO	Player C $200	
BTN	Player D $30	D's HUD Player D / (4) / -250 VP 50 / PF 0 / AS 0 / FB na 3B 0 / F3 na / AF na / na / na / na CB na / FC na / FT na W$F na / WtS na / W$S na
SB	You $194	
BB	Player E $218	

Situation: You are new to an online $200 NL 6-max table. Blinds are $1.00 and $2.00.

Your hand: A♣T♠

Action to you: The first three players fold and Player D opens for $4. The pot is $7.

Question: *What do you do?*

Answer: We're certainly not folding our ace-ten to a raise from the button. Still, let's analyze the situation and see where we stand.

We know essentially nothing about our opponent. He's played a couple of hands and lost some money in the blinds, hence his negative 'BB/100' score. All we can say is that a generic player made a min-raise from the button which is probably just a raise from a weakish hand that wants to see if it can take down the blinds. But it could also be a trap from a strong hand or it might just be the case that Player D likes the risk-reward ratio from min-raising, so he min-raises most of the time. We don't know, and we won't know that information until we're many hands along in the session. So for now, we'll have to respond in the dark.

Whatever his real raising range from the button, our ace-ten should do well. Let's use PokerStove to see exactly how well against various ranges.

Our Raw Winning Chances

Against a 20 percent range: 52%
Against a 25 percent range: 55%
Against a 30 percent range: 56%
Against a 35 percent range: 57%
Against a 40 percent range: 58%

And the answer is that we're doing well against all but the tightest button ranges. (We drop to even money if he's playing an 18 percent range, but that's very tight for the button.) What's more, our raw winning chances don't change much once his range expands past 25 percent. I like 3-betting for value once my hand is about 55 percent against his range and since a 30 percent raising range from the button is a good estimate for an unknown player, I'm happy 3-betting here. A good 3-bet size would be about $12.

Note that his stack size (15 big blinds before his raise) and our poor position makes me even happier to get the money in. This is a hand that will be decided either preflop or on the flop, and my two high cards should do well in this situation.

But if he responds by pushing, will we call? Yes. The pot would then be $45 (assuming the big blind has folded) and it would cost $18 to call. For that, we'd need a winning chance of 40 percent.

$$0.40 = \frac{\$18}{\$45}$$

Those are about our winning chances against a typical 11 percent range, and given his stack size and the likelihood that he sees himself as pot-committed if he calls, his real range should be wider.

Action: You 3-bet to $12 and the blinds and Player D fold.

Against a player who raises from the button 30 percent of the time or a little more, you can 3-bet for value with about 8 percent of your hands, a range consisting of

AA through 88
AK through AT, suited or unsuited

You'll also need to mix in some bluffs, ideally hands which have some value when your 3-bet is just called. And I like to use the suited connectors and suited one-gappers for this purpose. For instance:

JTs through 76s
QTs through 86s

These amount to another 3 percent of the hands, giving you a total 3-betting frequency of about 11 percent from the small blind against a button raiser.

One final point. Some players would argue for 3-betting even more often than this, but in the small blind you do have to consider the threat of the big blind, who's still free to act behind you.

Problem 5-8

Table layout:

UTG	You $220	
MP	Player A $330	A's HUD Player A / (60) / +8 VP 25 / PF 20 / AS 35 / FB 40
CO	Player B $130	B's HUD Player B / (140) / -3 VP 15 / PF 10 / AS 18 / FB 70
BTN	Player C $80	C's HUD Player C / (35) / -30 VP 40 / PF 18 / AS 80 / FB 20 3B 0 / F3 100 / AF 1.5 / 1 / 1 / na CB 60 / FC 0 / FT 100 W$F 25 / WtS 50 / W$S 25
SB	Player D $200	D's HUD Player D / (1) / -1 VP 0 / PF 0 / AS 0 / FB na
BB	Player E $405	E's HUD Player E / (60) / +12 VP 13 / PF 6 / AS 12 / FB 75

Situation: Online $200 NL 6-max table. Blinds are $1.00 and $2.00.

Your hand: A♥Q♠

Question: *What do you do?*

   Answer: Ace-queen offsuit is certainly a raising hand from under the gun (or anywhere else) so let's raise. But how much should we raise? Different players have different styles. Some like to raise three big blinds, others 3.5 big blinds, still others 4 big blinds. All are reasonable amounts. One approach that's often used is to observe what the other players do and copy it, which has the merit of not making you stand out from the crowd.

   The approach I prefer is to look at the characteristics of the other players at the table. If they seem tight, raise a smaller amount since that should be enough to get them to fold if they don't have a hand they want to play. If they do have a hand, it will tend to be a good hand, so by raising less you've invested less in a pot where you may be an underdog.

   On the other hand, if you're at a loose table, raise more. Your opponents will now tend to be playing weaker hands than you, so you're getting more money in the pot with what is often the better hand.

   When you're deciding on an opening raise size, pay special attention to the statistics of the big blind and weigh his tendencies more than the other players. Your raise size controls the pot odds that are offered to him, which is particularly important since he's already invested in the pot. Here's a quick chart of the most popular raise sizes and the pot odds that the big blind sees, assuming everyone else at the table folds:

Raise Size	Pot Odds Offered to the Big Blind
3 big blinds	2.25-to-1
3.5 big blinds	2-to-1
4 big blinds	1.83-to-1

Looking at our opponents, we can see that Player C looks loose, Player A is a little loose but aggressive, Player D is an unknown quantity, and Players B and E are tight. Since E is in the big blind, we'll consider the table tight and make a raise on the smaller end of our scale.

Action: You raise to $6. The next two players fold. Player C, on the button, calls the $6 and the blinds fold. The pot is now $15 and the effective stack is $74.

Flop: Q♣J♠2♦

Question: *What do you do?*

Answer: You've flopped top pair, top kicker, a fine hand so far and Player C is loose-passive with a relatively short stack. Note in particular that his 'fold to c-bet' number is zero. While you should sometimes check your top pair, top kicker hand to mix up your play, checking in this spot would be criminal. So you're going to make a continuation bet.

How much should you bet? The traditional amount for c-betting is about half the pot. This amount had the advantage of offering a good risk-reward ratio. If you bet exactly half the pot, your opponent only had to fold one-third of the time for your bet to break even. If he folded more often than that, your bet showed an immediate profit.

However, that bet size has the disadvantage of offering your opponent good pot odds to call. If the pot is $20 and you make a $10 continuation bet, your opponent needs to put up another $10 to see a pot of $30 which means he's getting 3-to-1 odds. Considering that many of your continuation bets are bluffs, those are good odds, and many experienced players would stick around to see a turn card. As a result, players began increasing the size of their continuation bets to two-thirds or more of the pot, cutting down on their opponent's pot odds.

In the absence of any information about my opponents, my preferred approach these days is to start off with half-pot continuation bets and gauge their reactions. If that bet size pulls down a lot of pots, I'll stick with it. If my opponents stick around too often, I'll raise my continuation bet size up to the two-thirds (or more) pot level. I like to bet the minimum that will get the job done, and determining that amount for a given table sometimes take a little while.

But in this situation, none of that reasoning applies. From his general looseness and his 'fold to c-bet' number (zero) we can be pretty sure that we hold the best hand and a bet here will be called. In this case, we're just making a great value bet and we want it to be as large as possible. With a $15 pot, a $12 bet seems about right.

Action: You bet $12 and Player C folds.

Unexpected, but that's how things go sometimes. No need to second-guess your bet amount. Given what you knew, it was the right play.

Problem 5-9

Table layout:

UTG	Player A $130	A's HUD Player A / (42) / -52 VP 36 / PF 8 / AS 18 / FB 60 3B 0 / F3 100 / AF 0.8 / 2 / 0 / 0 CB 33 / FC 67 / FT na W$F 44 / WtS 33 / W$S 33
MP	Player B $90	
CO	Player C $330	
BTN	Player D $210	
SB	Player E $225	
BB	You $290	

Situation: Online $200 NL 6-max table. Blinds are $1.00 and $2.00.

Your hand: A♠6♠

Action to you: Player A limps for $2 and then it is folded around to you.

Question: *What do you do?*

    Answer: You have a decent hand against a loose-passive player. As in a couple of previous examples, you don't have a lot of incentive to raise. While your hand is probably a slight favorite against his range, it's unlikely that a raise will do anything other than build a slightly bigger pot in a hand where you're out of position. Check, see the flop, and plan on winning the hand later.

Action: You check and the pot is $5.

Flop: K♥5♥4♣

    That's a pretty dry flop which missed most, but not all, of his range. The betting line you should choose depends on your opponent. Against a passive opponent, you have the option of checking now and possibly checking the hand all the way down to the river. If your ace high is currently good, it will mostly hold up and you'll win the pot without needing to risk much.

    Against an aggressive opponent, that line won't work. At some point he'll put in a bet to test you, and he may bet on a couple of streets if he thinks you're showing weakness and the hand is otherwise winnable. So to win the pot against such an opponent, you're better off taking the lead yourself on either the flop or the turn.

    Here we're clearly facing a passive opponent. His PFR, AS, and AF are all low, and his other statistics point to passivity as well. While you'll need to bet on occasion with a hand like ace-high just to avoid being predictable, a checking line should be your default option.

Action: You check and Player A checks behind you. The pot remains at $5.

Turn: 4♥

Question: *What do you do?*

    Answer: Nothing has changed. Check again and see what happens.

Action: You both check.

River: J♦

    That's not an especially good card, but it shouldn't change your approach. Check and try to reach a free showdown where your ace-high may be good.

Action: You both check, your opponent shows the T♦9♠, and you take the pot.

Problem 5-10

Table layout:

UTG	Sitting Out	
MP	Sitting Out	
CO	You $220	Your HUD You / (34) / +16 VP 26 / PF 21 / AS 27 / FB 0
BTN	Player A $130	A's HUD Player A / (34) / -38 VP 31 / PF 7 / AS 13 / FB 50
SB	Player B $245	B's HUD Player B / (42) / +2 VP 17 / PF 14 / AS 20 / FB 100
BB	Player C $110	C's HUD Player C / (32) / +11 VP 8 / PF 8 / AS 0 / FB 100 3B 25 / F3 na / AF inf / inf/ na / na CB 100 / FC na / FT na W$F 50 / WtS 0 / W$S na

Situation: Online $200 NL 6-max table. Blinds are $1.00 and $2.00. The table just went from 6- to 4-handed as two players decide to sit out.

Your hand: J♣9♥

Question: *What do you do?*

   Answer: You need to be playing a huge range of hands for jack-nine offsuit to be included, so there's no harm in folding here. However, two players have just left the table and we're down to four-handed, so an opportunity has arisen. Many players don't adapt quickly enough when the table gets short-handed, and a little extra aggression at this time can be profitable.

However, before deciding to raise, you need to look at the other players. Here we have a fairly typical mix: Player A is loose-passive and losing in the session. Player B seems to be tight-aggressive and he's breaking even so far. And Player C is extremely tight and up a little. Since we have a marginal play here, we'll weight our decision toward his tendencies, and it doesn't appear he defends his blind much, so let's raise.

Action: You raise to $6, Players A and B fold, and the big blind calls $4. The pot is now $13.

Flop: K♣6♦2♥

Action: Player C checks.

Question: *What do you do?*

Answer: That's a nice flop given that it didn't hit us in any way. It's dry and unlikely to connect with most of his calling range. So let's continue with our plan and make a continuation bet.

Note that our problem is fundamentally different from the last hand. There we held an ace-high hand against a passive opponent. The ace protected us against a scary overcard coming on the turn while his passivity meant we had a reasonable chance of checking the hand down. Here we have a jack-high hand so our chance of winning at showdown is less, and our opponent seems to be aggressive when he plays. Accordingly, we can't check this hand and expect to win. So to keep our equity, we need to bet.

With the dry board, a big bet shouldn't be necessary. We're representing a good hand, and if he has nothing, any bet of half the pot or more should do the job and chase him away.

Action: You bet $7. Player C raises to $20 and the pot is now $40.

Question: *What do you do?*
    Answer: We fold. Even if he's bluffing, he's probably bluffing with the best hand, and since we have nothing, it's time to go away.

Action: You fold.

Problem 5-11

Table layout:

UTG	Player A $100	
MP	You $220	Your HUD: You / (106) / +118 VP 24 / PF 20 / AS 32 / FB 60 3B 7 / F3 66 / AF 2.5 / 3 / 1.8 / 1.8
CO	Player B $120	B's HUD Player B / (88) / -44 VP 28 / PF 25 / AS 34 / FB 70 3B 8 / F3 70 / AF 2.4 / 2 / 1.5 / 2 CB 68 / FC 55 / FT 66 W$F 44 / WtS 26 / W$S 50
BTN	Player C $100	
SB	Player D $55	
BB	Player E $110	

Situation: Online $100 NL 6-max table. Blinds are $0.50 and $1.00.

Your hand: A♥J♣

Action to you: The first Player folds.

Question: *What do you do?*

Answer: Ace-jack, even offsuit, is certainly a strong enough hand to raise from middle position.

Action: You raise to $3 and Player B calls. All the other players fold and the pot is $7.50.

Flop: 8♣7♠5♣

Question: *What do you do?*
   Answer: That's an especially bad flop. In small stakes action, players with a profile like Player B (VP$IP/PFR of 28/15, 3-bet of 8) tend not to cold call a lot. When they do cold call, their hand range is fairly limited to medium pairs and medium suited connectors. While that flop missed you completely, it ended up squarely in the middle of B's range. You're not in a good situation and you're out of position besides. You don't need to continuation bet every flop, so let this one go.

Action: You check and Player B checks behind. The pot remains $7.50.

Turn: 9♥

Action: *What do you do?*
   Answer: You still have nothing and the board just hit a little more of his range while completing some straight draws. The fact that Player B checked the flop is helpful, although he could easily be trapping a big hand. Again, this isn't a favorable situation for betting, so you should check again.

Action: You both check and the pot remains $7.50.

River: A♠

Question: *What do you do?*
   Answer: His second check and the arrival of a good card for you has changed the situation. You still don't have a big hand

on this board, but it's no longer likely that he has a monster. The flush draws missed, and a straight or a set would have bet the turn fearing the arrival of a river card that would cool the action. If he made two pair by the turn he should have bet it. If he just made two pair with something like ace-nine or ace-eight, you caught a bad break. In short, his most likely hands right now are a single pair or no pair.

Question: *Can your bet make any better hands fold?*
Answer: No.

Question: *Can your bet make some weaker hands call?*
Answer: Yes, as long as it's not too big. If he has a single pair, he may think your bet is just a cheap attempt to take the pot with a hand like king-queen or king-jack, and look you up. This is the essence of a thin value bet: Based on what you know, it's likely to be slightly profitable, and at the small stakes, you need to take these profits.

Action: You bet $3, he calls and shows the 4♦4♠, and you take the pot.

Problem 5-12

Table layout:

UTG	Sitting Out	
MP	Player A $330	
CO	Player B $180	
BTN	Player C $220	
SB	You $215	
BB	Player D $200	D's HUD Player D / (50) / -3 VP 40 / PF 15 / AS 15 / FB 67 3B 0 / F3 na / AF 1.5 / 2 / 0.5 / 1 CB 50 / FC 50 / FT na W$F 50 / WtS 20 / W$S 50

Situation: Online $200 NL 6-max table. Blinds are $1.00 and $2.00.

Your hand: Q♥8♥

Action to you: One player is sitting out and everyone folds to you in the SB.

Question: *What do you do?*

    Answer: The big blind seems loose and not particularly aggressive. Your hand is slightly above average and has the merit of being suited. Hence, I would raise and expect to have a good chance of outplaying Player D if I don't win immediately.

Action: You raise to $6, the big blind calls $4, and the pot is now $12.

Flop: Q♠J♣9♦

Question: *What do you do?*

   Answer: You have top pair plus a gutshot. It's a hand that may well be best. However, you wouldn't like betting and getting raised by Player D with a random ten in his hand. Your top pair, weak kicker makes a far better bluff-catching hand than a value-betting hand. Check and try to keep the pot small.

Action: You both check.

Turn: A♠

Question: *What do you do?*

   Answer: That's a scary card since he might have checked an ace on the flop for the same reason you checked your top pair. Check again and see what he does. If he bets, you'll have a difficult decision.

Action: You both check.

River: 2♣

Question: *What do you do?*

   Answer: You could, of course, just check, and call a bet to see if your pair of queens are good. But before we check, let's think about the hand and see what Player D could have.

Our opponent has so far checked twice after seeing us check. Can he have a really big hand? He checked the flop which had plenty of dangerous drawing possibilities. A set or two pair would have bet to try and charge the draws, so a big hand is unlikely. Can he have an ace? If he hit a pair of aces on the turn, we'd again expect him to be betting, so an ace looks unlikely.

Does he have nothing? Maybe, but with nothing he might have tried a bet on either the flop or turn since we checked in front of him, and he would have seen a chance to take down an easy pot. (If we actually thought he had nothing we would mostly check the river and give him a chance to bluff.)

It looks like he has something like what we have, perhaps a jack, a nine, or even a low queen that he's trying to check down to the river. In that case, we're probably good, and we need to make a bet that's small enough for him to call and for you to extract a little more money from the hand.

With a $12 pot, the maximum you can bet and get called by a hand like third pair is probably something in the range of $4 to $8, a little less than half pot to a little more than half pot. Let's bet $6 and see what happens.

Action: You bet $6, he calls and shows the J♠8♠, and you take the pot.

Problem 5-13

Table layout:

UTG	Player A $110	
MP	You $145	Your HUD You / (54) / +30 VP 27 / PF 22 / AS 35 / FB 65 3B 8 / F3 60 / AF 3 / 3 / 2 / 1.5
CO	Player B $90	
BTN	Player C $190	
SB	Player D $120	
BB	Player E $105	E's HUD Player E / (106) / -4 VP 26 / PF 12 / AS 20 / FB 72 3B 3 / F3 70 / AF 1.2 / 1 / 1 / 2 CB 50 / FC 70 / FT 80 W$F 38 / WtS 20 / W$S 58

Situation: Online $100 NL 6-max table. Blinds are $0.50 and $1.00.

Your hand: A♥Q♠

Action to you: The first player folds.

Question: *What do you do?*
   Answer: There's no reason to do anything but raise.

Action: You raise to $3.50 and Players B, C, and D all fold. The big blind (Player E) calls $2.50 and the pot is $7.50.

Flop: Q♥8♦4♦

Action: Player E checks.

Question: *What do you do?*
   Answer: Again, there's no reason to do anything but bet. If you've been continuation betting a lot with nothing, it's especially important to bet as your more alert opponents will now be eager to call.

Action: You bet $5 and Player E calls. The pot is now $17.50.

Turn: 2♣

Action: Player E checks.

Question: *What do you do?*
   Answer: Just check. This looks like a pot control move, but it's not. Player E has some kind of hand because his 'fold to c-bet' number, 70 percent, is high, showing that he's willing to give up if he doesn't get something on the flop. We also notice that his 'fold to turn c-bet' is even higher at 80 percent, while his 'went to showdown' number (WtS) is only 20 percent, very low. This is a player who can pretty easily be pushed out of a pot if he lacks a strong hand and his opponent shows strength. But he checked and called the flop, so his hand has some value, but he didn't bet the turn, so he's not confident that his hand is best.

Player E's most likely holdings are a weak queen, something like QJ or QT, or a pair between jacks and fives, but not eights. If we're right about that, then he has only two or three outs to a hand that beats us.

So betting now will probably make these hands fold. Checking will indicate that we made a continuation bet with either nothing or something weak and we've now either given up on the pot or are trying to get to showdown. If he reads us that way our opponent might be inclined to either on the river make a bluff or make what he thinks is a value bet with whatever he has. Note that his 'river aggression' is 2, so he's capable of betting the river under some circumstances. Also, we don't have any notes to tell us exactly what those circumstances are, but we have a couple of bases covered. So let's check and see if we can induce a river bet which might double our profit on the hand.

Action: We check behind.

River: 4♣

Action: He bets $13.

Question: *What do you do?*
Answer: Call. Raising is silly because if we've read the hand correctly, he's unlikely to call a raise with the hands we think he has, and if he does call, he'll likely have us beat.

Action: We call $13, he shows the 9♥9♦, and we take the pot.

Problem 5-14

Table layout:

UTG	Player A $680	
MP	Player B $100	B's HUD Player B / (18) / -30 VP 43 / PF 14 / AS 10 / FB 75 3B 17 / F3 75 / AF 1 / 1 / 1 / na CB 50 / FC 75 / FT 100 W$F 25 / WtS 20 / W$S 50
CO	Player C $120	
BTN	You $460	Your HUD You / (95) / +67 VP 28 / PF 24 / AS 35 / FB 50
SB	Player D $320	D's HUD Player D / (40) / +19 VP 40 / PF 32 / AS 45 / FB 100 3B 22 / F3 100 / AF 6 / 8 / 2 / 1 CB 80 / FC 70 / FT 75 W$F 53 / WtS 67 / W$S 50 *Note: Extremely aggressive against weakness.* *PF: 3B=A9s,QJs.*
BB	Player E $140	

Situation: Online $200 NL 6-max table. Blinds are $1.00 and $2.00.

Your hand: A♠T♠

Action to you: Player A folds. Player B limps for $2 and Player C folds.

Question: *What do you do?*

    Answer: Your hand is reasonably strong, certainly better than most of the hands in Player B's limping range, so raise for value. You're hoping to isolate Player B and play heads-up after the flop, and you'll have position throughout the hand.

    The only difficulty on the horizon is Player D in the small blind who's extremely aggressive and has shown a propensity to 3-bet. However, his 3-betting range is so wide (22 percent) that your hand is actually a favorite against it, so you'll definitely be playing even if he chooses to 3-bet.

Action: You raise to $8. The small blind calls $7 and the big blind folds. Player B calls $6 and the pot is $26.

Flop: T♣T♦5♦

Action: Both your opponents check.

Question: *What do you do?*

    Answer: Player D did decide to play the hand, but he elected to just call your preflop raise rather than 3-bet. That's a little suspicious given the level of aggression he's shown so far in the session. His most likely hands at this point are low or medium pairs which he chose not to play strongly. Player B limped and called, but that doesn't really tell us much about his range.

    On the flop, we hit trips and our two opponents checked. We now have a monster which is almost certainly good, but we need to think about how to extract some extra value from the hand, even if that extra value is just one more bet.

If we were playing in a micro-stakes game, we'd just go ahead and bet. As we explained before, slowplaying in micro-stakes games is almost always a blunder since so many players will stick around with weak hands to see what happens. But as you graduate to small stakes games, the players are somewhat less likely to hang around. At these stakes, slowplaying starts to become a reasonable option, partly to allow opponents with nothing to catch up in the hand, but mostly to allow more aggressive players to bluff.

Therefore, in this case, our hand completely dominates this flop and slowplaying becomes a very reasonable choice for several reasons:

1. Betting now will most likely only take down the existing pot.

2. Checking may give both our aggressive opponents the idea that the pot is winnable on the turn with a bluff.

    It will also give a free card which might allow someone to draw out. But that chance is extremely small.

3. If either player has a pair, they're drawing to just two outs, or about a 5 percent chance of hitting (10 percent if both players have a pair).

4. From our previous distribution examples, the chance that either player has a flush draw is only about 5 percent, and the chance of then hitting that draw on the turn is only about 20 percent, for a total risk of about 1 percent.

In short, this is about as favorable a slowplaying situation as we could ask for.

Action: You check and the pot remains $26.

Turn: 2♥

Action: Player D bets $20 and Player B folds. The pot is now $46.

Question: *What do you do?*
    Answer: Player D did indeed take a stab at the pot. He may have something, or he more likely is just bluffing at a pot that no one seems to want. It's possible that you're beaten, but that's very unlikely.
    If you just call, your opponent will probably shut down on the river whether he has something or not. If you raise, you'll chase away his bluffs, but you may get action if he has a pair and thinks it's unlikely you have a ten.
    But before you raise, you need to decide your course of action if reraised since the stacks are deep. Therefore a little caution is required. However, given how aggressive he has been so far, and how aggressive you have been, it would be a mistake to try and get away from this hand. From the board and the flop action, either of you could be bluffing, and the stacks are not so deep that you'll be able to decide that you're really beaten before you get committed. So if you raise, be prepared to go all the way.

Action: You raise to $60 and he pushes all-in for another $292. The pot is $398 and it costs you $232 to call.

Question: *What do you do?*
    Answer: You have to call. You're getting 1.7-to-1 on your money and you beat most of the hands that could make this bet.

Action: You call and he shows the Q♥T♥. The river is the 4♥ and you take the pot.

Problem 5-15

Table layout:

UTG	Player A $210	A's HUD Player A / (20) / -36 VP 40 / PF 5 / AS 14 / FB 50 3B 0 / F3 100 / AF 1 / 2 / 0 / na CB na / FC 67 / FT na W$F 50 / WtS 33 / W$S 50
MP	Player B $310	
CO	Player C $145	
BTN	Player D $195	
SB	Player E $90	
BB	You $220	Your HUD You / (52) / +12 VP 41 / PF 35 / AS 50 / FB 50

Situation: Online $200 NL 6-max table. Blinds are $1.00 and $2.00.

Your hand: Q♦T♥

Action to you: Player A limps for $2 and the hand is folded around to you.

Question: *What do you do?*
Answer: Player A is clearly a loose-passive player who calls a lot and rarely raises. He does, however, raise some of the time. His 'attempt to steal' number (14 percent) is low, but it is a small sample of hands. He may not be positionally aware, but for now we'll assume he has some grasp of position.
Let's start by assigning him a range. His VP$IP is currently 40 percent, very loose. We're giving him credit for a little knowledge of position, so we'll shave that down to 30 percent since he's under the gun. His PFR is 5 percent, which is pretty tight, so we'll guess that he's limping with 25 percent of his hands which don't include the top 5 percent. His range therefore looks roughly like this:

> Pairs from 88 to 22
> All suited and offsuit aces except AK and AQ
> All other Broadway cards
> Suited connectors from T9s to 65s
> Suited one-gappers from J9s to 75s

How is our queen-ten offsuit doing against this range? Many players look at the sheer size of his range and assume that two Broadway cards must be doing pretty well, but in fact they're not. We're actually about a 55-to-45 underdog against that range. (Startling but true.) Remember that we're an underdog against all the aces and pairs, and we're also dominated by most of the Broadway cards. It's only against the suited connectors and suited one-gappers that we're actually favored, and there aren't very many of those hands.
We could raise here (and many aggressive players would), in which case we'll mostly get called and then have to play a bigger pot out of position. A better play is to just check, play a smaller pot, and try to outplay him after the flop which we should mostly be able to do.

Action: You check and the pot is $5.

Flop: J♣8♣3♦

Question: *What do you do?*

Answer: Not our worst flop, but certainly not our best. We do have some outs; nines are almost certainly an out, and queens are probably an out as well. Those two cards represent seven good outs. Tens may also be outs, but we can't be sure.

The flop connected reasonably well with the part of Player A's range that we used to be beating: the suited connectors and the suited one-gappers. A few of his suited hands now have a club flush draw, and ten-nine has become a straight draw. His aces are still beating us, but he can't know that. If he had a low pair it's still good, but again he can't know that. Against his preflop range and this board, we're now actually about a 62-to-38 underdog.

Hence we have no reason to bet. But given his general passivity and our outs, we can certainly call a bet.

Action: You check. He bets $4 and you call. The pot is now $13.

Turn: K♦

Question: *What do you do?*

Answer: The king is an interesting card. We postulated that KQ, KJ, and KT were all in Player A's range, so at first glance it would seem to hit a solid chunk of his range. But since we hold a queen and a ten, and the board contains a king and a jack, Player A can't hold as many hands containing a king as you might think. With a king and a queen now accounted for, only nine king-queen combinations remain for him (instead of 16), and the same is true for king-jack and king-ten. Actually that king hit less than 10 percent of his range, making it a reasonable scare card for us to use.

We can bet or check right now. A check isn't a bad play and may enable us to see a free river card. But a bet is slightly better for the following reasons:

1. It's a legitimate semi-bluff because we have eight cards (aces and nines) that give us a monster, while three more queens may give us a winning hand. A ten might also be a winner, but that's less likely.

2. A big chunk of his range consists of suited and offsuit aces and small pairs. A bet here has the potential to fold out a lot of hands that beat us.

3. If he has ace-jack, ace-eight, or ace-trey, we create the possibility of scooping his whole stack on the river if an ace hits, giving him two pair but giving us a very well-concealed straight.

The downside of betting is that we really don't want to face a big raise that chases us off our outs. However, the general passivity that we see in his HUD makes this possibility less likely.

Action: You bet $10 and Player A calls. The pot is now $33.

River: A♠

Question: *What do you do?*
   Answer: Sometimes good things happen to good people. We now have the nuts so we have to find the best way to extract some value. Given his general passivity, we have to bet. A huge number of hands in his range are callable, even for a

passive player, but we can't assume he would bet with any of those hands.

So how much should we bet? He may have hit top pair, or maybe even two pair with an ace, so we should assume he can call a fairly large bet, and this is a case where I like to err on the high side because of the possibility that he just hit a hand that can call quite a large bet. So let's overbet the pot a little and see if we can squeeze out some extra money.

Action: You bet $40, he calls and shows the A♥8♦, and you take the pot.

Problem 5-16

Table layout:

UTG	You $120	Your HUD You / (100) / +10 VP 26 / PF 22 / AS 36 / FB 66 3B 7 / F3 70 / AF 2.2 / 2.8 / 1.8 / 1.5
MP	Player A $100	
CO	Player B $179	B's HUD Player B / (100) / +35 VP 23 / PF 23 / AS 30 / FB 65 3B 12 / F3 60 / AF 2 / 3 / 2 / 1.5 CB 70 / FC 60 / FT 70 W$F 48 / WtS 24 / W$S 46
BTN	Player C $140	
SB	Player D $115	
BB	Player E $100	

Situation: Online $100 NL 6-max table. Blinds are $0.50 and $1.00.

Your hand: 9♣8♣

Question: *What do you do?*

   Answer: A medium suited connector is right at the bottom of our opening range under the gun. Playing these occasionally gives your game good diversity and makes you hard to read.

Action: You raise to $3 and Player A folds. Player B 3-bets to $10 and the other players all fold.

Question: *What do you do?*

   Answer: Player B has been an active 3-bettor and we've had to lay down to him a couple of times. Our hand is only about 37 percent to a typical 12 percent range, technically not good enough to call. But he's been throwing his weight around and we feel like getting involved. He certainly won't read us for this hand, so we may be able to maneuver after the flop.

Action: You call for $7 more and the pot is now $21.50.

Flop: Q♠T♦3♣

Question: *What do you do?*

   Answer: We have a gutshot and a backdoor flush draw, so there is no reason to lead. Let's check and see what happens.

Action: You check and Player B checks behind.

   That's an odd check since this seems to be a flop where a 3-bettor would routinely take a stab. The most likely explanation is that his range is now polarized between very strong hands (set, two pairs) and weak hands where he chooses not to continue. (Polarized ranges don't only happen on the river!)

Turn: Q♥

The queen doesn't hurt us, but our backdoor flush draw has gone away. Furthermore, with two queens on board, it's hard for us to represent a queen, so we'll check again.

Action: Both players check.

This check is even more peculiar since he needed to bet whether his hand was strong or weak. This was his best chance to take the hand down.

River: J♥

We hit our straight on the end. Since the board is paired, we could be beaten, but it's not likely given the betting so far unless he has exactly ace-king. We should bet on the assumption that he has some sort of weak made hand, and he'll look us up if the bet isn't too big.

Action: We bet $10, he calls and shows the J♦8♦ for a pair of jacks, and we take the pot.

Our opponent checked the flop with exactly the same hand we had, a gutshot and a backdoor flush draw. Perhaps he didn't bet for fear of losing those small shots at a big hand, although his bet would have won the pot either there or on the turn. Moral: be aggressive when you have the initiative!

Problem 5-17

Table layout:

UTG	Player A $280	A's HUD Player A / (41) / +40 VP 51 / PF 27 / AS 60 / FB 0 3B 0 / F3 50 / AF 5 / inf / inf / 1 CB 0 / FC 86 / FT na W$F 36 / WtS 29 / W$S 50
MP	Player B $40	
CO	Player C $160	
BTN	Player D $220	D's HUD Player D / (70) / +7 VP 26 / PF 23 / AS 39 / FB 50 3B 21 / F3 67 / AF 2.3 / 4 / inf / 0 CB 60 / FC 0 / FT na W$F 67 / WtS 67 / W$S 50
SB	Player E $440	E's HUD Player E / (46) / +61 VP 13 / PF 9 / AS 27 / FB na 3B 0 / F3 83 / AF 4 / inf / 0 / inf CB 100 / FC na / FT na W$F 33 / WtS 33 / W$S 100
BB	You $552	Your HUD You / (120) / +66 VP 26 / PF 22 / AS 31 / FB 67 3B 9 / F3 71 / AF 3.3 / 2 / inf / 2 CB 57 / FC 100 / FT na W$F 60 / WtS 30 / W$S 67

Situation: Online $200 NL 6-max table. Blinds are $1.00 and $2.00.

Your hand: J♥8♥

Action to you: Player A raises to $8 and the next two players fold. Player D (the button) calls the $8 and Player E (the small blind) calls for $7.

Question: *What do you do?*
> **Answer:** The pot is now $26 and it costs $6 to call. You're getting 4.3-to-1 on your money with a speculative hand and moderate to deep stacks around the table. Easy call at that price.

Action: You call $6. The pot is now $32 and four players are involved.

Flop: 8♣6♣5♦

Action: The small blind checks.

Question: *What do you do?*
> **Answer:** You were looking to flop a big draw, but instead you've hit top pair, weak kicker. It's a hand, but you're not happy.
>
> Two other players are yet to act. Player A is loose and aggressive, but having three other players in the pot may slow his aggression down. But if he decides to stick in a bet, you shouldn't mind calling, especially if Player D and the small blind fold. Also, Player D looks like your standard tight-aggressive player, but his aggression factors on the flop and turn are higher than usual. This means he may be inclined to stab at the pot if Player A checks. Therefore, since your position is poor and you'll have trouble calling a big raise if

you open the betting, just check and be prepared to call a bet from either of the players behind you.

Action: You check as do Players A and D, and the pot remains at $32.

Turn: T♥

Action: The small blind checks again.

Question: *What do you do?*
   Answer: No one bet the flop which tells us a few things.

1.   No one has a set. A player with a set would definitely have bet with three opponents and a somewhat wet board.

2.   No one has two pair for the same reason.

3.   Flush draws and straight draws are certainly possible. Semi-bluffs are less effective in multiway pots since the folding equity usually goes down faster than the size of the pot has gone up, so the lack of betting doesn't indicate no draws are present. This is true even though the players are aggressive.

4.   Players A and D probably have overcards or underpairs. Both are aggressive, have favorable position, and neither bet. In addition, Player A was the preflop raiser and should have bet this flop with a high pair, while Player D called in position, so those hands make sense for him as well.

5. The small blind called two players preflop and has now checked twice. Two overcards or an underpair make sense for him as well.

The checking on the flop made the value of our hand go up a bit, but the overcard on the turn knocked us down again. Since we think that overcards are the mostly likely hand for all of our opponents, the arrival of the ten on the turn hits everyone's range. Thus our hand is now a bluff-catcher and we should check again and see what happens.

Action: All remaining players check and the pot remains at $32.

River: J♠

Action: The small blind bets $22.

Question: *What do you do?*
Answer: Interesting. Just as you hit a pretty good hand, the small blind wakes up and bets. His HUD statistics (13/9, with an aggression factor of 4) mark him as a very tight player with an aggressive streak. Would he bet into three players with nothing? Probably not. Still, he's seen two complete rounds of checks so far, so he probably doesn't believe that there's a lot of strength out against him.

Let's start by narrowing his hand range down a bit, and see what we can conclude. First, let's note that without three cards of a suit or a pair on board, the best possible hand is a straight and three holdings make a straight on this board: Q9, 97, and 74. Note that the latter two made a straight on the flop, so if he had one of those he checked both the flop and the turn against three opponents with either the nuts or the second nuts. That's a non-standard play to say the least.

On the other hand, queen-nine, probably suited, fits the action fairly well. He calls preflop with a speculative suited hand, (unusual, but not impossible given his numbers), checks the flop with two overcards, checks the turn with a double belly-buster draw, and then hits the nuts on the river.

What about the sets? If he called preflop with either a pair of eights, sixes, or fives, then he hit a set on the flop. Would he check a draw-heavy board against three opponents? That's just possible because he might have been hoping for a check-raise. But it's not likely since it would be difficult to believe from the preflop action that there are a lot of hands out that could bet this board. Player A, who raised preflop under the gun, might have a high pair, but Player D and you in the big blind almost certainly don't. Two pair on the flop is an unlikely holding on this board since most players won't call a preflop raise with small connectors, and a single pair is unlikely to bet. So playing for a check-raise on the flop with a set doesn't look like a good play, and we can tentatively eliminate those sets from his hand range.

Two other sets are possible: tens and jacks. Jacks are the least likely both because we have a jack and because he didn't reraise with jacks preflop after an opening raise from a very loose player (Player A) and a call from a somewhat loose player (Player D). That's a perfect spot for a value raise with jacks, but he only called. He also could have bet with an overpair on the flop or the turn, so we can pretty much discount jacks from his range.

Tens aren't likely for the same reason. There was no raise preflop, no bet on the flop with an overpair, and no bet on the turn with a set and a board that was still drawish.

Hence, there's not a single possible set that makes sense for the small blind, or for any other player at the table. Now let's take a look at the two pair hands.

There are ten hands that could have two pair on this board. They are: JT, J8, J6, J5, T8, T6, T5, 86, 85, and 65.

Since the small blind was facing a raise and a call, it's probably safe to say we're only looking at suited combinations of these hands. Let's start by eliminating four hands: J6, J5, T6, and T5. Even when suited, these holdings aren't going to be in the range of a tight player facing a raise and a call preflop. So throwing those away leaves us with these six: JT, J8, T8, 86, 85, and 65.

We can eliminate the last three combinations next. Those hands (86, 85, and 65) hit two pair on a draw-heavy flop, so anyone holding one of these would have been inclined to bet the flop. And if they didn't bet the flop, they'd have certainly been inclined to bet the turn. Since neither bet happened, we eliminate these hands and are left with just three: JT, J8, and T8.

Let's consider T8 (probably suited) next. Calling preflop is reasonable enough. Checking the flop with top pair, weak kicker and three opponents is also reasonable. But checking the turn with top two pair and three opponents is about as unlikely as checking a set. Again, we can eliminate this hand which reduces his candidate two pair hands to JT and J8.

Jack-eight is our hand, and checking it this far makes as much sense for him as it did for us, so that's a possible hand in his range. Jack-ten works the same way, so we have another possible hand.

Could he have an overpair? Only three are possible: aces, kings, and queens. But all of these hands should have been brought in with a reraise preflop and a bet on the flop, so we eliminate them.

Could he have AJ, KJ, or QJ? These are all hands that could have called preflop, could have checked the flop and turn, and now just hit top pair on the river. However, many players would have treated them as bluff-catchers on the river and just checked. But given the lack of interest shown in the pot so far, it's not unreasonable to bet with one of them hoping to get called by a weaker pair, while planning on folding to a raise.

So after considering all the hands in the small blind's range that could have checked the flop and turn and bet for value on the river, we're reduced to only a handful: Q9, JT, our own J8, and possibly AJ, KJ, or QJ. We're losing to the first two, splitting with the third, and beating the last three.

Could he be bluffing? His HUD shows that he prefers betting to calling on the river, and in this session he's won whenever he got to showdown. However his hand sample is too small to assign any importance to those numbers. We're really on our own.

But given that everyone checked the flop and turn, there's always some chance that a decent player would bluff the river. But out of position against three players makes this a generally poor spot to try this. So I'd say the chance of facing a bluff here is pretty minimal.

What about the two players yet to act? Here our decision is a little easier. Player A raised under the gun preflop. With an overall PFR of 27, his under the gun raising range is probably about 15 to 20 percent. Once we eliminate the possible sets (for the same reason we eliminated them for the small blind) only two hands beat us: Q9 and JT, probably suited. Certainly jack-ten suited is in his range, while queen-nine might make it. However, the betting action on the flop and turn haven't narrowed his range at all, so these two hands make up just a tiny percentage of his possible hands at this point.

The same reasoning holds for Player D. While the small blind's range was narrowed *because he just bet*, the other two players still have the same wide ranges as before, so it's unlikely they'll be involved in the hand any more. At any rate, we can make our decision without worrying much about them.

So we believe that we are facing a small subset of the small blind's range, some of which we beat (AJ, KJ, QJ), some of which we're losing to (Q9, JT), and one hand with which we're splitting the pot (J8). Also notice that the number of hands we're beating is larger, but we're less confident that the small blind would always have bet those hands since they're really just bluff-catchers at this point. He certainly, however, would bet those holdings that beat us.

Finally, we want to consider the pot odds. The pot was $32 and the small blind bet $22, so we're getting pot odds to call of 54-to-22, or about 2.5-to-1. That's good enough, under the circumstances, to call, so we'll at least do that.

Should we raise? Not really. Raising is unlikely to make any money. The top pair hands that we beat will almost always fold to a raise, while the hands that are beating us will stick around: Q9 is the nuts and will reraise, while JT will at least call. So our decision is clear; we should call.

Action: You call, Players A and D fold, and the small blind shows the Q♦9♦ and takes the pot with the nut straight.

If this hand had occurred at micro-stakes, with all the actions up to the river being identical, the last decision would have been more difficult. The probability that the small blind was betting the river with a pair would be higher, and the probability that a pair somewhere would have called a river raise would also be higher. Therefore, the right play would now be to raise the small blind.

Glossary

Poker has always had its own terminology and the growth of online poker and poker forums has added even more terms to the traditional lingo. So here is a useful collection of terms, phrases, and examples that will help you navigate the world of poker talk.

3-bet: The first pre-flop reraise. *Example*: Pre-flop, the under the gun player raises and the player in middle position folds. The cutoff reraises. His reraise is called a 3-bet. Historically, 3-bets were rare and indicated a very strong hand, often aces or kings. In medium to high-stakes 6-max play, 3-bets are more common and are often an attempt to push a tight player off a good but not exceptionally strong hand. This type of move is also known as '3-betting light.'

4-bet: The second pre-flop reraise. *Example*: Pre-flop, the under the gun player raises and the player in middle position folds. The cutoff reraises (a 3-bet), and the button and the blinds fold. If the under the gun player now raises again, his reraise is called a 4-bet.

5-bet: The third pre-flop reraise. If the effective stack is about 100 big blinds, a 5-bet will often be an all-in move.

6-max: In cash games, a table with a maximum of six players.

ABC poker: The most straightforward style of playing poker in which you bet your good hands, check your medium-strength hands, and fold your weak hands. That is the only plays you make reflect the true strength of your hand. For instance, if your ABC opponent makes a large bet or raise, you assume they have the hand they represent. This strategy is close to optimal against tables of weak, loose, passive players who play too many hands and go to far with their hands.

AF: See *aggression factor.*

aggression factor (AF): A measure of post-flop aggression calculated as follows: AF = (bet% + raise%) / call%. The aggression factor is not influenced by checks or folds and therefore has to be evaluated in conjunction with other statistics like PFR.

ATS: See *attempt to steal.*

attempt to steal (ATS): In either full ring or 6-max games, an open raise from the cutoff or button position. As a HUD statistic, the percentage of times a player attempts to steal when possible.

auto-rebuy: A feature on many sites which allows you to have the site automatically move money to your stack to give you a full buy-in whenever your stack dips below that amount.

bluff: A bet made with a weak hand designed to chase your opponent out of the pot. Players mix appropriate numbers of bluffs along with their value bets to achieve a balanced strategy that is difficult for their opponents to categorize.

button: The player to the right of the small blind who acts last on each betting round. The button is the seat with the maximum positional advantage in each hand.

calling station: A player who will frequently call every street post-flop with a made but very marginal hand such as second or third pair. Calling stations are targets for relentless value betting with a good hand, and are difficult to bluff.

CO: See *cutoff*.

cold-call: A pre-flop call of a raise from a player who hasn't yet put any money into the pot, as opposed to a call from the blinds or a player who has already limped in.

continuation bet: A bet made on the flop after a player has taken the lead by raising preflop. On average, good players will make continuation bets on 60 to 70 percent of their hands where they were the first one to raise preflop.

cutoff (CO): In both full ring and 6-max games, the cutoff is the player who acts just before the button.

datamining: The process of using various software applications to collect data on opponents online. The term usually only applies to applications which collect data when the user is not actually online. On the other hand, PokerTracker and similar database programs are not considered datamining applications since they collect data while the user is actually playing. Many sites ban datamining applications.

deep stack: A stack which is more than about 150 big blinds. Deep stacks offer high implied odds which allow players to play more hands.

donk bet: A lead-off bet on the flop made by a player who didn't take the betting lead preflop. **Example**: Preflop, the under the gun player makes a standard opening raise and everyone folds but the big blind, who calls. After the flop, the big blind acts first and, rather than checking to see what the under the gun player does, instead leads with a bet. At micro-stakes or small stakes, donk bets are generally considered a mark of a weak player ("donk").

double barrel: A bluff where you miss the flop but make a continuation bet, get called, and then make another bet on the turn.

dry board: A flop which does not offer any possible draws. For example, on a flop like the K♥8♦2♣, no one can have a straight draw or a or flush draw.

equity: See *expected value.*

expected value (EV): The exact value of a particular action in a hand. Expected value can be positive (+EV) or negative (-EV) depending on whether a particular action is expected to make or lose money in the long run.

Fancy Play Syndrome (FPS): Describes a player who likes to make clever exotic plays when simple plays should make more money.

fit or fold: An excessively conservative style where a player will fold on the flop unless he makes a good hand (medium pair or better) or has a strong draw. Fit or fold players rarely, if ever, bluff.

float: Call a continuation bet with nothing aiming to take away the pot away with a bluff on the turn. Floating is effective against players with a high continuation bet percentage and a low turn aggression percentage.

full ring: In cash games, a 9- or 10-handed table.

heads-up (HU): A pot with only two players.

information bet: A bet made to get information about the relative strength of your hand compared to your opponent's by gauging his response. Also known as betting "to see where you stand." Such bets are often mistakes.

implied odds: Money which you expect to win in the future as a result of making a particular play. For instance, when you call a bet to draw to a flush, the value of your call is based partly on the immediate odds being offered by the pot and partly on whatever money you expect to win, on average, if you hit your flush. That future money makes up your implied odds.

LAG: See *loose-aggressive*.

leak: A persistent type of error in one's play which allows equity to slip away. Plugging leaks is a goal of improving players.

limp: Calling, instead of raising, the big blind preflop. Players who subsequently call are also known as limpers.

line: How a player elects to play a hand; his sequence of bets.

loose-aggressive (LAG): A player who enters a lot of pots but usually plays them aggressively by raising rather than calling. His typical VP$IP/PFR stats might be something like 30/24 or 35/27. He likes to take control of the pots he enters.

loose-passive (LP): A player who enters a lot of pots, usually by calling instead of raising. He will typically continue after the flop with weaker hands. (See *calling station*.) This is a losing style of play at almost any stake.

metagame: That part of poker which goes beyond the play of individual hands to the aspect of what you know about the other players and what they know about you. The higher the stake and the better the players, the more metagame should play a role in your decision making.

nit: An extremely tight player who will typically have VP$IP/PFR statistics in the range of 10/8, 8/6, or 4/4. He wants to have a very strong hand before he gets involved in a pot.

open raise: A pre-flop raise after all the players in front of you have folded.

opposite player: A player who consistently plays his hands in a way opposite to their true strength.

out: A card which will give you the winning hand if it hits. For example, if you have A♥K♥ and the flop comes J♣T♥4♥, any heart on the turn will give you the nut flush, and any queen which is not the queen of hearts will give you the nut straight. You have nine outs from the hearts and three more from the queens, for a total of 12 "sure" outs. In addition, an ace or a king might give you a winning pair for six more possible outs.

overpair: On the flop, a pocket pair higher than any of the board cards.

PFR: See *pre-flop raise*.

Polarized range: A range consisting only of very strong hands and bluffs. Many players will bet on the river only with a very polarized range, betting their nuts for value and occasionally bluffing, but checking their medium strength hands.

pot-committed: Having so few chips in your stack relative to the size of the pot that any all-in move by your opponent will require a call because of the favorable pot odds that are being offered. If making a normal-sized bet will leave you or your opponent pot-committed, then an all-in move is likely preferable.

pot control: Making plays to limit the size of the pot with a good but not great hand. **Example**: On the flop, a player makes a hand like top pair, good kicker. He bets and his opponent calls. The turn does not improve his hand. So he elects to check. Although his holding is reasonably strong, the possibility that his opponent may be trapping makes him unwilling to create a big pot with this hand. Instead, he prefers to keep the pot somewhat small and perhaps make one final bet on the river if his opponent has not shown strength. It's an important concept although passive players will take this idea to extremes.

pot odds: The money odds offered by the pot if you call a bet. For example, if the pot contains $20 and it costs $5 to call, the pot odds are 4-to-1.

Pot-sized bet (PSB): A bet that's the size of the pot.

pot-sized raise (PSR): A raise that's the size of the pot. If someone has acted and bet in front of you, a pot-sized raise will be the amount required to call the first bet, plus the size of the pot at that point. **Example**: The pot is $40 and your opponent bets $30. A pot-sized raise on your part would be $30 (to call his bet) plus ($40+$30+$30, the size of the pot at that point), or an additional $100 for a total of $130.

preflop raise (PFR): Any raise made before the flop. The PFR statistic measures your preflop raises as a percentage of the total hands played. A PFR of more than about 20 marks a player as aggressive; under 12 is tight. A normal range is about 12 to 20.

push: Move all-in.

pwn: To dominate an opponent by continually winning hands where you both are involved; a variation of "to own," favored by players who can't afford to buy a vowel.

rake: The portion of the pot taken out as a fee by the online site. Rake is usually not charged on hands that never see a flop. Rakes are generally capped at a certain amount and you should check the documentation of your online site to see the rake cap for a given stake.

rakeback: A portion of your rake may be returned to you if you join an online site through an intermediary site which offers rakeback. Typical arrangements will return about 30 percent of your actual rake as rakeback.

range: The set of hands with which your opponent might take a given action.

raw winning probability: The probability that you win the hand if the board was dealt out to the river with no further betting.

reverse implied odds: Your expected loss if a hand is played out. If you have a hand with little chance to improve, your expectation may be negative from that point forward if the hand is played to the river.

semi-bluff: A post-flop raise with a drawing hand which is almost certainly not best now but which has outs to become the best hand. For example, you have the 8♥7♥ and the flop comes Q♥J♥4♣. Your opponent bets and you raise. Currently you only have eight-high which is probably not the best hand right now (although it might be). However, any of the nine remaining hearts give you a flush, and any of the six remaining eights or sevens will give you a pair which might possibly be the best hand. Notice that your raise may win the hand outright, and if it doesn't, you may still make the best hand. Semi-bluffs differ from true bluffs by having outs to a winning hand, whereas a true bluff usually has no outs or very little chance to improve to the best hand.

short stack: A stack much smaller than the normal buy-in amount. A typical full buy-in for an online cash game session is 100 big blinds. A short stack player might buy in for 20 to 30 big blinds. Some short stack players attempt to play normal poker, but many adopt a specific *short stack strategy* which calls for waiting for premium hands, and then getting all-in as quickly as possible.

slowplaying: Playing a strong hand in a deceptive manner by checking and calling rather than betting and raising. Good players know to slowplay some of the time; bad players tend to slowplay either too much or not at all.

small ball: A style of play that involves making small bets and raises rather than large ones, putting pressure on the opponent and gaining information at small cost. Small ball also provides more opportunities to outplay your opponent on the later streets rather than being all-in or pot committed.

stack to pot ratio (SPR): The ratio of your stack to the existing pot. If you have $100 in your stack and the pot after the preflop betting is $25, your SPR is 4. Low SPRs favor hands like overpairs or top pair, top kicker which may be able to get all-in while they are still a favorite. High SPRs favor drawing hands.

suck bet: A small bet which offers tempting pot odds, made with the idea of luring an opponent into the pot with the worst hand.

TAG: See *tight-aggressive.*

tagfish: A tight-aggressive player who plays mechanically and without insight.

tight-aggressive (TAG): A style of play where you play relatively few hands but play them aggressively either by betting or raising instead of calling or checking. Most good players are some variation of this type.

triple barrel: A bluff which is an extension of a double-barrel in which you make a third and final bluff bet on the river.

underpair: On the flop, a pocket pair lower than any of the board cards.

value bet: A bet made to get more money in the pot when you are fairly sure you have the better hand and will be called by a worse hand.

valuetown: A happy destination where value bets are paid off by weaker hands. Also known as "valuetowning" or "taking your opponent to valuetown."

variance: The inherent variability of poker results. Players who are inadequately bankrolled for the stakes they are playing can be destroyed by variance. It is high in no-limit hold 'em, and loose-aggressive styles have more variance than tight-aggressive styles.

voluntarily put money in pot (VP$IP): A statistic which measures the percentage of time a player puts money in the pot pre-flop. The normal range is 15 to 30 percent. Outside of this range a player is either too loose or too tight.

VP$IP: See *voluntarily put money in pot.*

wet board: A board with many flush and straight possibilities. An example would be a flop like the T♥9♥8♥. Players may have hit a flush or straight already, or they could easily have a strong draw.

Index

Note: Following the style of the text, "we" and "you" refers to you, and "he" refers to your opponent.

NOTES